Defending the Faith

SUNY Series in Religious Studies

Robert Cummings Neville, EDITOR

Defending the Faith

NINETEENTH-CENTURY AMERICAN JEWISH WRITINGS ON CHRISTIANITY AND JESUS

George L. Berlin

State University of New York Press

BM
648
.B46
1989

Published by
State University of New York Press, Albany

© 1989   State University of New York

For information, address State University of New York
Press, State University Plaza, Albany, N.Y., 12246

Library of Congress Cataloging-in-Publication Data
Berlin, George L., 1938–
    Defending the faith : nineteenth-century American Jewish writings
on Christianity and Jesus / George L. Berlin.
        p.   cm. — (SUNY series in religious studies)
    Bibliography: p.
    Includes index.
    ISBN 0–88706–920–7.   ISBN 0–88706–921–5 (pbk.)
    1. Judaism—Apologetic works.   2. Jesus Christ—Jewish
interpretations.   3. Judaism—United States—History—19th century—
Sources.   I. Title II. Series.
BM648.B46   1989
296.3'872—dc19   88-15440
                                                                             CIP

10 9 8 7 6 5 4 3 2 1

In Memory of my Father,

Joseph Berlin

CONTENTS

Preface

The relationship between Jews and Christians today is a matter of interest and concern to informed members of both religions. During the past twenty-five years, a number of significant developments have occurred. Beginning with the Second Vatican Council under the guiding spirit of the late Pope John XXIII, the Catholic Church began a reexamination of its relationship with the Jewish people and Judaism. Similar reevaluations have taken place in a number of Protestant denominations. Numerous denominational statements and papers have been issued announcing major and minor modifications of traditional theological positions regarding the Jews. Jews, too, although in a more restrained manner, have begun to reassess their traditional attitudes towards Christianity. At its best, contemporary Jewish–Christian dialogue is an honest attempt on the part of the two sides to understand each other by maintaining a stance of respect and granting legitimacy to each other's religious expression.

During the nineteenth century, Christians and Jews also spoke to each other about religious matters. However, they did not speak as equals, and frequently there was little genuine respect for the other's religious convictions. American Jews often had to defend Judaism and their loyalty to it in the face of both a triumphalistic Protestantism that sought to Christianize America, and liberal Protestants who denied the religious value of Judaism in the post-Jesus era.

For American Jews, these Christian attitudes posed not only a challenge to Judaism, but seemed likely to undermine their cherished security in America as well. Faced with these threats, they devised a variety of defensive strategies which, in turn, reflected the different religious views among them. Of necessity, when responding to Christian challenges, American Jews had to deal with Christianity and Jesus. The following chapters relate how they did this as they attempted to defend their faith.

The book is divided into two parts. The first analyzes nineteenth century American Jewish writings on Christianity and Jesus. Part Two is a collection of primary sources extracted from books no longer in print and from periodicals that are not readily accessible.

Chapter Two is a revised version of a paper, "Solomon Jackson's *The Jew*: An Early American Jewish Response to the Missionaries," originally published in *American Jewish History* 71 (September, 1981), pp. 10–28.

It is a pleasure to thank Professor Jonathan Sarna for having read an earlier version of the first part of the book and for having offered many helpful suggestions. I would also like to thank my children, Joseph and Miriam, who, through their forbearance, have demonstrated that they, too, appreciate the search for knowledge. Most important of all, to my wife, Adele, who has been a constant source of encouragement and support to me in this project, as in all else, my gratitude and much more.

PART ONE

Defending the Faith

1　Introduction

Jews and Christians have been arguing over religious questions since the earliest period in Christian history. The main issues were delineated long ago: Was Jesus the messiah? What is the nature of the messiah and what was he to accomplish? Has the revelation of Jesus embodied in the New Testament superseded the covenant that God made with Israel at Sinai? Has God rejected the Jewish people and has the Church replaced the Jews as God's chosen people? Are Christian doctrines such as the trinity foreshadowed in the Hebrew Bible? What is the meaning of Jewish existence in the post-Jesus era, and what will be the ultimate destiny of the Jews? Some or all of these questions have been the subject of Jewish–Christian controversy in every century since the birth of Christianity. For centuries the answers to these questions were viewed by both sides as mutually exclusive. Either Jesus was the messiah or he was not. God's chosen people could not be represented by both Israel and the Church. Either the Jews were correct in their religious assumptions or the Christians were right in theirs. It was thought impossible that both could share the absolute truth. Only in recent years have more complex answers been presented, answers such as the dual covenant theory which attempts to grant legitimacy to the religious claims of both Christians and Jews. During the long past, however, the debate was fought in absolutist and mutually exclusive terms. Theologically, Christians were motivated by the need for legitimation that would be provided by confirmation of their supersessionary claims, and by a missionary impulse to convert the Jews. For their part, the Jews were impelled by a need to defend their faith in a world that contained far fewer Jews than Christians.[1]

Historians have recognized, however, that Christian–Jewish polemics should not be understood merely as a continuing theological debate having relevance only to the development of theological ideas. Religious polemics are very much a reflection of the historical environment in which they take place. The particular issues stressed by a polemicist, the emphasis, nuances and innovations that are brought to bear should be understood as a product of the historical forces at work

1

in a particular time and place. Polemical writings, therefore, may be used as a valuable source for understanding a historical situation. Nineteenth century American Jewish writings on Christianity and Jesus provide us with a useful tool for understanding the historical situation of the American Jewish community.

The nineteenth century is the formative period in the history of American Jewry. In the early decades, the Jewish community was quite small; in 1830 it numbered only 4,000–6,000. However, it grew steadily, its size increasing to 125,000–150,000 by 1860, and to 230,000–280,000 by 1880, the eve of the great migration from eastern Europe.[2] Along with the growth in numbers came the establishment of religious, communal, educational and cultural institutions. However, the creation of overall national organizations to harness the energies of the community nationwide for any of these purposes was a slow and sometimes painful task. The first major national Jewish organization, the Board of Delegates of American Israelites, was not established until 1859. The creation of umbrella rabbinical and congregational organizations and the founding of a rabbinical seminary took even longer. Lacking a rabbinical seminary, the community was without trained religious leadership until the 1840's when European rabbis, mostly from Germany, began to arrive in America. This small decentralized community, lacking trained rabbinical leadership until mid-century, faced critical and unprecedented challenges. The freedom which America granted to her Jews, the openness of the new country geographically and economically, the prevailing democratic spirit and social fluidity, and the absence of ghetto restraints combined to stimulate the processes of assimilation and acculturation. Yet, while seeking to participate fully in American life, most Jews also manifested a desire to remain Jews. How to accomplish both became the fundamental challenge for nineteenth century American Jewry.

Assimilation was not the only challenge confronting American Jews. During the early decades of the nineteenth century a vibrant and confident evangelical Protestantism was making its mark on American life. In the wake of the wave of evangelical religion that had been unleashed by the Second Great Awakening, many American Protestants optimistically believed that it was possible to create a godly society in America. To many, Americanism and Christianity blended together and the terms Christianity, democracy, and civilization became synonymous. This religious feeling was characterized by a strong missionary thrust. The goal was to spread Christianity throughout the country and to all segments of society by attaining the willing compliance of the American people to live a personal and national life in accordance with Christian standards. As Winthrop

S. Hudson has noted, in a country like America "where neither a Christian prince nor a Christian elite has the power to command, there is no substitute for a voluntary obedience to the laws of God. By no other means can the Christian faith find expression in the total life of the community."[3] The means through which America was to be transformed was the voluntary (often interdenominational) society. These societies proliferated during the second and third decades of the century. The American Education Society and the American Bible Society, both founded in 1816, were followed by the American Sunday School Union in 1824, the American Tract Society in 1825, and the American Home Missionary Society in 1826. The blending of Americanism and Christianity, the guiding spirit behind all of these groups, was captured in a circular announcing the establishment of the American Home Mission Society which declared that "we are doing a work of patriotism, no less than that of Christianity."[4] Missionary work among the Jews became one of the causes in the struggle to create a godly America.

Adding impetus to the optimistic pulse of early nineteenth century American Protestantism and particularly to the missionary effort among the Jews was a strong millenarian strain. Millenarian expectations were widespread in early nineteenth century America among a wide variety of Protestants. Many viewed the work of Christianizing society as preparation for the coming of the Lord. Typical of this frame of mind was the Memorial to the General Conference of the Methodist Episcopal Church issued by the New York Methodist Conference in 1808. The Memorial declared:

> The fields are white unto harvest before us, and the opening prospect of the great day of glory brightens continually in our view; and we are looking forward with hopeful expectations for the universal spread of Scriptural truth and holiness over the inhabitable globe.[5]

Many American Christians believed that the restoration of the Jews to Palestine and their subsequent conversion were essential ingredients leading to the advent of the millennium. This was a time of widespread millennial speculation and expectations. Momentous events were taking place that seemed to be fulfilling Biblical eschatological prophecies. The shattering of the power of the Roman Catholic church during the French revolution, the political and social dislocations resulting from the rise and fall of Napoleon, the spread of infidelity in the form of Deism, and the great religious revivals of the times fueled speculation that the end of days was approaching. The time was ripe for Christians to come forward and do their part in the working out of God's plan for history.

The American Board of Commissioners for Foreign Missions caught the spirit of the times when it declared in 1811 that "prophecy, history, and the present state of the world seem to unite in declaring that the great pillars of the Papal and Mahometan impostures are now tottering to their fall . . . Now is the time for the followers of Christ to come forward boldly, and to engage earnestly in the great work of enlightening and reforming mankind."[6] Jedidiah Morse, pastor of the Congregational church at Charlestown, Massachusetts, declared in an 1810 sermon that the western and eastern Antichrists (i.e., the Papacy and the Ottoman Empire) would fall in the year 1866.[7] William Miller, one of the most famous millenarian figures in America at the time, predicted that the millennium would dawn in 1843. The feeling that the present stage in history was coming to an end, and the feeling that it was the responsibility of Christians to help in the working out of God's plan gave impetus to the missionary movement in early nineteenth century America.

According to many millenarians, the Jews had a special role to play in the eschatological scheme. Jedidiah Morse predicted that they would be restored to Palestine in 1866 as a necessary prelude to the millennium. Other American millenarians shared this view of Jewish destiny.' It was widely felt in these circles that the conversion of the Jews and the conversion of the heathen peoples were inextricably intertwined. Some, like John H. Livingston, believed that the heathen would be converted after the conversion and restoration of the Jews. Others felt that the conversion and restoration of the Jews would be the climactic step leading to the millennium, and that it would therefore follow the conversion of the heathen. Still others believed that only a portion of the Jews would be converted prior to the Second Coming and that the remainder would convert later.[8] Whatever the sequence of conversions, the Jews were crucial to the scheme. To be sure, not all American millenarians advocated a restoration of the Jews to Palestine. William Miller declared that "the theory of the return of the Jews was not sustained by the Word." The Biblical promises of the restoration of Israel were to be applied to the spiritual Israel, that is, the Church.[9] In his opposition to the restoration of the Jews to Palestine, however, Miller was going against the tide of American millenarian thought on the subject.

America, it was believed, had a special role in bringing about the restoration and conversion of the Jews. In 1814, John McDonald, an Albany, New York Presbyterian minister, published a new translation and interpretation of Isaiah 18 in which he sought to prove that the prophetic charge was directed to American clergymen to convert the Jews:

Nation and churches of New England, cradle and nurse of the American churches, exert yourselves with your learned and venerable Pastors, to train up messengers for God! By your influence, and by multiplying your prayers prepare your sons and your posterity by your exertions, as legions of angels to unite with your Redeemer, in bringing back to him, his kindred according to the flesh.[10]

According to McDonald, the conversion of the Jews at the hands of American missionaries would be followed by the restoration of the Jews to Palestine. The forces of anti-Christ would then gather and the battle of Armageddon would be fought. With 1866 as the approximate date of that battle, American missionaries had little time to lose since the converted and restored Jews were to be part of the Messiah's army at Armageddon.[11] Thus, converting the Jews was seen as a worthy endeavor by a significant segment of American society.

For the Jews, the problem of how to respond to those who felt that they should become Christians was a difficult one. To be sure, not all Christians wanted to convert the Jews. There were groups, both religious and secular, that opposed missionary work among Jews for a variety of reasons. Nevertheless, the activities of the missionaries and the prevailing opinion among Christians, even those who did not favor missionary work, that Judaism was an inferior religion to Christianity, necessitated Jewish responses. The large amount of a polemical material to be found in nineteenth century American Jewish periodicals and sermons is an indication of how keenly the Jews felt the need to respond.

American Jews faced difficulties when they wrote about Christianity. First of all, there were pragmatic considerations. The Christian challenge had to be answered, but at the same time, Christian sensibilities had to be respected. Although separation of church and state and liberty of conscience were basic principles of the American state, American Jews were occasionally reminded that they were living in a Christian country. Given the widespread support that the missionary movement enjoyed, would an assault on it cause an anti-Jewish backlash? Moreover, which arguments should be used against Christians and who should present them? Was it preferable to take a confrontationalist or an accommodationist posture? These were primarily pragmatic considerations involved in developing a strategy that would not undermine Jewish security in America. In addition, however, there was also an important ideological factor. In responding to Christian missionaries or negative Christian evaluations of Judaism, Jews were defining for themselves their relationship to the Christian majority. The issue was not an easy one and it involved important choices. A new era had dawned in western history in which religious toleration and freedom of conscience were accepted norms. America was in the forefront of the new trend. It was increasingly difficult for Jews to dismiss the religious claims of Christianity simply by pointing to Christian persecution of Jews as a symptom of Christian failure. America presented a new kind of Christian society which granted full rights and equality of opportunity to the Jews. Jews and Christians interacted well in America, and while antisemitic incidents occurred, they were nowhere as prevalent as in most parts of Europe. What did all of this mean for the Jewish-Christian relationship? Did the new relationship between Jews and Christians mean that a reevaluation of traditional ideas about the relationship between Judaism and Christianity was in order, and if so, what would this entail?

Through their writings on Christianity and Jesus, American Jews, were, in effect, defining their relationship to American society and culture. This definition can be analyzed as that of insider and outsider. Jewish spokesmen who emphasized the differences between Judaism and Christianity and stressed the need for religious and social separation from the Christians were reflecting an outsider stance which maintained that the Jews must keep their distance from American culture. On the other hand, those who emphasized the commonalities between Judaism and Christianity were expressing an insider view which saw little or no conflict between Judaism and American society and culture, and even sought to identify Judaism with Americanism. In the following pages we shall discuss examples of both of these approaches to Christianity and see how they shed light on the Jewish community's attempt to define its own identity in the world of American freedom.

The following three chapters present examples of nineteenth century American Jewish writings on Christianity and Jesus. The first deals with early Jewish attempts to counter missionaries. The next chapter discusses Isaac Leeser's polemics and attempts to show how they reflect Leeser's traditionalist religious position and his outsider stance concerning the relationship of American Jewry to American culture and society. The last chapter analyzes late nineteenth century Reform Jewish writings on Christianity and Jesus, and demonstrates how these writings constitute an important element in the Reformers' insider definition of the place of the Jews in American society.

2 Early Confrontation with the Missionaries

American Christian missionary interest in the Jews goes back to the seventeenth century, although it was not until the first quarter of the nineteenth century that organized attempts to convert Jews were undertaken. In June, 1816, the writer and author of the first history of the Jews written in the United States, Hannah Adams, founded the Female Society of Boston and Vicinity for Promoting Christianity amongst the Jews. The inspiration for Miss Adams' effort was the London Society for Promoting Christianity amongst the Jews that had been established seven years earlier. The Boston society was followed in December, 1816, by the American Society for Evangelizing the Jews, which became in April, 1920, the American Society for Meliorating the Condition of the Jews (ASMCJ). This organization, founded by the German Jewish convert Joseph S. C. F. Frey, had as its professed goal the founding of a colony in America where Jews, who already had converted to Christianity in Europe, would be able to live and support themselves. Frey was appointed agent of the ASMCJ in 1822, and during that and the following year he travelled through the South and New England collecting money and establishing many local chapters. By 1824 nearly two hundred local chapters were in existence. The officers and board of directors of the ASMCJ consisted of a number of important Presbyterian and Dutch Reformed clergymen as well as some prominent laymen who were active in various areas of public life. In January, 1823, the ASMCJ began publishing a periodical called *Israel's Advocate*. The periodical continued until the end of 1826 and contained exhortations to Christians on the necessity to convert the Jews; reports on the activities and progress of the ASMCJ; frequent accounts of European missionary activities, especially those of the London Society; accounts of European Jews who had converted; and occasional descriptions of Jewish life in Europe and Asia which indicated that the Jews were in desperate need of Christianity and that the time was ripe for their conversion.[1]

The emergence of the ASMCJ and the considerable support that it had within the Christian community was a cause of concern to the Jews, and they responded to it. The first Jewish literary response to the missionaries came in 1816, the year that Frey had arrived in America, with the publication of an American edition of Jacob Nikelsburger's *Koul Jacob*. Nikelsburger had published his booklet in Liverpool in 1814 as a rebuttal to a series of pamphlets, written by Frey and published by the London Society, on the subject of the messiah. The work contains a refutation of the christological interpretations of a number of messianic sections of the Bible. Nikelsburger couched his argument in a moderate tone, and assured his readers that he had not written his booklet in order to engage in religious controversy, but only because Frey had challenged the Jews to answer his arguments. Declaring that he did not seek to write against Christianity, Nikelsburger affirmed his belief "that there are good men of all religions," and that "we all serve One God at last, though in different ways." Nikelsburger, drawing a contrast between himself and Frey, disclaimed any wish to convert anyone, and branded as reprehensible attempts to proselytize others.[2]

For American Jews *Koul Jacob* seemed an appropriate answer to Frey who had resumed his missionary activities shortly after his arrival in America. It was a well-tempered but firm refutation of Frey's arguments. Moreover, its author was an English Jew, and if American Christians were to take offense at it, its European authorship distanced American Jews from it.

The same year saw the publication of a vehement attack against Frey and his activities entitled *Tobit's Letters to Levi*. This work, authored by a non-Jew, is an example of the opposition to missionary activity that was felt in some circles, both religious and nonreligious. A number of Baptist and Methodist groups, Hicksite Quakers, and Unitarians as well as free thinkers feared that the benevolent societies that were proliferating in America at the time might lead to a centralization of religious authority through which one denomination or a group of denominations could become strong enough to effect a practical union of church and state. Their opposition to the missionary societies is symptomatic of their fear of the benevolent societies in general.[3]

"Tobit" attacked Frey's missionary efforts on ideological grounds and Frey himself on personal grounds. Frey's missionary work, wrote "Tobit," "borders on a spirit of persecution" and thereby violates the spirit of American religious toleration. The American people were genuinely fair and tolerant and would even elect a Jew president of the country if they found him to be the most qualified candidate for the office. Creedal conformity was not the measure of man for "Tobit." It was the morally upright man who found favor in God's sight, he asserted, "and such a man would I rather be even though I were a Jew withal, than the most rigid observer of the forms and ceremonies which the wisdom, superstition, or religion of mankind (call it what you will) have invented from the commencement of the world to this hour.[4]

"Tobit" went beyond a defense of religious toleration in his attack against Frey. He questioned both Frey's character and his motives. He charged that Frey was a man of questionable morality who had sought release from the strict system of Jewish law so that he could more easily lead a looser moral life in what he misunderstood to be the "holy liberty" of Christianity.[5] Frey had converted not out of conviction, but because he saw a chance to make money as a missionary to the Jews. Seeing in his abandonment of the Lutheran for the Baptist church proof of his lack of genuine religious conviction, "Tobit" accused Frey of being "an adventurer in the doctrines of the Christian world, ready to accept any offer which might promise emolument," and, addressing himself to Frey, charged that the missionary would "turn Jew again provided you had a subscription sufficient to build you a synagogue."[6] Frey's lack of principles could also be seen in his own admission that he was unfamiliar with the doctrines of Christianity at the time of his conversion. Indeed, declared "Tobit," Frey was still probably a Jew at heart, for after all, instead of marrying a Christian woman, he had married a Jewish woman whom he had converted in London. "Tobit" sought to cast further doubt on Frey's character by questioning the somewhat mysterious reasons why Frey had left London and why he did not bring with him any recommendations from Jews whom he had converted there.[7]

In addition to his attack on Frey's character, "Tobit" also defended the Jews and Judaism against what he considered to be the defamatory statements of Frey. He cited his own observation of Jewish life in both England and America to refute Frey's negative description of Jewish religious life. Jews were not narrow in their knowledge and did not confine their reading to Hebrew books, as Frey had written. American Jews possessed books that had Hebrew printing on one side of the page and English on the other, and well informed Jews had Bibles containing both the Old and New Testaments bound together. Against Frey's description of Jewish religious ceremonials as "vain" and "burdensome," "Tobit" praised the Jewish dietary laws as humane and declared that many Christians purchased kosher meat believing that it was of a higher quality.[8]

"Tobit" also defended the Jews against Frey's charges of moral laxity. Frey was wrong when he wrote that Jews felt free to cheat Christians. If indeed Jews did have a negative attitude toward Christians that was due to centuries of Christian maltreatment of Jews. In America, where "the Jewish nation have been treated with the characteristic humanity of the Christian religion . . . you find them good citizens, and with full as much morality as any other sect of believers." There were Christians who cheated Jews just as there were Jews who cheated Christians, but, concluded "Tobit," that was no reason "to condemn, in masse, their creed, their doctrine, and their congregations." Moreover, Jews were not addicted to material concerns as Frey had claimed. The Jews's adherence to their religion despite physical hardship and deprivation was well known. Concern for material gain was probably more the trait of Jewish converts than of those Jews who remained loyal to their faith.[9]

"Tobit" further stated that Frey had distorted Judaism when he alluded to its superstitions. Frey's critic saw no qualitative advantage for Christianity in the matter of superstition:

> Is the Jewish religion then the only religion which can be accused of superstition? How stands the Christian religion . . . in this particular? Does not the Protestant accuse the Catholic of superstition—while the Catholic accuses the Protestant of impiety? Does not one sect of the Protestant Church accuse the other of idle ceremonies and mockeries, while it retorts in return upon its accuser for a want of proper decorum and respect?[10]

Indeed, it was these divisions among Christians that actually gave an advantage to Judaism over Christianity. "Tobit" averred that there was only one version of Judaism while there were many versions of Christianity. If consistency is the test of truth,

> is it not more natural to believe, that the various Christian sects now existing, together with the various other sects which shall grow out of them in every succeeding age, shall after innumerable divisions and subdivisions, unite in one faith—and that faith be the religion of the Jews, than that the Jews should be converted to believe in the doctrines of Christianity, while it is disputed by so many expounders, and gives birth to passions even diametrically opposite to those inculcated by Christ himself?[11]

The identity of Tobit is unknown. However, his claim that Frey's missionary work violated the spirit of American religious toleration and his criticism of Christianity for its multiplicity of sects and its doctrinal controversies are similar to arguments used by free thinkers.

Tobit's *Letters* was followed four years later by the appearance of another work which attacked the missionaries in even harsher tones. The name of the book was *Israel Vindicated*. The identity of its author is not certain. The title page designates the author as "An Israelite." The book has been attributed to Abraham Collins, the New York Jewish printer who published it, or to George Houston, the non-Jewish writer and editor of the literary magazine, *Minerva*. Recently, the probability of Houston's authorship of *Israel Vindicated* has received new support. It has been suggested that Houston, a free thinker who had attained a reputation for his views even before he had come to America from his native England, received the active support of American Jews in the publication of *Israel Vindicated*. The book sharply attacked the missionary activities of the ASMCJ and claimed that they undermined the legal equality of America's Jews. The major thrust of the book was an attack on the authenticity of the New Testament and on Christian beliefs. American Jews in 1820 saw in Houston's defense of religious toleration and in his assault on Christian religious beliefs a proper and articulate answer to the missionaries. However, they were as yet unwilling to enter openly into religious polemics with Christians. Although *Israel Vindicated* contained some disparaging remarks about Talmudic Judaism, the Jews chose the cautious path of collaborating with a freethinker and having his book serve as their weapon against the missionaries.[12]

Regardless of the authorship of *Israel Vindicated,* and the probability of a temporary antimissionary alliance between Jews and the freethinker George Houston, the American Jewish community soon produced its own authentically Jewish response to the ASMCJ. In March, 1823, just three years after the publication of *Israel Vindicated,* the first issue of the first American Jewish newspaper appeared. The paper was called *The Jew,* and its editor was Solomon Henry Jackson.[13]

Jackson played an active role in New York Jewish affairs until his death on February 13, 1846. Born in England, he came to America around 1787 and settled in Pike County, Pennsylvania. There he married Helen Miller, the daughter of a Presbyterian minister. They had five children, all of whom were raised as Jews. After his wife's death, Jackson moved to New York. In March, 1823 he began publication of *The Jew* which came out in twenty-four monthly issues through March, 1825. In addition, Jackson made several other literary contributions to American Jewish history. In 1826, he published the first American Jewish prayerbook in both Hebrew and English. Jackson himself prepared the English translation. In the same year, Jackson declared his intention to produce a new literal English translation of the Pentateuch that would be noncontroversial and would be of use to members of all religious denominations. He even appealed to the Episcopalian bishop of New York, John Henry Hobart, to become a sponsor. The project, however, was never completed. A little more than a decade later, Jackson published the first American edition of the Passover services in Hebrew and English.[14]

In addition to these literary activities, Jackson also played a significant role in the communal and religious life of New York Jewry. In 1825 he was one of the founders of the Hevra Hinuch Nearim which soon developed into B'nai Jeshurun congregation. He was also active in the establishment of the Anshe Chesed and Shaarei Zedek synagogues. Jackson served a number of New York synagogues as clerk, a position of some power in those days, which consisted of secretarial and bookkeeping responsibilities. In 1837 he became president of the Zeire Hazon Society, an organization whose goal was to settle German Jewish immigrants on cooperative agricultural settlements. Jackson made his living as a printer. He was the first Jewish printer in New York, and during the 1830's he enjoyed a near monopoly on printing for New York synagogues.

The Jew represents a new stage in American Jewish self assertion. This first Jewish newspaper to be published in America did not provide its readers with information on current affairs in the world, national or local Jewish communities, nor did it present Jewish cultural material. Its purpose was quite narrow: to confront and rebut the ASMCJ and its periodical Israel's Advocate. It is important that the first American Jewish newspaper was a defensive instrument against the missionaries, for it shows the threat to their security that American Jews perceived in the missionary endeavor. Jackson, who possessed a fair amount of Jewish learning, felt that the missionary activity was a form of anti-Semitism and had to be confronted head-on. American Jews could defend themselves and, according to Jackson, had an inherent right to do so based on the principle of freedom of expression. Previously American Jews had depended either upon works imported from Europe or upon American non-Jewish opponents of the missionaries. Koul Jacob was a work that had been produced in England. The author of Tobit's Letters was non-Jewish. The Jewish authorship of Israel Vindicated is doubtful. Indeed, if it had been written by George Houston at the behest of the Jews, that would demonstrate that the Jews in 1820 still did not feel secure enough to engage in a direct confrontation with the missionaries. The Jew undertook this task with vigor under an editor who sought to hide neither his name nor his Jewishness.

Jackson based his endeavor on the right of every American to freedom of speech and freedom of religion. Those in the Jewish community who believed that his writing might arouse Christian antagonism were counseling the way of retreat and defeat. Jackson was a confrontationalist in his attitude towards Christianity. He displayed a strong anti-Christian animus. He never used the word "Christian" in The Jew, preferring instead to write " . . . ian." In 1829, he strongly condemned a New York Jewish charity for accepting money from Christians, stating "It is not allowed to accept charity from them." To those New York Jews who urged caution, Jackson responded in the preface to the first issue of *The Jew:*

> . . . caution is now fear, and instead of being a virtue, is in truth a weakness. In the present enlightened age, not to defend Judaism would be considered a tacit acknowledgement that it was indefensible, or at least that we thought so. Not to defend our character as a people, as Jews, by repelling detraction, would be a dereliction of duty, and might be considered as a proof either that we had not a character worth defending, or that we despised the good opinion of our fellow citizens and of the world . . . [15]

Jackson pointed to a number of past Jewish polemicists who had defended Judaism against Christian attacks and who had not suffered for their efforts, including: Isaac of Troki, Yom Tov Lippman Mullhausen, David Levy, Jacob Nikelsburger and Isaac Orobio de Castro. Of these, only the last had experienced danger because of his polemical writings. David Levy and Jacob Nikelsburger, both of whom had lived in England, wrote their works in English. It would be insulting to America, argued Jackson, to think Americans less tolerant or enlightened than Englishmen.[16]

Jackson's anti-missionary campaign consisted of three elements: 1) a defense of Jews and Judaism against the misrepresentations of the missionaries and of *Israel's Advocate,* 2) an attack on both the motives and methods of the ASMCJ, and 3) a polemical assault against Christianity.

Jackson felt that one of his major tasks was to defend the good name of the Jewish people against the slanders of *Israel's Advocate.* He ridiculed the missionary periodical and held it up to contempt. Despite his pledge that *The Jew* would maintain a tone of moderation and would never use offensive or derisive language, Jackson's characterization of *Israel's Advocate* was harsh and bitter. It was, he wrote, made up of "Ends and scraps of bad composition," was "barren of anything like argument," reflected a "slightly covered enmity towards Israel," and contained "lame attempts at misrepresentations of the Jewish religion." While these attempts at misrepresentation may have been lame, they were nevertheless a source of both outrage and danger as far as Jackson was concerned. Some of his sharpest barbs were directed against articles in *Israel's Advocate* that purported to describe Jewish habits and attitudes. The June, 1823 issue of *The Jew* contained a commentary by Jackson on the first annual report of the ASMCJ that had been issued a month earlier. In that report, Reverend Alexander McCleod, minister of the First Reformed Presbyterian Church in New York and the

ASMCJ's Secretary for Foreign Correspondence, stated that Jews destroyed Christian tracts and abused converts to Christianity. Jackson considered these charges defamatory and feared that they would help to create a gap between the Christian and Jewish communities in America. Christian missionary societies distributed thousands of religious tracts among Jews, but this had not led many Jews to convert. According to Jackson, the missionaries falsely attributed the failure of their tracts to win many converts to the hostility of the Jewish community. The missionary literature failed, not because the Jews destroyed the tracts, but because the arguments presented in them were weak and unconvincing. Jackson dismissed McCleod's charge that the Jews publicly vilified converts. Jews would not dare do this in Europe even if they wanted to, and there was no record of this kind of behavior in New York. On the contrary, Jackson claimed to know of instances where converts in New York were able to maintain friendly relationships with their Jewish relatives and friends. McCleod had portrayed an attitude of hostility towards Christians on the part of Jews. That, for Jackson, was defamatory and would harm the Jews.[17]

On another occasion, Jackson quoted an article from *Israel's Advocate* that had described the hostility of the Jews to the convert Joseph Wolf. He referred to the missionary periodical as the "Adversary of Israel" for printing material that could only result in arousing animosity against the Jews within the Christian community. Although he would continue to decry such misrepresentations, Jackson expressed pessimism about being able to change the situation. He concluded that Christian religious leaders, pretending love for the Jews "have ever soured the mind of their poor flocks against their innocent Jew neighbors, causing all the persecutions that have occurred from the first establishment of Christianity to the present day, and this I fear is inherent in the spirit of Christianity; it must be deplored, but I fear cannot be altered."[18]

In another column, Jackson not only railed against a misrepresentation of Jewish attitudes, but also sought to identify those attitudes with American ones. When the Albany clergyman, John McDonald, described the mass suicide at Masada as an act born "more of the desperation, the despair of the coward, than the courage of the collected and brave," Jackson appealed to enlightened American opinion to reject this calumny. He identified the sacrifice at Masada with American ideals: "The Jews fought for liberty; for political independence; for personal freedom." The Jews, like the Americans, were a people that valued liberty and would make great sacrifices for it.[19]

In addition to countering the misinformation about Jews that the missionaries were spreading, Jackson also attacked the ASMCJ by questioning its methods and its motives. It was not the Jews who displayed ill will or bigotry in their relations with Christians, asserted Jackson. Rather, the hostility that existed was a result of the unethical means used by the missionaries in their attempt to convert Jews. The missionaries had to use these means because they could not convert Jews through argumentation. With more feeling than accuracy, Jackson wrote that there had never been a Jew who had converted to Christianity out of religious conviction. Whatever meager success the missionaries had enjoyed resulted from their bribing Jews to convert.

Jackson focussed much of his criticism on the ASMCJ's plan to establish a settlement in America where European converts could live. In Jackson's view, this was nothing more than a grand scheme to bribe Jews to convert. The settlement project was the idea of John David Marc, a German Jew who had converted in 1817 and served as missionary of the London Society in Frankfurt. There he was aided in his work by Count Adalbert von der Recke, a young nobleman. In 1819, Marc wrote to Frey proposing the establishment of a settlement in America for converted Jews. After some initial hesitation, Frey accepted Marc's idea and it became the basis upon which the ASMCJ was founded. In 1821, under the urging of Marc, Count von der Recke established a settlement for converts at his estate in Duesselthal which was to serve as a training school for converts who would be sent to the American settlement.[20]

The professed goal of the ASMCJ was, therefore, not to convert American Jews, but to provide a refuge for European converts who had severed their connections with the Jewish community but who had not been fully accepted within the Christian community. Jackson, however, viewed this as a means of bribing Jews to convert, and also felt that the settlement scheme allowed the ASMCJ to hide its real goal which was to convert American Jews. Indeed, the original name proposed for the ASMCJ had been the American Society for Colonizing and Evangelizing the Jews. This name clearly proclaimed the twofold program of the founders of the organization. It was only when the New York state legislature balked at granting incorporation to an organization formed specifically for religious purposes that the name was changed to ASMCJ and the founding of the settlement was declared to be the goal of the organization. As far as Jackson was concerned, however, the change in name and the emphasis on the settlement plan could not hide the real intent of the ASMCJ.

In the opening issue of *The Jew*, Jackson challenged the ASMCJ to forego its plan for settling European converts in its proposed settlement and instead to devote its energies to the task of converting American Jews.[21] The ASMCJ could not agree to this, wrote Jackson, because American Jews were not impoverished and, therefore, would not be ready prey to the material blandishments of settling in the colony. Jackson taunted the ASMCJ for its concentration on European converts and its seeming lack of interest in American Jews:

> Are we not as interesting as Poles? We understand your language—it is, indeed, our own; we are in a manner one people. We are also the children of Abraham, descended from the same stock as the Polish and German Jews;—indeed, many of us are Poles; many of us are Germans. Why not, then, undertake us? Why not try to convert us? You will have no occasion to manufacture Hebrew tracts, at a vast expense, and which you do not yourselves understand; a little plain English will answer your purpose with us.

The ASMCJ, however, would not accept this challenge, according to Jackson, because it realized that it would lose more than it would gain. Addressing the ASMCJ, Jackson asked:

> Are you afraid you will be paid in your own coin? That you will receive as good as you send; and that when you gain one, (if you should gain any) you might lose one hundred? You, in that case, must be conscious of the weakness of your cause, and you fear and avoid the trial.

In the June, 1823 issue of *The Jew*, Jackson added a new element to his attack on the settlement plan when he argued that it would impose a financial hardship on the American Jewish community. The settlement would attract from Europe those Jews "who hold that God owes them a living, and the world must afford it for them." They would soon tire of the novelty of America, and the work regimen that was to be part of life at the settlement would not suit them. Finding no profit in their new religion, these opportunists would return to Judaism. Jackson described the situation that this would create:

> And now comes our trouble, now our benevolence is to be taxed; droves of apostatized Jews will be coming back to our cities, crying in sincerity Laman Hasham, Laman Harachamim; (this no Jew can withstand) we repent, we repent, and repent they truly will in sackcloth and ashes, for they will have nothing but rags to wear, and hardly anything but bread to eat. There will be no entering our synagogues but over the bodies of prostate miserables; . . . thus will you empty Europe of paupers and inundate our cities with them. Thus, gentlemen, you would take the comfortable morsel out of our mouths and out of the mouths of our children, and oblige us to divide it with the beggars of Europe . . . [22]

A few months later, Jackson attempted to make the financial argument more relevant to the Christian community by suggesting that the proposed settlement would prove to be a financial burden not only to

American Jews, but would also engulf the ASMCJ in a financial quagmire. The settlers would lack occupational skills and would require training. In the meantime, the ASMCJ would have to support them. The ASMCJ would do well to follow the example of the London Society, which had refused to provide financial support to Count von der Recke's settlement. Jackson cited a letter from a student at the seminary for converts at Stockhamp that had been published in *Israel's Advocate* as proof for his contention that the proposed settlement would be a financial drain on the ASMCJ. The letter had been addressed to Bernard Jadownicky, a Polish Jew who had been converted by Marc, and sent by him to Count von der Recke's farm at Duesselthal. In 1822, Count von der Recke dispatched Jadownicky to America in order to give the leaders of the ASMCJ a first hand account of the progress of the count's settlement. The letter proposed that the ASMCJ pay the travelling expenses for one hundred poor converts to come to America. Jackson ridiculed the proposal, pointing out the enormous financial cost involved. Moreover, warned Jackson, the travel expenses of the converts was only the tip of the iceberg. The settlement would perpetuate a kind of welfare dole for the converts. Receiving financial support from the ASMCJ, the converts would have no incentive to leave the settlement and try to support themselves. It would be more sensible, wrote Jackson, for the converts to learn a trade in Germany. Then, if they chose to come to America, they would be in a position to find employment and would be a burden neither to the ASMCJ nor to society at large.[23]

As part of his campaign against the ASMCJ, Jackson took aim at the converts employed by the ASMCJ and tried to show that they were not sincere converts. He described Erasmus Simon, a Dutch convert who had arrived in America in 1823 and who was employed by the ASMCJ as a fund-raising agent, as an opportunist who used his conversion as a path not to spiritual fulfillment but to material security. Jadownicky was a puppet in the hands of the ASMCJ. Unfamiliar with American ways and not yet fluent in the English language, he read speeches that had been written for him by the ASMCJ which he did not understand. Jackson, however, reserved his sharpest criticism for Frey. He had met Frey on at least two occasions. Once, in either 1820 or 1821, Jackson had visited Frey at his home, eaten with him there and spent the better part of a day discussing religious matters. The second meeting took place shortly thereafter when Frey called upon Jackson. Both meetings apparently took place in a cordial atmosphere although the two men were unable to resolve their differences. Jackson used the pages of *The Jew* to attack Frey as a charlatan who was using the ASMCJ as a means to earn a living. He advised the board of directors of the ASMCJ to examine closely the career of Frey. If they did so, they would see that Frey, as a missionary, had moved from one position to another basing his moves on where he felt he had most to gain materially. Now he had brought the Christian public in America "into a pack of trouble with a western settlement for Jewish converts, who he knows well will be unmanageable." Meanwhile, Frey himself had no intention of settling in the colony because he would never allow himself to fall into a life of obscurity and hard work. Rather than settle in the colony, Frey would sooner return to Judaism even though he would not gain any profit by doing so.[24]

While Jackson attacked the character and questioned the motives of converts like Simon, Jadownicky, and Frey, who worked for the ASMCJ, he did not impugn the integrity of its Christian directors. Arguing that the ASMCJ's missionary activity was misguided, that it reflected an anti-semitic bias, that it spread misinformation about Jews and Judaism, and that it was harming Jewish-Christian relations in America, Jackson nevertheless refrained from personal attacks on ASMCJ leaders. He did not, however, refrain from publishing an article questioning their real goal.

The November, 1823 issue of *The Jew* carried the charge that the ASMCJ was trying to impose Presbyterianism as the established religion in America. This charge, accompanied by no real substantiation, was meant to discredit the ASMCJ and to deprive it of some of its considerable support within the Christian community. It may well be another example of Jews using the arguments of free thinkers to bolster their antimissionary protest. We have already noted the threat that some Christian groups as well as free thinkers felt that missionary and other benevolent societies posed to religious liberty in America. Separation of church and state was a fundamental American principle, one that conformed to the reality of American religious life in which a variety of different sects existed side by side with none having sufficient numerical weight to assume a position of legal domination. The article evoked the threat of an "un-American" plot on the part of the Presbyterian leadership of the ASMCJ to undo the country's religious balance. It warned that while Jews might be the first victims of this plot, they would not be the only ones to suffer from it. American society would be torn apart by religious strife.

> The fall of the Jew is but the preliminary stroke intended as a token to the establishment of an order of things in this country, which (God avert) will cause many a bleeding heart. We are but a small people here, and our oppression would be accounted of but little note in the scale of society in the U.S.; still our fall would be the prelude to the establishment of some one predominant sect, or rather, for that state of affairs, much worse than

such predominance, the strife for the mastery; when father will be mar-
shalled against son, the son against the father; the mother against the
daughter, the daughter against the mother, that state wherein a man's
worst enemies will be those of his own household.[25]

There is no evidence to support this charge against the ASMCJ.
Although a significant number of its leaders were Presbyterian, others
were members of the Dutch Reformed and Congregationalist churches.
The article tried to substantiate its allegation by citing the fact that the
ASMCJ did not publish and distribute tracts among the Jews although
this was one of its stated purposes, and that it had not answered the
charges and arguments that Jackson had levelled against it in *The Jew.*
The article's author saw this as an indication that the real interest of
the ASMCJ was not the conversion of the Jews. These things, however, can be explained by the fact that the ASMCJ was preoccupied
with its settlement project and raising funds for it. Its publication, *Israel's Advocate,* addressed a Christian rather than a Jewish audience and
tried to convince it of the necessity and feasibility of converting the
Jews. Its missionaries—Frey, Simon, and Jadownicy—spoke to Christian audiences attempting to elicit their support for the cause. At this
stage in its development, the ASMCJ directed more of its energies towards winning support within the Christian community than in gaining converts. This, too, explains why the ASMCJ did not respond to
Jackson. *Israel's ADvocate* explained that the ASMCJ wanted to avoid
religious controversy. It was interested in converting the Jews, not in
engaging in religious controversy or dialogue with them. It may well
be that Jackson published the sensationalist charge against the Presbyterians not only to discredit the ASMCJ, but also in order to force it to
take notice of him and to answer him.[26]

Jackson did not accept the silence of the ASMCJ and *Israel's Advocate* as an attempt to avoid religious controversy, but chose instead to
interpret it as tacit acquiescence. *Israel's Advocate* did not respond to
him because it could not. Jackson placed himself in the company of
previous Jewish polemicists who had silenced their opponents.

> The philosophical, the learned, the wise, the potent Dr. Priestly has been
> silenced, together with all the clergy of England, by David Levy. The
> Reverend J. S. C. F Frey has been awe-struck by M. Nikelsburg, and even
> myself, the least of the little ones, and as to abilities, the humblest of my
> fellows and brothers, have literally silenced *Israel's Advocate* . . . [27]

The aggravating silence of *Israel's Advocate* notwithstanding, Jackson
filled the pages of *The Jew* with anti-Christian polemics. Indeed, it is
as a polemicist that he may have made his most noteworthy contribution to American Jewry. He is the first American Jewish writer to

present some of the main arguments of the Jewish literary polemical tradition to the American public, while at the same time adding a few touches of his own to that tradition.

Jackson was familiar with Jewish polemical literature. He quoted from the writings of Isaac of Troki, Moses Mendelssohn, David Levy, and Jacob Nikelsberger. He was also aware of the works of Saul Levy Morteira and Isaac Orobio de Castro, and possessed a copy of the Amsterdam edition of Yom Tov Lippman Mullhausen's *Sepher Nitzahon*. Interestingly, however, he did not mention *Israel Vindicated*. Jackson was undoubtedly aware of this work, which had been published in New York in 1820, and which had created a stir because of its strong anti-Christian tone. Although *The Jew* also contained sharp polemical attacks against Christianity, it is likely that Jackson did not want to be associated with a work that had already aroused controversy. Perhaps, even more importantly, he did not want to be associated with a book that had been authored by a freethinker. Jackson himself had been a freethinker in his early days, but later in life had returned to religious Judaism. *The Jew* was to be the response of authentic Judaism to the arguments of the missionaries.[28]

Jackson himself penned much of the polemics carried in *The Jew*. However, he also published a number of features that were polemical in character. One of these was a series of letters by a correspondent "Abraham." These letters took the form of a running commentary on a speech delivered by Reverend Truman Marsh on April 14, 1823, to the Litchfield, Mass. Auxiliary Society for Meliorating the Condition of the Jews. "Abraham" denounced Marsh for professing kind feelings towards the Jews and criticizing past persecutions while at the same time portraying the Jews as ignorant, possessing a false zeal, and the objects of God's wrath. Such vilification bespoke not friendship but anti-Semitism, and, charged "Abraham," were it not for the liberal institutions of America, Marsh would "go as great lengths in reviling, abusing and persecuting us, as the Europeans, whom you charge with being influenced . . . by 'prejudice and bigotry.' " "Abraham" then proceeded to a critical analysis of Christian beliefs. He contested the messianic claim for Jesus because Jesus was not of Davidic descent, the genealogies in Matthew 1 and Luke 3 notwithstanding. Moreover, whereas the messiah was supposed to be a human being, Christians claimed that Jesus was a divinity. The strongest objection, however, was that neither during his own lifetime nor anytime afterwards did the peace and harmony that the messiah was supposed to bring to the world come. "Abraham" then turned his attack against the authority of the New Testament and the historicity of Jesus. No mention is made of Jesus in the writings of Tacitus, Philo or Josephus. The Christian argument that the belief of millions of people in Jesus was proof of his historicity and divinity was fallacious because if the number of believers was to settle the question, "it must follow that the idols of the Chinese, of the natives of Hindostan, of the Persians . . . would all have equally well founded claims with your Jesus to be acknowledged the true and only Deity that ought to be adored." In fact, the only evidence for the historicity of Jesus is the New Testament, and that source, according to "Abraham," was unreliable. The four gospels were composed long after the events they describe, and they are merely four accounts out of a much larger number that existed in the early Christian centuries. Moreover, the contradictions between the four gospels removed from them any claim of being divine revelations.[29]

More important than Abraham's letters was a second polemical feature that Jackson serialized in *The Jew,* from July, 1823 through February, 1825. This work, entitled "Dea's Letters," appeared without introduction and without comment by Jackson. The *Letters* were, in fact, the greater portion of a book entitled *A Series of Letters on the Evidences of Christianity* authored by Benjamin Dias Fernandes. Fernandes was an eighteenth century merchant of Portuguese origin who migrated from Jamaica to England where he wrote his *Letters.* It is not known how Jackson came across the manuscript, for the book was not published until 1859, when Isaac Leeser published it in Philadelphia. Leeser, whose interest in the *Letters* was first aroused when he read it in the pages of *The Jew,* traced its history and discovered that only two manuscript copies of the work had existed prior to its appearance in *The Jew.* One manuscript copy had made its way into the hands of Solomon Simson shortly before the American Revolution. Jackson's version of the *Letters* was based on the copy of that manuscript that had been made by Simson's clerk, a Mr. Jacobs. In the late eighteenth century, the Simson family attempted to publish the *Letters* in Philadelphia, but were unable to find a printer who was willing to undertake the job. Presumably the members of the Simson family made the work available to Jackson for inclusion in *The Jew.*[30]

Through the serialization of the *Letters* in *The Jew,* Jackson made available to American Jewish readers many of the arguments that had been developed in the body of Jewish polemical literature. Fernandes had used as his sources Isaac of Troki's *Hizuk Emunah,* the most important late medieval Jewish polemical work; Saul Levy Morteira's *Tratado de la Verdad de la Ley;* and Isaac orobio de Castro's *Prevenciones Divinas Contra la Vana Idolatria de las Gentes.* Fernandes' was a thorough and systematic assault on Christianity. He challenged the authority and accuracy of the New Testament; refuted the christological interpretations of Old Testament messianic prophecies; demonstrated that Matthew had misunderstood and misapplied Old Testament verses; disputed the messianic qualifications of Jesus; argued against the Christian view of the sinfulness of man and the Christian method of obtaining atonement, and attacked the belief in the trinity as an absurdity. By reproducing the Letters, Jackson presented to the American Jewish public a coherent and forceful attack on the fundamental beliefs of Christianity. In so doing, he demonstrated his belief that the best defense was a good offense. He had argued that if the missionaries hoped to win Jewish converts, they would have to prove the superiority of Christianity as a religious system. Now he had presented to the Jewish community a sharply reasoned attack against Christianity, and had thus given to it a powerful weapon with which it could defend itself against the missionaries and their arguments.[31]

Jackson added his own polemics to those of "Abraham" and Fernandes. His tone was always challenging and often abrasive. Some of his polemical writings were aimed at refuting Christian polemics published in Israel's Advocate. On four occasions Jackson used the pages of The Jew to answer addresses to the Jews that had been published in Israel's Advocate, which contained Christian explanations of Biblical sections that were the subject of differing interpretations by Jews and Christians, and which presented reasons why the Jews should convert. By responding to these articles, Jackson hoped to open a dialogue with their Christian authors.

The first article to draw Jackson's comment was an address "To the Jews," published originally in Israel's Advocate in January, 1824, and reproduced by Jackson in the May, 1824 issue of The Jew. The author of the address, identifying himself as "Camden," presented a series of questions on Jewish messianic and eschatological beliefs. Jackson answered these questions and complimented "Camden" on his moderate tone and fairness. He expressed his hope that this would be the beginning of honest argumentation between Jews and Christians and declared:

> This is as it should be. This is the only legitimate method . . . Christians can take to convince, and consequently to convert Jews. We hail it as a promising sign of the commencement of a more liberal method of procedure on the part of our opponents . . . [32]

Jackson's hopes for a dialogue were disappointed. "Camden" did not respond to his invitation to keep the discussion going. Months later, a correspondent in Israel's Advocate complimented Jackson for the "friendly spirit" and candor of his response to "Camden," but explained that "Camden" was "indisposed to reply to objections made by the Jews because controversy is liable to be unpleasant and do more harm than good." For his part, Jackson interpreted "Camden's" silence as an admission of defeat. Jackson's comments on the other three articles also failed to elicit responses.[33]

Jackson's own polemical writing was a regular feature in The Jew. His most extensive polemics were his critique of the gospel of Matthew and his commentary on the fifty-second and fifty-third chapters of Isaiah. The former was primarily a restatement of the Jewish argument that Matthew had misused Old Testament verses because he did not understand them. The latter was a rebuttal of the Christian identification of the "suffering servant" of these texts with Jesus. After presenting the objections of Fernandes and Nikelsburger to the Christian explanation of these chapters, Jackson published his own fifteen page interpretation in the last two issues of The Jew. In typical exegetical form, he saw in the prophet's words allusions to his own time as well as a view of the future. Thus, for example, when the prophet spoke of those who ruled over the Jewish people and continually blasphemed God's name (52:5), this was a reference to the Christians who identified Jesus with God. On a triumphalistic note, Jackson proclaimed that in the future the Christians would admit the falseness of their doctrines and acknowledge the truth of Judaism. In accordance with one of the traditional Jewish interpretations of Isaiah 53, Jackson identified the Jewish people as the suffering servant. Until that time in the future when the Christians would acknowledge the truth of Judaism, they were being used as God's instrument to inflict suffering on the Jews. This suffering was a necessary forerunner to Israel's eventual vindication and exaltation. Jews should therefore, understand and patiently bear Christian persecution for it was all part of God's plan. In the face of Christian hostility, Jews should always act with candor toward Christians and be ready to explain to them in a forthright manner why Jews had to remain loyal to their faith. Jackson thus assured his Jewish readers that their continued faith in the religion of their fathers would not go unrewarded. The Jews were a small and despised people, but they would be vindicated for their loyalty to God and the suffering that that loyalty entailed. The arguments of the missionaries were baseless and rested on a faulty exegesis. No Jew who understood the Bible properly would fall prey to them. Instead he would remain loyal to his religion with the knowledge that someday God would prove him right.[34]

In October, 1824, Jackson announced that The Jew would cease publication at the end of the current volume. He explained this by claiming that the paper had accomplished its main goal: "Religious publications are now conducted more liberal than heretofore." By this, Jackson apparently meant that The Jew had broadened the horizons of the American religious press. However, in the last issue of *The Jew* Jackson indicated that financial difficulties were the real reason. The paper undoubtedly had been opposed by some Jews who recoiled from its strident tone and felt that it could provoke an antisemitic backlash in the Christian community. The paper must have had a limited circulation. There is no independent substantiation of Jackson's claim that *The Jew* enjoyed a larger circulation than *Israel's Advocate,* whose readership was estimated at two thousand. At a time when the Jewish population of New York was still less than one thousand and when the total Jewish population of the country was around three thousand, this claim seems exaggerated. If true, it would mean that *The Jew* probably had more Christian readers than Jewish ones, an unlikely occurrence given the lack of response evoked by *The Jew* within the Christian community.[35]

Despite its short life, *The Jew* marked a significant milestone in American Jewish history. It is the first major direct effort on the part of American Jewry to counter the American Christian missionary impulse. Missionary work was a popular cause in early nineteenth century America. Some even believed that America was the divinely appointed instrument to bring about the conversation of Israel. Jackson thus set himself against a popular impulse. In so doing, he fortified America's small Jewish community with the means to defend itself against missionary arguments by providing it with the literature of the Jewish polemical tradition. By justifying his endeavor on the principles of freedom of speech and of conscience, Jackson insisted that American Jews should make use of the civil rights guaranteed them by the United States constitution to protect their interests, even in such a controversial area as religious argumentation. He boldly pointed out some of the anti-Jewish statements and themes used by the missionaries. By exposing and countering misstatements about Jews and Judaism, Jackson served as a one man antidefamation agency. In all of this, Jackson was a worthy predecessor of nineteenth century American Jewry's later defenders and polemicists.

3 Isaac Leeser:
A Traditionalist's Approach

The most outstanding nineteenth century traditionalist American Jewish leader who wrote on Christianity was Isaac Leeser. Born in Westphalia in 1806, Leeser was orphaned and moved to Dulmen near Muenster and there received his Jewish education at the hands of rabbis Benjamin Cohen and Abraham Sutro. He studied secular subjects at the Muenster Academy, a Catholic school where several of his teachers were Jesuits. In 1824, Leeser immigrated to America where he settled in Richmond and worked for his uncle. He came to the attention of Philadelphia's congregation Mikveh Israel in 1829 after responding in print to the antisemitic statements contained in an article that had been published in the *London Quarterly*. The congregation invited Leeser to serve as its hazzan, and he did so until 1850 when he resigned because of differences with the congregation over his extra-synagogal community activities.[1]

Despite a difficult life that was marked by illness, the death of a brother with whom he was close, his failure to marry, and an unimpressive physical bearing described by his friend Rebecca Gratz as "awkward and ugly," Leeser poured his determined energy into strengthening American Jewry. During his public career of nearly four decades, Leeser contributed significantly to the development of American Jewish life in a number of areas. In the area of Jewish education, he helped to establish the Philadelphia Hebrew Sunday school, and was instrumental in the opening of Maiminides College in 1867, an abortive attempt to establish an American rabbinical seminary. His activities in the area of journalism included the founding, in 1845, of the first American Jewish Publication Society whose goal was to disseminate Jewish knowledge to the American Jewish community. His journal, the *Occident,* which ran from 1843 to 1868, was the first major American Jewish periodical. Its purpose, too, was to spread Jewish knowledge and also to counter antisemitic sentiments. Among Lesser's literary endeavors, the most significant was his translation of the Bible

(1853) which he undertook in order to provide American Jews with an English translation of the Bible that was free of Christological overtones. In the area of liturgy, Leeser produced English translations of both the Portuguese (Sephardic) prayer book (1837) as well as the German (Ashkenazic) one (1848). All in all, a remarkable list of achievements in religious and cultural life which laid the foundation for future growth of the community.[2]

Among Leeser's most urgent concerns were the spread of Jewish knowledge and the safeguarding of Jewish rights in America. American Jewry in the mid-nineteenth century was still a tender shoot acclimating to the soil of a free and open society. American Jews enjoyed full legal equality with the exception of the right to hold office in certain states. Yet, Leeser expressed a certain ambiguity about American freedom. On the one hand, he contrasted the favorable status of American Jews with the less favorable conditions of Jewish life that still prevailed in most parts of Europe, and frequently expressed his gratitude for the freedoms enjoyed by American Jews. On the other hand, those freedoms were neither complete nor fully secure. Leeser spoke out against the remaining bars to Jewish office holding and battled against what he perceived to be infringements of Jewish legal equality, such as the Sunday laws and prayer in public schools. At times he seemed disheartened and even alarmed. When the United States failed to pressure the Swiss government to alter the terms of an American-Swiss commercial treaty that allowed Swiss cantons to refuse entry to American Jews, Leeser wrote that "it would appear that we are too unimportant as a class to render it worth the while of the conservators of the liberty of the state to prevent our rights being damaged, provided only those of the majority remain intact."[3] More alarming to Leeser than the seeming uncertainty of freedom in America, was the high toll in assimilation and the breakdown of traditional Jewish religious observance that freedom exacted. In the past, Jews had drawn closer together in the face of persecution. Now, however, in a more liberal age, Jews were becoming less observant. He warned that the key to Jewish well-being did not lie in the enlarged liberty of the new era. The better treatment accorded to Jews in recent times did not mean that Christians had learned to love Jews. Rather, it had become unfashionable, in the modern world, to persecute people because of their religious beliefs. Men now tolerated each other, at least outwardly. There was, however, no certainty that the fashion would not change once again. Instead of viewing present Jewish liberty as the product of a drastic change in the history of mankind, Leeser thought it wiser to understand it simply as a gift from God.[4]

Leeser's concerns about American freedom along with his strong traditionalist bent in religious matters help to explain his strong attachment to the idea of the restoration of the Jewish people to the land of Israel. He saw no contradiction between his gratitude and loyalty to America and his desire to see a Jewish state restored. Such a state would be a place "where the Jew would not and need not receive his rights as a favor, where there would be no talk of toleration, where there would be no fear of abridgement of privileges, where, in short, the Israelite would be free, not because the stranger grants it, but because his laws, his religion, his faith, constitute him a part and parcel of the state itself." Under the best of circumstances, even in free America, Jews who wanted to observe their religion fully could not hold office and faced difficulties in commercial life because of the problems posed by Sabbath observance. Leeser lamented the willingness of so many American Jews to sacrifice their religious practices in order to attain worldly gain. A restored Jewish state would obviate the need for such sacrifices. Asserting that Jews could be good American citizens and obey the law of the land, Leeser nevertheless maintained that opposition to the restoration of a Jewish state "is asserting that it is preferable to expose us to constant diminutions, to the caprice of nations, and the will of tyrants, to the end of time."[5]

For Leeser, America was the most beneficent land in which Jews could find a home. However, the liberties which she gave to the Jews were neither fully assured nor free of dangers to Judaism. Leeser fought to see those liberties guaranteed and the dangers they posed to Judaism reduced. America, however, could be no substitute for a restored Jewish state. Leeser thus assumed an outsider stance in his view of the proper Jewish relationship to American culture and society. America was home, but from Leeser's theological perspective, it was a temporary one. While America provided the opportunity for a free Jewish expression, its national life was Christian, in fact if not in law. This outsider stance is an important key to understanding Leeser's anti-Christian polemics.[6]

Despite, or perhaps because of, his qualms about Jewish life in America, Leeser constantly strove to provide a more solid footing for the American Jewish community. For him, the dangers of antisemitism and assimilation were compounded by two complementary factors. The first was the low level of Jewish knowledge among American Jews. The second was the constant misrepresentation of Judaism that was contained in the writings and statements of Christian writers and missionaries. These misrepresentations spread erroneous ideas about Judaism among the Christian population, and therefore constituted a potential source of antisemitism. In addition, they could cause confusion among Jews who had little knowledge of Judaism and thus make them easier prey for the missionaries. Much of Leeser's communal activity and literary output were aimed at overcoming Jewish ignorance and countering Christian misrepresentations of Judaism. His earliest work, and the one which he felt best expressed his views, *The Jews and the Mosaic Law* (1833), presents an explanation and justification of the traditional Jewish understanding of the Pentateuch. In his preface, Leeser states that he wrote the book in order to present a systematic and rational explanation of the Jewish religion that would counter Christian misunderstandings of Judaism, and also to show the fallacy of those Jews who were abandoning tradition in the false belief that the laws of Moses were no longer obligatory.[7] Leeser felt it essential to protect the good name of Judaism in order to insure that Jewish rights in America would not be undermined. In his mind, Jewish legal equality was intertwined with the acceptance of Judaism as a respectable religion.[8] In order for this to happen, American Jews had to be educated to a proud affirmation of their religious tradition, and Christians had to be corrected in their mistaken views of Judaism. This concern for attaining equality for Judaism in America provided the second key to understanding Leeser's statements on Christianity.

Leeser began his polemical career with self-professed reluctance and a seeming lack of confidence, despite the apparent help and coaching that he received from certain Richmond Jews. He bemoaned the lack of others in the American Jewish community to take up the struggle in defense of Judaism and decried the dearth of polemical works available to American Jewry.[9] Time and again Leeser emphasized that he was not writing to attack Christianity, but to give American Jews the means to defend their religion against the arguments of missionaries. On one occasion, he expressed a distaste for religious argumentation declaring it convinced no one to change his views and only served to arouse antagonism. He defined the defensive nature of his polemics when he stated that Jews did not have to refute the ideas of Christianity, because they based themselves on a system that predated Christianity. The burden, therefore, was upon Christianity to disprove Judaism. Clearly sensitive to the danger of fueling antisemitism, Leeser announced that he wished "not to attack the opinion of others, to inflict a wound upon a tender conscience which we may not be able to heal. . . . " Nevertheless, he warned his readers in the *Occident*: "We must not lose sight of the fact that we do not live in the midst of barbarous idolators . . . but amidst a highly civilized people, in many respects far better educated than we are, and in possession of the Scriptures no less than ourselves." The Christians, however, had their own beliefs and they sought to convert the Jews. Leeser recognized the problem that was created when two religions basing themselves on the same sacred scripture maintained opposing and mutually exclusive interpretations of that scripture. He understood the urge of every sincere Christian to convert the Jews because as long as the Jews did not convert, Christianity's claim to truth could not stand firm. This placed Leeser in a difficult position, for while he might not wish to attack Christianity, he felt that the Jews had to be instructed to understand the correctness of Judaism and to see the perversions in Christian Biblical interpretation.[10]

Although Leeser may have preferred the defensive posture of an apologist for Judaism to the more aggressive stance of a polemicist against Christianity, he could not maintain the rather fine line that separated the two positions. It is difficult to defend Judaism against the claims of Christianity without attacking those claims. The difficulties involved in Leeser's defensive posture became evident in his earliest forays into the arena of polemics.

Leeser's earliest polemical attempts came in response to antisemitic articles that had appeared in British journals. In 1829, encouraged by a group of prominent Richmond Jews, he published a rejoinder in the Richmond *Whig* to an antisemitic essay that had appeared in the London *Quarterly Review* and had been reprinted in America. Leeser's piece was followed by an exchange of letters with a Quaker correspondent which the *Whig* also published. In 1833, Leeser republished the essay along with the letters as the second part of his *The Jews and the Mosaic Law*. Eight years later, in 1841, Leeser published his *The Claims of the Jews to an Equality of Rights*. This work consisted of Leeser's letters that had been previously published in the Philadelphia *Gazette*. The letters had been occasioned by new antisemitic articles in British periodicals. Along with the letters, the *Claims* contained extracts from an offending article as well as Leeser's rebuttal. The British articles that had aroused Leeser's ire were attacks on the Jewish religion, its ethical standards, and the alleged unfitness of Jews to be free and equal members of society. They suggested conversion as the best solution to the Jewish problem. Although these articles had been published in Britain and were part of the current debate in that country over Jewish emancipation, Leeser felt that they posed a threat to the security of American Jews because they provided ammunition to anyone hostile to Jews. He therefore felt compelled to respond. In both of these early works, Leeser strikes a defensive pose; his concern is to refute the charges made against Jewish ethics and spirituality, and to expose the futility of the missionary endeavor. However, he found it impossible to remain defensive, and while he professed in his exchange with the Quaker that he would say as little as possible about Christianity, and that whatever he might say should "be considered as extorted from me in defense of my faith," his defense of Jewish ethics slid into a frontal attack on Christian ethics.[11]

By the time Leeser began publishing the *Occident* in 1843, and certainly by 1850, we note a change in his tone. We now find a more confident and aggressive combatant, boldly attacking Christian beliefs as he continues to staunchly defend Jewish ones. Instead of reluctance to engage in religious controversy with Christians, we find almost an eagerness to do so. Leeser filled the pages of the *Occident* with polemical articles by both Christian and Jewish spokesmen. He even granted that it would be all right for Jews to pay occasional visits to churches as long as they refrained from engaging in worship. Such visits would serve to familiarize Jews with Christian doctrines and arguments so that they could better defend Judaism. They would also demonstrate to Christians that Jews were not merely "blind believers" who were unwilling or afraid to hear the views of others. Leeser confidently exclaimed, "our religion is emphatically one that can bear the test of exposure and has millions of arguments to prove its truth and holiness."[12] It is not entirely clear what prompted this change in Leeser's approach. It may have been due to a growing maturity which yielded greater confidence as the years passed, or, it may have been stimulated by a sense of frustration with the continued activity of the missionaries and the threat that he felt they posed to American Jewry. In the face of his ongoing efforts to defend Judaism against its detractors, Leeser may have concluded that the best defense was a good offense. Whatever the reason for the change in Leeser's tone, it was clearly and perhaps best expressed in the controversy surrounding the invitation issued by the New York Synod of the Presbyterian Church to the Jews to convert.

The Synod issued its call in October, 1849, and Leeser published it in the January, 1850 edition of the *Occident* along with rejoinders by himself and Rabbi Wolf Schlessinger. The Presbyterians based their appeal to the Jews on the claim that the governmental structure of the Presbyterian church was fashioned after that of the Synagogue and that the Presbyterian church was, therefore, the true heir of the synagogue. As God's purpose in establishing the synagogue had been to spread His truth throughout the world, the Presbyterians were now facilitating this purpose through their churches, which they referred to as "Christian synagogues," and by distributing Bibles throughout the world. It was now time for the Jews to help the synagogue fulfill its mission by joining the Presbyterian church. Recognizing that the greatest objections that the Jews had against joining the Presbyterians were over doctrinal matters, the Presbyterian call made no attempt to convince the Jews of the correctness of Presbyterian theology but asked only that the Jews read the New Testament and then consider the validity of Presbyterian teachings. The latter part of the Presbyterian statement dealt with the problem of Jewish suffering. Here the Presbyterians found themselves caught on the horns of a dilemma created by the difficulty involved in maintaining a traditional Christian theological stance and, at the same time, trying to extend what they considered to be a friendly hand to the Jews. On the one hand, they justified Jewish suffering theologically as validation of the curses of the Old Testament applied to a sinful Israel. On the other hand, aware of Jewish sensibilities, they dissociated themselves somewhat from this stand by deploring the oppression of the Jews in the past and by claiming that the Presbyterians had never been guilty of persecuting Jews.[13]

Leeser took up the Presbyterian challenge with uncharacteristic relish. He dismissed the call to convert as "neither warranted by propriety nor common sense" because it had failed to provide any new or convincing arguments. The issue of church government was irrelevant since it was not the structural apparatus of the church that the Jews objected to in Christianity, but Christian doctrine. Then, assuming an assertive tone, Leeser turned the tables on the Presbyterians. He told them that they had things backwards. Instead of the Jews becoming Presbyterians, the Presbyterians would become Jews. He welcomed the fact that the Presbyterians had adopted the Jewish form of church government and expressed the hope that they would borrow more from Judaism. On other occasions Leeser had declared his belief that ultimately the Gentiles would realize the truth of Jewish monotheism. Then, however, he seemed to be merely expressing a conventionalized Jewish hope. This time, Leeser professed to be speaking in earnest as he proclaimed his triumphalistic hope:

> We say this in sober seriousness—we never jest on sacred subjects—and we mean what we say, that the world will be ultimately converted to our doctrines, and to the law in the manner the Lord will clearly reveal it for the gentiles . . . [14]

This future vindication of Judaism would come about through the spirit of inquiry awakened by Jewish-Christian encounters such as the one presented by the Presbyterian call for the Jews to convert. We no longer find a reluctant Leeser. The hesitation is gone, the apologetic posture abandoned. Now Leeser welcomed the opportunity to discuss the comparative merits of Judaism and Christianity, fully confident that this would not only strengthen the faith of Jews but would lead Christians to question their own beliefs.

In line with this new readiness to engage in religious debate, Leeser filled the pages of the *Occident* with both Jewish and Christian responses to the Presbyterian call. The Presbyterians, however, seemed less enthusiastic, and Leeser complained when they failed to respond to Rabbi Schlessinger's rejoinder. Apparently wishing to keep the matter alive, Leeser invited his acquaintance, the Presbyterian minister Matthew R. Miller, to enter the discussion in the pages of the *Occident*. Miller responded by sending a letter which Leeser published in the July edition. This letter, which contained a defense of the Presbyterian call to the Jews, initiated a correspondence between Miller and Isaac M. Wise which Leeser published. In addition, Miller, an enthusiast for converting the Jews, also asked Leeser to send to his subscribers a pamphlet that he had written as an answer to Schlessinger. Leeser turned down this request because he felt that the Christian press had been unfair in its refusal to publish Schlessinger's letter. Miller then published his pamphlet under the title *The Identity of Judaism and Christianity,* and promised Leeser that any Jewish response to it would be published in the Presbyterian press. Leeser accepted Miller's challenge, but once again the Christian papers shied away from publishing the Jewish side of the theological argument. Leeser sent a sermon on Zechariah 2:10 to Miller in the hope that it would appear in the Presbyterian press, but it did not. Meanwhile, Leeser's correspondent in England, J. R. Peynado, had sent Leeser a response to the Presbyterian call to the Jews which, at Peynado's request, Leeser had transmitted to reverend John M. Krebs, Clerk of the Presbyterian Synod of New York. Leeser complained to Krebs that the Presbyterians now had two Jewish answers and had ignored both of them. He attacked the Presbyterian reluctance to keep the discussion going, and proclaimed that no one could now say that the Jews were afraid to debate with Christians on religions questions.[15] Leeser kept the matter alive by publishing a series of articles by Schlessinger in late 1850 and early 1851 under the title *The Difference between Judaism and Christianity.* As the title indicates, the articles were intended as a refutation of Miller's pamphlet.[16]

Like previous Jewish polemicists, Leeser employed a variety of polemical weapons. We may categorize them as exegetical-theological, ethical, and historical. Interestingly, unlike other Jewish writers, Leeser rarely engaged in historical or textual criticism of the New Testament. He was aware of New Testament criticism through his familiarity with previous Jewish polemical literature that had contained it, and he even published some of this material in the *Occident.*[17] Nevertheless, he himself shied away from this method of attacking Christianity, perhaps because he saw in it a threat to Judaism. Casting doubt on the historical veracity and textual reliability of the New Testament was a useful weapon, but it could easily be turned against the Hebrew Bible just as well. Eighteenth century Deists and skeptics had levelled sharp critical attacks against the Bible, and although Deism had passed its peak in America by the 1820's, Leeser was keenly aware of the threat that rational skepticism posed to Judaism. He felt that its danger was even greater than that of the missionaries. Leeser was familiar with the defense of the Hebrew Bible that the eighteenth century English Jewish polemicist David Levi had written as a response to the slashing attack on the Bible contained in Tom Paine's *The Age of Reason*. For Leeser, belief in the Bible, as divine revelation, was the bedrock upon which Judaism stood. Although he may have taken comfort from critical attacks on the New Testament, he was reluctant to employ a weapon that could be turned against the Hebrew Bible. Similarly, Leeser rarely discussed either the historicity or the personality of Jesus. In an 1845 sermon in which he rejected the Christian contention that Isaiah 40:3 referred to John the Baptist, Leeser declared that this was his first mention of a Christian religious personality in his sermons. He apparently felt that while arguments against Christian doctrines were necessary in order to bolster Jewish faith and resistance, negative statements about Jesus were apt to arouse antisemitic feeling.[18]

The starting point in Leeser's polemics was his assertion that Judaism was true in and of itself, and not only in contrast to the falseness of Christianity.[19] By this he meant that Judaism was based on divine revelation and that this was its validation. Leeser accepted the revelation at Sinai as a historical fact. The truth of the Bible was, therefore, inviolable and its commandments remained obligatory upon the Jews. The revelation at Sinai had never been superceded by any other, and religious claims that either contradicted it or professed to supercede it were false. Christianity did both. Leeser's weapon of choice against Christianity was to show that its teachings contradicted the Bible. While he occasionally attacked Christian doctrines on the grounds that they violated either reason or ethics, the argument that he used most often was the Biblical one.[20] This may be clearly seen in his treatment of the Christian beliefs in an atoning mediator, human sinfulness, and the trinity.

Leeser expressed grudging admiration for the Christian concept of a loving God who sacrificed himself for man, describing it as "highly poetical." Nevertheless, it was a concept that was foreign to the Bible. Instead it was "an invention of heathen poets, whose works teem full of reports of incarnations, and of bodily appearances of divinities on earth, and of divisions of the gods. . . . " This appropriation of heathen themes was necessary because Christianity found that the concept of one God was too abstract for the heathen mind to accept.[21] All

Christian attempts to prove the necessity of a mediator failed because they contradicted the Bible. Christians claimed that God had rejected the Jews because they had not accepted the salvation offered to them through Jesus. However, countered Leeser, the Bible contained no reference to a mediator or any other means of atonement aside from personal repentance. He dismissed Christian Biblical exegesis which found inferences and allusions to a mediator in the Bible on the grounds that it was inconceivable that God would leave such a weighty matter clouded in obscurity. Since it was something that concerned the ultimate fate of man, the need for a mediator should have been spelled out explicitly, and should even have been included in the Ten Commandments. If, on the other hand, Christians were to concede that the Hebrew scriptures did not speak of a sacrificial mediator, but that he was proclaimed in a new and purer revelation superceding the Hebrew scriptures, Leeser contended that no new dispensation from God would differ from the original one, since God would not lie or change His mind, certainly not on such a crucial matter. If it were true, Leeser argued, that the Hebrew Bible foreshadowed a new revelation, this could only apply to the Biblical laws but not to basic religious truths. However, even this could not be granted since God was not inconsistent; he would not issue laws and then revoke them for no reason.[22]

Leeser believed that the concept of an atoning mediator derived from Christianity's unbiblical view of human nature. While the Bible taught that man could overcome his own evil through repentance, Christianity stressed the evil nature of man, the inadequacy of his repentance, and the need for the intercession of a divine mediator to effect man's salvation. This mistaken understanding of human nature had led Christianity to commit its greatest error, one which demonstrated in boldest form the divergence of Christianity from the religion of the Bible. Christianity could not reconcile its negative view of human nature with Biblical monotheism. The need for a saving mediator created a plurality in the Godhead, "one part of which assumed the human form to suffer the penalty of sin, as an atonement to the other that accepted the sacrifice." This was a clear violation of monotheism since "there can be no unity of purpose . . . if a sacrifice can be accepted by one part of the Deity from the other. . . . "[23] On a later occasion, Leeser again lashed out at the idea of a plurality in the Godhead when he graphically described Catholics as " . . . praying to what they call the mother of God, to intercede with her son, with whom she is said to be all-powerful, while he is equally influential with the father, thus having three male gods, the spirit being one, and the fourth adjunct, and this a female god." This belief was a polytheistic absurdity. The burden of proof rested on the Christians to bring convincing Biblical evidence to support their beliefs. Such evidence, for Leeser, simply did not exist. And furthermore, he charged, since Christians had been unable to answer Jewish objections to their beliefs, they had sought to silence the Jews through persecution.[24]

While Leeser polemicized against the lack of Scriptural basis for Christian teachings of human depravity, a saving mediator, and the trinity, he felt that an even weaker point in the Christian argument concerned the messiah—a question that lay at the heart of the difference between Judaism and Christianity. His views on the subject were presented in a series of lectures that he delivered in 1836–1837. In conformity with his early defensive posture, Leeser explained that the purpose of these lectures was to provide information to the Jewish community on a vital religious question, since Jewish written material on the topic was not readily available. His goal was not to display Jewish views to Christians. While this may have been the case, the lectures nevertheless present a systematic refutation of the Christian view of the messiah.[25]

As in all other points of issue between Judaism and Christianity, the conflicting views on the messiah had to be judged according to their agreement with the Biblical text. Accordingly, Leeser reviewed the various Biblical sources that Christians used to prove that Jesus was the foretold suffering messiah. He tried to show, in painstaking detail, that Christian exegesis of these passages distorted the true meaning of the text. Repeating traditional Jewish polemical points, Leeser noted that Jesus did not conform to the characteristics specified in the Bible for the messiah. The claim to divinity for Jesus contradicted the Bible which nowhere referred to the messiah as a divine being. The Bible stated that the messiah was to be a descendant of David in the male line. This was not true of Jesus no matter how much text-twisting the Christians brought to bear in order to prove that it was true. Nowhere the Bible states that the messiah would have the authority to alter the Biblical commandments, let alone to abrogate them. Since this is what Jesus had done, he could not have been the messiah. According to the Bible, the messiah was to possess unusual wisdom and an extraordinary sense of justice, characteristics that Leeser did not find in Jesus. The most decisive factor for Leeser in the argument over the messiah was that those occurrences that the Bible had predicted would accompany the coming of the messiah had not taken place with the appearance of Jesus. According to the Bible, the messiah's coming would bring about the restoration of the Jews to the land of Israel where they would live in peace and prosperity, and man-

kind at large would enjoy an era of universal peace as the knowledge of
the Lord spread among all men. Since these things did not come to
pass during the time of Jesus, he could not have been the messiah.

Leeser buttressed his assertion that the Bible alone was the only
proper arbiter between the truth claims of Judaism and Christianity by
rejecting the Christian contention that such claims could also be vali-
dated by miracles. In conformity with his tendency to refrain from
critical or historical analysis of the New Testament, Leeser did not
claim that the miracles of Jesus were unhistorical. Instead he argued
that they simply were not impressive enough. If Jesus were really the
bearer of a new revelation from God, his validating miracles should
have been greater than those which accompanied the revelation at
Sinai, and they should have been witnessed by the whole nation rather
than by small groups of people. Leeser, proposed, in addition, a more
decisive argument. Once again reverting to the Bible as the fountain-
head of religious truth, he claimed that Christians misunderstood the
nature of Biblical miracles. They were intended to impress upon the
minds of men certain truths that had already been enunciated; their
purpose was not to alter any religious or moral truth or to abolish any
precept of the Bible. This, however, is what the miracles of Jesus did.
No miracle performed by Jesus or by anyone else could make truth
"what common sense and the Bible declare as not true." No miracle
could abrogate the unity of God or abridge His ability to save sinners.
Jesus' miracles were not authentic ones because Biblical miracles "took
place to glorify the Creator before His works, not to elevate creatures
to an even rank with Him." Hence Jews could not admit "that any
number of miracles can attest to that which is not true from the very
nature of the terms." For Leeser, the New Testament miracles of Jesus
were one more example of Christianity's divergence from the Bible.[26]

While Leeser's main argument against Christianity was that it was
not true to Biblical teaching, he also argued against Christianity from
an historical-theological point of view. The historical argument focussed on the question of Jewish suffering and the purpose of continued Jewish existence. The traditional Christian view was that the Jews
had undergone centuries of suffering, and continued to exist as a
downtrodden people, because God had rejected them and was punish-
ing them for their failure to accept Jesus. Eventually, with the aid of
Christian instruction and concern, the Jews would recognize their error. The argument was a potent one because it touched a raw nerve for
Jews—why had God allowed His chosen people to suffer so much and
for so long? For Leeser, of course, Jewish history in the Christian era
had a very different meaning. God had not rejected the Jews. His covenant with them remained intact. Had it been God's intent that Chris-

tianity should supersede Judaism, the Jews would have disappeared long ago. Indeed, their very survival through so much persecution was a miracle, and proof of God's continuing concern for them. Jewish suffering was due to the failure of the Jews to obey the commandments of the Bible; it had nothing to do with their rejection of Jesus. The continued existence of the Jews as a distinct people was proof of the truth of the Bible and of Jewish claims. The Bible had foretold Jewish suffering as a consequence of Jewish disobedience to the Biblical laws. It had, however, also promised that God would never destroy the Jewish people, and that eventually their suffering would end with their restoration to their homeland. Jewish suffering was a validation of the word of God, and as such, it carried with it the comforting assurance of future consolation. Jewish responsibility now lay in obeying the Biblical commandments and awaiting God's redemption. While Christians argued that God's covenant with Israel no longer existed and that Jewish adherence to the Biblical laws was therefore meaningless, Leeser declared that God had given the Biblical laws to the Jews as a means to assure their survival as a distinct people whose purpose it was to bear the message of God's unity to a reluctant and unreceptive world. Christians who called upon the Jews to cease observing the Biblical commandments were thus urging a course that ran counter to God's wish to preserve the Jews.[27]

A second historical argument used by Leeser centered on the fragmentation within contemporary Christianity. One of the major characteristics of nineteenth century religious life in America was the proliferation of denominations.[28] While this fragmentation did not prevent various Protestant denominations from banding together for joint action in a number of social and religious causes, Leeser saw in it a weakness in Christianity. Which denomination represented true Christianity? If the Jews were to convert, which one should they join? Leeser undoubtedly agreed with his English correspondent J. R. Peynado who wrote in a letter to the *Occident* that disagreements over questions of dogma created divisions among Christians and posed a great danger for Christianity. Speaking of the dispute over the trinity, Peynado wrote that some Christians who felt that the trinity was not to be understood in a literal sense were afraid to say so openly lest all other Christian dogmas be subjected to critical examination. He concluded that "the greatest enemies of the Church are in her bosom, and in the discussion which will arise from each person wishing to maintain his own interpretation of its tenets, and to oppose all others, they will show on what a frail foundation the doctrine is built."[29]

There was, of course, a danger in turning Christian divisiveness against the Christians because nineteenth century American Judaism also conformed to the pattern of denominational fragmentation. Christian missionaries were of two minds about the orthodox-Reform split among American Jews. Some missionaries looked with disfavor upon Reform either because they felt that it was a step towards atheism or because it showed that Jews could modernize without becoming Christians. Other Christian conversionists, however, pointed to the split between Jewish Reformers and traditionalists as an encouraging sign and viewed the Reformers' denial of Talmudic authority as movement away from Jewish stubbornness and spiritual blindness and as a step towards Christianity. Leeser was painfully aware of this, and although he was a staunch opponent of Reform, he denied that Reform represented movement towards Christianity. Nevertheless, he had to concede, and often bemoaned, the encouragement that the traditionalist-Reform split within Judaism was giving to Christians intent on converting the Jews.[30]

Although he pointed to the divisions within Christianity as a sign of weakness, Leeser's main concern was not with any individual denomination, but with Christianity as a whole. His evaluation of Christianity was largely negative. Granting that Christianity taught morality and honor of God, Leeser noted that these were borrowed from the Hebrew Bible. Anything in Christianity that was not taken from the Hebrew Bible was worthy of neither respect nor obedience. Leeser did, however, allow that Christianity had accomplished some good. While it was Judaism that had given the Bible to mankind, it was Christianity that had spread the Bible throughout the world. Moreover, according to Leeser, since Christianity professed belief in Providence, "we must suppose that the step it presents between the darkness of the heathen and the light of Israel is one in the progress of mankind towards a high perfection." Protestantism represented that step better than Catholicism. The Protestant rejection of the worship of Mary and the intercession of the saints showed that Protestant Christians, at least, were "approaching daily nearer to the standard of our faith and the absolute unity."[31]

Despite these statements, Leeser rarely talked about the commonalities between Judaism and Christianity. His desire was to enunciate clearly the essential differences between the two religions and to point out the fallacies of Christianity. Leeser insisted that the Jews maintain their own religious traditions although this created a barrier which prevented full Jewish integration into American life. Jews could live as free and loyal citizens in America, but this did not and could not mean sacrificing their religious traditions. While he did not oppose minor religious reforms and even introduced a feature of the Protestant worship service into the synagogue—the English sermon—Leeser resisted any attempt to blur the essential differences between Judaism and

Christianity, for this could only serve to further weaken the already tenuous hold of tradition among American Jews. Jewish survival required that American Jews retain their own distinct identity differentiating them from other Americans. This "outsider" stance explains Leeser's insistence upon stressing the differences between Judaism and Christianity. In an 1853 sermon, he insisted that the creeds of Judaism and Christianity were incompatible. After listing the thirteen principles of faith of Maimonides, Leeser proclaimed, "how utterly subversive the features of our creed are of all dogmas and beliefs held by other persuasions, although they profess to be based on the revelation of God."[32] On another occasion he attacked the Reformers' claim that Christianity represented a step in the spread of Judaism throughout the world. Whatever religious progress mankind had made had been depressingly slow. Dividing the Christian world between Protestant countries in which "the son whom they allege to have proceeded from God the father, has usurped the honors due to the last," and Catholic lands where "worship of Mary has almost replaced worship of God," Leeser asked, "where is there in all this the slightest evidence that the theory . . . of our faith is progressing among the men with whom we live?"[33]

Although Leeser felt that Protestant Christianity represented an advance over Catholicism, he generally did not distinguish between Christian denominations in his polemics; however, in his effort to emphasize the distinction between Judaism and Christianity, he had to counter in particular those Christian groups that claimed an affinity with Judaism. Thus, he argued against millenarian Protestants even though many of them, like the Jews, interpreted the Biblical prophecies of Israel's restoration to the land of Israel in a literal sense. The literal or figurative interpretation of Biblical prophecy was not the issue. Since Christians who accepted the literal interpretation of Biblical prophecy also accepted Jesus' role as a mediator, they shared no common ground with Judaism.[34] Similarly, Leeser protested vigorously against the Anglican plan to build a church on Mount Zion in which the service, which was to consist largely of the recitation of Psalms, would be in Hebrew. The missionary sponsors of this project hoped that it would attract Jews to Anglicanism not only because of the language of the service, but because its simple ritual and emphasis on scripture would present to the Jews "an inviting contrast to the idolatry and superstition of the Latin and Eastern churches." In response to this proposal, Leeser wrote that if Catholicism and Protestantism were to be compared, Protestantism was less objectionable to Jews because it had rid itself of image worship. However, this comparison was meaningless since "all divisions of Christians are alike unscriptural."

As for a Christian religious service in Hebrew consisting largely of psalms, Leeser retorted that Jews had been reciting psalms long before civilization had come to England.[35]

Jews in nineteenth century America were also subject to appeals from both sides in the Trinitarian–Unitarian controversy. Unitarians argued that their rejection of the trinity showed that they were true to Biblical religion, and therefore closer to Jews in religious spirit than any other Christian denomination. On the other hand, Trinitarians, especially Presbyterians, tried to prove to the Jews that the concept of the trinity was rooted in the Hebrew Bible. Leeser dismissed the claims of both Unitarians and Trinitarians. Although Unitarianism may have represented a less objectionable form of Christianity, its emphasis on Jesus created an unbridgeable gap separating it from Judaism. Nor could Jews take seriously Trinitarian assertions that Trinitarian Christianity was identical with Biblical Judaism. As we have already seen, Leeser dismissed Christian Biblical exegesis that sought to prove the existence of Trinitarian doctrine in the Hebrew Bible, and charged that the doctrine itself was a violation of monotheism.[36]

There was yet another form of Christian appeal to Jews that Leeser sought to challenge. As far back as the seventeenth century, certain English Protestant writers, in urging the Jews to convert, held out what they thought to be a considerable enticement. They stated that after their conversion, the Jews would be ale to continue to observe the Biblical laws and thus form a separate Jewish church within Christianity. In the late eighteenth century the English scientist and Unitarian, Joseph Priestly, had urged this course on the Jews, and in the nineteenth century, the proposal was raised in America, too. In 1850, Leeser's Presbyterian friend, Matthew R. Miller, argued that if the Jews were to convert they could continue to observe the Biblical commandments and thus remain a separate people. In rejecting Miller's suggestion, Leeser pointed out a logical inconsistency; since Christianity taught that the Biblical commandments were no longer to be observed, if the Jews were to convert, there would be no point in observing the commandments. Furthermore, noted Leeser, Jews observed these laws as testimony to their belief that the entire scheme of revelation had been given to Moses at Sinai, a belief that Christianity obviously did not and could not accept.

Leeser also pointed out a practical difficulty caused by Miller's proposal. If an individual Jew were to convert, it would be impossible for him to continue to observe the Biblical laws since no Jewess would marry him, and if he were to marry a Christian woman, such observance would be impossible. With an uncharacteristic touch of humor, Leeser suggested that the only way Jews could convert and still observe the Biblical laws would be for all of the Jews to convert at once so that they could marry among themselves. Then they would be able to observe dual religious celebrations like Passover-Easter and circumcision-baptism. However, mass conversion was not likely to take place, and Leeser suggested, perhaps with tongue in cheek, that until it did, Christians should stop trying to convert individual Jews.[37]

The third major argument that Leeser used in his polemics was the ethical one. For Leeser, this argument was crucial because it involved the good name of Judaism. Popular misconceptions about Jewish ethics could easily foster antisemitism and undermine Jewish security in America. As in other areas of Leeser's polemics, a defense of Judaism and an attack on Christianity sometimes merged. While Leeser's goal was to defend Jewish ethics against Christian misrepresentation, the method he used was to contrast Jewish and Christian ethics thereby showing how they differed and to demonstrate the superiority of the former. The discussion over the comparative merits of Jewish and Christian ethics was to continue in the late nineteenth century, but then it was to take on a new meaning. As far as Leeser was concerned, the main goal of the discussion on ethics was to defend Judaism and to prevent antisemitism while at the same time underlining the differences between Judaism and Christianity.

Leeser's use of the ethical argument came early in his polemical career. It first arose in his 1829 exchange with the Quaker letter writer in the Richmond *Whig*. The Quaker had written that Jewish ethics did not match the standard of Christian ethics because they were particularistic and reflected hostility towards non-Jews, and because they sanctioned and even encouraged warfare. Basing his analysis of Jewish ethics on his understanding of the Hebrew Bible, the Quaker concluded that the New Testament offered a higher morality based on nonresistance and pacifism. Leeser responded by trying to prove that the Quaker had misunderstood the Biblical passages upon which he based his conclusions, and then went on to argue that on precisely those issues cited by the Quaker, Jewish ethics surpassed Christianity. Jewish ethics were not particularistic because Judaism posited a belief in universal salvation whereas Christianity held out salvation only to Christian believers. As for pacifism, Leeser declared that Judaism acknowledged that warfare was necessary on occasion in order to combat evil. Pacifism in the face of aggression amounted to surrender to evil. In addition, Leeser, repeated the traditional Jewish polemical argument that Christians had never lived up to the ideals of pacifism and nonresistance. Jesus' teaching of nonresistance "has not been fulfilled by fifty men from all Christendom ever since Christianity was established." Even Quakers did not conform to the New Testament ideals. While not directly contradicting the Quaker's assertion that William Penn had established a commonwealth in Pennsylvania based on the ideals of love and pacifism, Leeser pointed to the Inquisition and to the New England Puritans as examples where Christians had flaunted these New Testament ideals by persecuting both Jews and Quakers in the name of the New Testament.[38]

In his later sermons and writings, Leeser expanded his critique of Christian ethics. Not satisfied with reminding his Christian contemporaries of past and present Christian mistreatment of the Jews, Leeser declared that this was symptomatic of the larger failure of both Christianity and Islam to ameliorate the ethical conduct of mankind. Between them, Christianity and Islam had converted the pagan nations, but the sword still ruled the world. Leeser sought to discredit Christianity not only by citing its failure to bring peace to mankind, but highlighted this failure by contrasting Jewish and Christian behavior. Wrapping himself in the robe of moral self-righteousness, Leeser declared that unlike Christianity and Islam, Judaism really was a religion of love, tolerance, and free thought, and that Jews would not have persecuted Christians had they ruled over them.[39]

Leeser also cited the unoriginal nature of Christian ethics as a flaw. Christianity had added nothing of value to the ethical teachings of the Hebrew Bible. Utilizing an argument that was to take on great significance in later nineteenth century American Jewish polemics against Christianity, Leeser claimed that anything worthwhile in Christian ethics had been borrowed from Judaism, and that those elements of Christian ethics not taken from the Hebrew Bible were of questionable value. He expressed the point in a sermon delivered at the fifth anniversary of the Hebrew Sunday School in Philadelphia:

> We shall not claim to be more instructed in worldly sciences than our gentile friends, which we are not; we will not say that as a people we are more moral, more honest then they are, which, though surely true in some respects, is not so in others; but this we will say, we are more acquainted with the basis of all truths than they are, we are blessed with a treasure from which, despite of the pride of human opinion, they have been compelled to borrow most of their moral principles, and whatever they have of their own, independently of this source, is either not practical or of a very questionable usefulness.[40]

In his contrast of Jewish and Christian ethics, Leeser faulted Christianity for its emphasis on dogma over action. Unbiblical and irrational Christian dogmas detracted from whatever good Christian ethics may have provided to mankind. Judaism, on the other hand, was a religion of works in which dogmas were few and uncomplicated. Its belief in the unity of God was so simple that it obviated the need for theological casuistry. Unfortunately, this belief was too abstract for the Gentiles to accept, and they fell into the trap of trying to arrive at an adequate formula that would define the impossible, the compound nature of the unity of the Godhead. This, along with an overly pessimistic view of man's ability to overcome his sins, and the formulation of a scheme of salvation that relied on a divine mediator drained Christian spiritual energies so much that there was too little left for an adequate emphasis on deeds.[41]

Aside from this critique of Christian ethics, Leeser found grounds for complaint on a more immediate and practical level. He charged that the Christian missionary effort to convert Jews was unethical, as were the motives of the few Jews who converted. A small number of these Jews converted out of religious conviction; most did so out of the desire for material gain or career advancement. Such people were dishonorable and represented a small loss to Judaism while they provided Christianity with no worthy gain. Missionary societies were unethical since they utilized bribery and misrepresentation of Judaism as their means to attract converts. They were always exaggerating their success in order to fool the Christian community into giving them financial support. Leeser expressed wonderment and dismay at the large sums of money that were spent on the missionary effort, and delighted in pointing out the meager success that such sizeable expenditures achieved. It all seemed to him like a grand farce. However, at the same time, it infuriated him and he considered it to be dangerous to the Jewish community.[42] The missionaries sought to entrap unsuspecting Jews by distributing Hebrew Bibles to them. The problem was that these Bibles contained Christological marginal notes. It was the need to provide American Jewry with a Bible text free of Christological influences that induced Leeser to produce his magnum opus, an English translation of the Bible.[43] Leeser also questioned the ethics of the missionary assertion that the conversion efforts grew out of Christian love for the Jews, which had replaced the earlier spirit of persecution. As far as Leeser was concerned, the missionary endeavor was not the product of any new found spirit of friendliness towards the Jews. On the contrary, by their constant distortions of Judaism, the missionaries were holding up the Jews and Judaism to ridicule and contempt, and were thus fueling antisemitism. If Christians really wanted to demonstrate friendly concern for the Jews, they should grant respect to Judaism. Now that the Jews had attained political equality, genuine Christian good will should insure religious equality to Judaism as well.[44]

Leeser's outrage at the missionaries was so great that it led him to make a rather bold threat. If Christians persisted in their attempts to convert Jews, the Jews might begin to missionize Christians. Leeser acknowledged that Judaism was not a missionizing religion. It taught that the upright among all the nations would share in God's reward for the righteous. Non-Jews could live a righteous life without observing the ceremonial laws of the Bible since these were meant only for the Jews. However, despite this live-and-let-live characteristic of Judaism, if Jews were to compete with Christians in missionary work, the Jews would come out ahead. On one occasion he even told of receiving three or four unsolicited requests from Christians who wished to convert to Judaism during a one year period. He remarked that, were the Jews to actively proselytize, the number of Christians that would convert to Judaism would far outweigh the small number of Jews who had converted to Christianity. While Leeser never pushed for Jewish missionary activity, he did include a number of articles in the *Occident* on the Jewish attitude towards conversion. Nevertheless, for Leeser, Jewish missionary work remained a dormant threat. If Jews were to missionize among Christians, they would forfeit their argument that Judaism was more tolerant than Christianity because it granted the possibility of salvation to non-Jews. Probably a more weighty consideration was the fear that a competitive struggle for converts between Jews and Christians might arouse anti-Jewish feelings.[45]

Isaac Leeser broke little new ground in his anti-Christian polemics. Most of his arguments were derivative, and he showed little creativity in formulating new ones. Nevertheless, his writings on Christianity provide us with a valuable insight into mid-nineteenth century American Jewry. At a time when the Jewish community was virtually leaderless, Leeser shouldered the responsibility of serving as its defender. As the outstanding representative of traditional Judaism in America during his time, Leeser was determined to preserve Jewish tradition. At the same time, he sought to insure Jewish legal equality in America. As a traditionalist, Leeser felt that at-homeness for the Jews in America precluded full Jewish integration into American life. The barriers against assimilation posed by the Jewish religious tradition had to be preserved in order to assure Jewish survival. Jews had to know how and why they differed from Christians, otherwise, in the open and free environment of America, they could disappear. Leeser, therefore, stressed the differences between Christianity and Judaism. In addition, Christians in America had to be shown that Judaism was a respectable religion. In this way, Jews would be respected and Jewish security would be enhanced. These two goals: the survival of traditional Judaism in America, and gaining Christian respect for Judaism shaped Leeser's writings on Christianity.

4 Late Nineteenth Century Reform: A New Look At Jesus

The latter part of the nineteenth century witnessed an outburst of Jewish expression on Christianity; books, journal articles, and sermons proliferated. However, unlike earlier in the century, much of this literature focussed on the relationship of the Jews to Jesus rather than on theological questions. Reform rabbis did most of this writing and preaching. Both the abundance as well as the content of the Reformers' material attest to the need they felt to clarify the relationship between the two religions, for this clarification was an important aspect of their difficult struggle to define an American Jewish identity.

Many contemporaries and some later historians have sought to explain the Reformers' often favorable evaluations of Jesus as the result of a more enlightened Jewish attitude caused by the improved treatment of the Jews in the western world in modern times. Typical of this view is a recent study on Jewish attitudes towards Jesus in which the author states that "the Jewish attitude has varied with almost mathematical certainty according to the precise degree in which Christians have shown themselves real followers, in spirit and deed, of their Savior."[1] This statement, while partially true, is nevertheless too simplistic. It is similar to the belief of many missionaries that the most important obstacle standing in the way of Jewish conversion was Christian mistreatment of the Jews. It seems more reasonable to assume that better Christian treatment of the Jews in the nineteenth century should have resulted not so much in a more generous Jewish view of Jesus but rather in a more favorable Jewish evaluation of Christianity. However, we do not find this. As we shall see, there is an almost paradoxical attempt on the part of the Jewish writers to mute the differences between Judaism and Christianity and emphasize their commonalities, and at the same time to condemn Christianity on theological and ethical grounds. Indeed, rather than fostering a greater receptivity to Christianity, the improved status of the Jew in the Christian world in the nineteenth century, and especially the freedom that Jews enjoyed in America, created the environment for a new and sharp Jewish polemic against Christianity. The Jewish reevaluation of Jesus is a crucial part of that polemic.

American Jews were not the only ones who wrote about Jesus in the nineteenth century. European Jewish scholars such as Abraham Geiger and Samuel Hirsch wrote about Jesus from a historical perspective, and their work influenced the American Reformers.[2] Equally important influences were exerted by nineteenth century Christian New Testament scholarship as well as by the emergence of the study of comparative religion and the impact of Darwinism. Nineteenth century New Testament scholarship was, at least in part, an attempt to rediscover the historical Jesus, a Jesus who was unencumbered by later creedal accretions. The writings of scholars like David F. Strauss and Ernst Renan had a profound effect in America as well as in Europe. In America, they helped to feed a liberal stream in American Protestantism. Known as the New Theology, this form of liberal Protestantism represented a denial of significant elements of traditional Calvinist theology. Its spokesmen rejected the concepts of original sin and of election and damnation. Instead, the New Theology emphasized a more positive view of human nature and of man's potentialities, emphases that were in accord with an era characterized by economic expansion and an almost dogmatic belief in progress. The spirit that informed the New Theology was derived from the Christian concept of the incarnation. The belief that God's presence pervaded the world and that it manifested itself in contemporary culture was the basic premise of the New Theology. This premise lent a theological underpinning to the pervasive cultural optimism of late nineteenth century America.[3]

The emphasis on the incarnation placed Christian liberals in a difficult position. If God's spirit infused human culture, then all cultures (and their religious systems) should be deemed of equal worth. This left Christian liberals confronting the uncomfortable question: what, then, is unique about Christianity? Egbert Smyth, liberal Congregationalist clergyman and professor at Andover Theological Seminary, was on the mark when he declared the fundamental religious question of the time to be "the claim of Christianity to be the one perfect and final religion for mankind." Christian liberals struggled with this problem. A typical response was that of the Baptist minister and theologian William Newton Clarke who wrote in his Outline of Christian Thought, published in 1898, that "religion is natural to man, being natural to man, religion is universal among men." He then sought to obviate the religious relativism implicit in this position by arguing that a judgment could be made concerning the value of specific religions. Granting that no religion lacked worth, Clarke declared that a religion's value was determined by how close it came to a complete grasp of the truth. For Clarke as well as for other liberal Protestants, there was no doubt that Christianity's grasp of the truth was the most complete. Clearly, personal inclination and loyalty dictated this conclusion. There remained the problem of validating it through some clear-cut proof.[4]

Liberal Protestants found the proof they needed in the ethical teachings and personality of Jesus. The outstanding expositor of this position, the German scholar, Adolf von Harnack, set forth his argument for the uniqueness and superiority of Christianity in his famous series of lectures delivered in 1899–1900 entitled *Das Wesen des Christentums*. The lectures were translated into English in 1901 and published under the title *What is Christianity?* Harnack maintained that Jesus' teaching concerning the kingdom of God as a spiritual force that operates within the individual went beyond previous religious conceptions. In addition, Harnack claimed that the emphasis of Jesus on the fatherhood of God suggested a divine love for man that raised man's worth in a way that no other religion had done, and that Jesus' stress on ethics over ritual transcended previous ideas. For Harnack and other liberal Christians, therefore, herein lay the uniqueness and superiority of Christianity—the personality and the message of Jesus.[5]

Like their liberal Protestant counterparts, late nineteenth century Reform leaders were under pressure to clarify their religious stance.[6] Traditionalists like Leeser and somewhat later Alexander Kohut accused the Reformers of abandoning traditional Jewish practice and of adopting a too willing accommodation with American culture that would surely lead to the destruction of Judaism. In addition, Ethical Culture, Christian Science, and various forms of spiritualism were attracting a disquieting number of Jews. And, of course, the Reformers had to respond to the challenge posed by the liberal Protestants. The Reformers shared some important ground with liberal Protestants. Both rejected ceremonialism and emphasized ethics as the essence of religion, and both held a positive view of human nature and were optimistic about man's capabilities. The implications of critical Bible scholarship, and the study of comparative religion and evolutionary theory were generally accepted in one form or another by most Reformers and liberal Protestants. Moreover, on a practical level, members of the two groups joined forces in the battles against prayer in public schools, Sunday Blue laws, and the campaign to amend the constitution to designate America as a Christian country. While some welcomed the apparent coming together of liberal Protestantism and Reform Judaism, it was precisely this apparent closeness that required each side to articulate a rationale to justify its own religious system and to demonstrate its superiority over the other. By demonstrating the superiority of Judaism, the Reformers accomplished two things. In the first place, by distinguishing themselves from liberal Protestants and showing the inherent worth of Judaism as the religion that best met the needs and aspirations of modern man in general and of America in particular, they provided a rationale for continued Jewish group existence. In addition, in the face of a disturbing rise in antisemitism in late nineteenth century America, the Reformers hoped that by showing the consonance of Judaism with Americanism they could forge a weapon that would undermine the antisemites. Since Protestant liberals based their claim for Christianity's superiority on the uniqueness of Jesus and his message, the Reformers had to deal with Jesus, and had to do so in a way that would undermine the liberal Protestant position.

II

The main thrust of the Reformers' argument was to prove that Christianity had misunderstood both the personality and the teachings of Jesus. Here we see an interesting reversal in the positions of the two religions. Since for Christianity, Jesus represents the fulfillment of the Hebrew scriptures, Christian polemicists have contended for centuries that the Jewish rejection of Jesus was the result of the failure of the Jews to understand their own scripture. The Reformers now turned this weapon against the Christians by maintaining that they understood the nature, mission, and message of Jesus better than the Christians did. The goal of the Reformers was to deprive Christianity of Jesus by placing him and his message within the context of first century Palestinian Judaism. By demonstrating that Jesus operated fully within the system of Judaism and that his teachings did not diverge from Jewish doctrine, the Reformers hoped to show that Jesus' message was a Jewish one, and therefore the uniqueness and superiority that liberal Protestants claimed for Christianity really belonged to Judaism.

In their reconstruction of the historical Jesus, the Reformers insisted upon the significance of rabbinic sources. The New Testament sources were inadequate to provide an accurate picture of Jesus because they were later than the events they purported to describe, and were contradictory and tendentious. While New Testament critical scholarship had progressed during the nineteenth century, and the difficulties posed in using New Testament sources to reconstruct a picture of the historical Jesus had become clear, Christian scholars for the most part still ignored the rabbinic sources. Isaac M. Wise claimed to have translated several hundred rabbinic passages from the original in preparing his book *The Origins of Christianity.* By bringing rabbinic sources to bear, Wise hoped " . . . to have opened an entirely new avenue of research to Christian theology and criticism."[7] This emphasis on the part of Wise and other Reformers on the prerequisite of familiarity with rabbinic sources for a correct understanding of Jesus was not merely an attempt to establish their own credentials as authoritative scholarly voices who could speak about Jesus, but was an assertion that their scholarly credibility was greater than that of Christian writers who ignored the rabbinic sources. Reform writers claimed that Christian scholars who paid no heed to rabbinic sources were engaged in a tendentious attempt to separate Jesus from his people. For the Reformers, to borrow a Paulinian image, the time had come to graft Jesus back on to the trunk from which he had sprung.

While all of the Reformers insisted that Jesus had to be understood within the context of the first century Palestinian Judaism, they differed over which Jewish religious group he had adhered to. Most followed the German Jewish scholar Abraham Geiger and placed him in the Pharisaic camp.[8] Typical of this approach is Wise's reconstruction of the historical Jesus: Jesus was a Pharisee and a Jewish patriot who was determined to rescue the Jews from Roman rule. He believed in the imminent dawning of the kingdom of heaven, which meant the reestablishment of the theocratic rule of God over the Jewish people. John the Baptist had led a rebellion against Roman rule with the hope of restoring the theocracy. Jesus was his disciple and successor. Jesus did not claim to be the messiah, and he accepted this designation only reluctantly when it was suggested by Peter in order to stimulate popular support for the revolt. Jesus' followers devised a plan in which Jesus, fortified with the messianic title, would appear in Jerusalem for the Passover festival. His appearance there would energize the crowds, who packed the city for the festival, the Romans would be overthrown and the kingdom of heaven restored. Jesus, however, realized that a popular demonstration would result in carnage, and he understood that the only way to prevent this was to give himself up to the Romans. His followers, carried away by their own enthusiasm, did not allow this, and Jesus became a captive in the hands of his extremist followers. Therefore, in order to avert calamity, Jesus ordered Judas to betray him to the Romans. Jesus willingly died so that his countrymen would be spared from Roman wrath. This was the real vicarious atonement involved in the death of Jesus. Thus, for Wise, Jesus was a loyal Jew, a Pharisee, and a martyred nationalist patriot.[9]

In contrast to the nationalist patriotic messianic rebel of Wise, Kaufmann Kohler, one of the outstanding intellectual leaders of Reform Judaism of his day, offered an alternative interpretation of Jesus.

Kohler portrayed Jesus as a wonder working Essene. However, unlike the Essenes who had cut themselves off from society in order to keep wholly pure, Jesus associated with the poor and the outcasts of society. Expecting the imminent dawn of the kingdom of God, Jesus preached an Essene-like life style of voluntary poverty, chastity, asceticism and passivity in the face of evil. Also, like an Essene, he opposed the house of the high priest and he overturned the tables of the money changers in the temple. As a result, the priests handed Jesus over to the Romans who executed him. Belief in the messiahship and resurrection of Jesus came only after his death and were the result of the apparitions that his followers had of him.[10] While his view of Jesus differed from that of Wise, Kohler, like Wise, stressed that Jesus was a product of the Jewish religious environment of his day. Kohler insisted that Jesus could only be understood within the context of the eschatological concepts and the apocalyptic and Essene literature of the times along with the legendary accounts of saints in rabbinic literature.

III

Jewish reconstructions of the historical Jesus paid special attention to the crucifixion story. An essential part of the attempt to prove the Jewishness of Jesus entailed denial of Jewish guilt for the crucifixion. The gospel accounts of the death of Jesus had been a major source of anti-Jewish sentiment through the centuries, and the Reformers were anxious to dispel this source of prejudice since even in free and tolerant America they felt it to be a threat. Their feeling was heightened by the rising tide of antisemitism in late nineteenth century America. Jewish religious leaders railed against the continued proclamation of Jewish guilt for the crucifixion that emanated from Christian Sunday schools and pulpits. The apparent lack of sensitivity, on the part of even responsible Christians, to the harm that the crucifixion accounts caused was a matter of concern to Jewish spokesmen. In the Spring of 1890, the traditionalist periodical, the *American Hebrew* conducted a survey in which it questioned over fifty prominent non-Jews, including many Christian religious figures, asking them whether or not they thought that Christian teaching concerning the crucifixion was the root cause of antisemitism.[11] The vast majority of those queried responded in the negative. According to these respondents, the causes of antisemitism were not religious. Instead, they cited such factors as racial antagonism, resentment of Jewish "exclusiveness," the ostentatious manners of lower class Jews, and unethical Jewish business practices as the real causes of antisemitism. Only nine respondents granted that the crucifixion story might be a contributing factor to antisemitism, and of these only two, Robert G. Ingersoll, "the great agnostic," and George W. Curtis, the writer and proponent of liberal social views, agreed that it was the main cause. Of the others who conceded that it might be a factor, most downplayed its significance. They explained that it was only one factor among many, and that while anti-Jewish prejudice might be transmitted when the crucifixion story was taught, this was done unwittingly, and was, in any case, less of a problem in the present than it had been in the past. Or, as the liberal R. Heber Newton wrote, it might be a factor among the lower classes and the ignorant, but certainly not "among the cultivated people, the classes who for the most part attend our Protestant churches and Sunday Schools."[12] Clearly there was a significant difference between Jewish and Christian perceptions of the damage that the crucifixion story had caused to Jewish-Christian relations in the past and its potential for continued harm.

Among the most extensive treatments of the crucifixion story are those of Isaac M. Wise, Joseph Krauskopf, and Emil G. Hirsch. The purpose of all three was to show that the Jews were not responsible for the death of Jesus. Wise devoted an entire book to the subject. In his *The Martyrdom of Jesus of Nazareth,* Wise maintained that the gospel accounts of the crucifixion were unhistorical and that they amounted to nothing more than "a conglomeration of contradictions and improbabilities."[13] Their purpose was to exonerate the Romans and to implicate the Jews in an attempt to increase the appeal of Christianity to Greek pagans. However, the truth was that it was the Romans who killed Jesus because they viewed him as a political threat. The only Jewish role in the affair was played by the chief priests and the scribes. They, too, acted not out of religious antagonism to Jesus, but out of political motives, which, although not commendable, were, at least, understandable. The priests feared that the Romans would crush the uprising that would result from Jesus' appearance in Jerusalem and his disciples' proclamation that he was the messiah. They wanted to avoid the ensuing carnage and confiscation of property that would be the fruit of the revolt. Wise's account of events, as we have already noted, even exonerated Judas. By doing this, Wise hoped to remove the venom from the old motif—Judas-traitor-Jew—which continued to recur periodically in new forms.[14]

Probably the most systematic and best known example of the Jewish defense against the crucifixion charge is Emil G. Hirsch's essay "The Crucifixion Viewed from a Jewish Standpoint" which he delivered in 1892 before the Chicago Institute for Morals, Religion and Letters. In it, Hirsch posed the crucial question: who would gain by the death of Jesus? His answer was that it was not the Jews. There was nothing in the gospel accounts of Jesus to indicate that he did anything "which could have aroused religious opposition on the part of even the most punctilious among the Jews." His controversies with the Pharisees and scribes "reveal not even one single trait that would countenance the assumption of a departure on his part from the well-recognized principles and standards of Jewish orthodox practice," and his moral teachings did not differ significantly from those of the Synagogue of his day. Nor was Jesus' messianic claim an adequate explanation of Jewish antagonism to him. The Pharisees anticipated a messiah who would free the Jews from Roman oppression, and the Sadducees, who did not share this belief, nevertheless would not have killed Jesus because they shared the revulsion against bloodshed that characterized all Jews of the time, except the fanatical zealots. There was, therefore, no party among the Jews that sought the death of Jesus, since he represented a threat to none of them. Only the Romans felt threatened by Jesus and his messianic claims. Hirsch does allow that there was one small group of Jews who did view Jesus as an enemy. The priests who monopolized the sale of pigeons and money changing in the temple were alienated by Jesus' attack on them. They complained of Jesus to Pilate who, viewing Jesus as a political threat, ordered the crucifixion. However, while conceding that the priesthood played a role in the events leading to the crucifixion, thus providing an element, albeit a small one, of Jewish culpability for the death of Jesus, Hirsch insisted that the Jews had not played any direct role. He, like other Reformers, went to considerable lengths to disprove the New Testament accounts of a Jewish trial of Jesus. They pointed to the contradictions in the gospel accounts of the trial, to the fact that Jewish courts at that time had no power to impose capital punishment, and to the violations of Jewish judicial procedure that the Gospel accounts require, as proof of the impossibility of a Jewish trial.[15]

Perhaps the most extreme example of exonerating the Jews from any guilt in the crucifixion may be found in the account of Joseph Krauskopf. Rabbi of Philadelphia's Congregation Knesset Israel, Krauskopf had witnessed the emotional impact of the crucifixion story when he attended the 1900 presentation of the Oberammergau passion play. Upon his return to America, Krauskopf delivered a series of lectures detailing his impressions of what he had seen. The lectures proved so popular that he published them in a book entitled *A Rabbi's Impressions of the Oberammergau Passion Play*. Krauskopf took the position that no guilt at all could be ascribed to the Jews for the death of Jesus. Not only did he affirm the impossibility of a Jewish trial of Jesus, but he also denied the historicity of the temple scene and of Judas. The temple scene of the New Testament was incredible because it portrayed Jesus, who preached love of one's enemies and nonresistance to evil, in a highly uncharacteristic manner. In addition to portraying Jesus out of character, the temple scene lacked authenticity because Jesus, as a typical Jew of his time, had from his earliest years, "drunk in the Jews' reverence of the teacher in Israel, of the judge who judges in God's stead," and according to Krauskopf, there was never an age in Israel's history that had a religious leadership more worthy of reverence than the age of Jesus. In Krauskopf's view, the New Testament's description of the villainous Judas was even more implausible than its temple scene. Since Jesus' crucifixion had been preordained as a necessary step for the salvation of mankind, it would have occurred even without Judas' betrayal. Moreover, if Judas really was a villain, the New Testament account would have been more morally instructive had Jesus converted Judas from his evil. In any case, Krauskopf dismissed Judas as a creation of third century Christian anti-Jewish polemics. Christian writers created Judas to represent the Jewish people and its betrayal of Jesus, and to assign responsibility for his death to them.[16]

These Jewish accounts of the crucifixion had as their goal the exoneration of the Jews. The Reformers thus sought to remove what they considered to be a root cause of antisemitism. Their weapons were New Testament criticism and an insistence that Jesus and the Jews of his day were not antagonistic to each other.[17] The Reformers' approach to the crucifixion, therefore, represents another example of their attempt to deprive Christianity of Jesus.

While seeking to free the Jews from any responsibility for the death of Jesus, the Reformers, at the same time, appropriated the rich religious symbolism of the crucifixion for their own purposes. The Reformers had not only deprived Christianity of its Jesus by stressing his Jewishness, but they also sought to deprive Christianity of the crucifixion by claiming that it was a more appropriate symbol for the Jewish religious experience. Thus, for the Reformers, it was not Jesus who suffered on the cross because of the cruelty of the Jews, but the Jews who were the martyred people who had suffered at the hands of Christians throughout the centuries. In a new application of the Isaianic suffering servant motif, some Reformers saw the Jews as the messiah people who had undergone great suffering as the result of the sins of the world. According to Kaufmann Kohler, one of the most articulate expositors of this theory, the central idea of Judaism was that the Jewish people was "the man of sorrows from whose wounds flow the balm of healing for the nations." Israel was to Judaism what Christ was to the Church. "The Jews are a people of Christs. Not A Jew but THE Jew is the God-chosen mediator between the nations and creeds and classes of men whose life blood has so often to atone for the sins of the world. This is the solution of the Jewish question, this is the explanation of the perplexing puzzle concerning the wandering Jew."[18] The transference of the potent religions symbolism of the crucifixion from Jesus to the Jewish historical experience underlined the Reform concept of the mission of Israel in a very striking way. It gave a formulation that was easily translatable to Christians while at the same time, it brought home the reality of Christian antisemitism in a dramatic manner.

IV

Along with their attempt to prove that Jesus did not stand apart from the main streams of first century Palestinian Judaism, the Reformers also contested the liberal Protestant assertion that the ethics of Jesus surpassed those of Judaism. The argument over ethics was extremely important for both the Reformers and the liberal Protestants. Since their version of Judaism deemphasized the national and halachic aspects of Judaism and was defined by ethics, the Reformers not only had to defend Jewish ethics but they had to demonstrate their superiority over Christian ethics or be left with no justification for continued Jewish existence. Christian liberals, on the other hand, based their claim to Christian religious superiority on the ethics of Jesus. If Jesus' ethics were not superior to those of Judaism, then there would be no basis for the claim that Christianity had superseded Judaism. Therefore, the crucial battleground between Jewish and Christian religious liberals was over the question of ethics.

Rabbi Alex Lyons of Albany succinctly summarized the Jewish position when he remarked that "Unitarianism, Ethical Culture, or any other liberal religious denomination cannot offer ethical or moral values that are not more abundantly furnished by Judaism."[19] The Reformers insisted that Jesus did not depart from the accepted Jewish ethical norms of his day. Emil G. Hirsch and others declared that the majestic sentiments expressed in the Lord's Prayer, the Sermon on the Mount, and the Golden Rule were all echoes of sentiments found in contemporary rabbinic sources. Time and again the Reformers pointed to parallels between the teachings of Jesus and those found in Jewish sources. Typical of this approach was Joseph Krauskopf who devoted a ten page appendix to his book on the Oberammergau passion play to a detailed listing of Jesus' ethical teachings, and in adjoining columns cited the rabbinic parallels. The problem was that Christian scholars refused to acknowledge the Jewish roots of Jesus' ethics. Reformers complained bitterly that most Christian scholars were either ignorant of the rabbinic material or, if aware of it, sought to create artificial differences between it and Jesus out of a preconceived wish to demonstrate the superiority of Christianity.[20]

The Reformers, of course, were unable to escape the fact that some of the ethical teachings of Jesus simply could not be reconciled with Jewish values. In such cases, the Reformers either historicized Jesus' teaching or tried to show that it was inferior to Jewish ethical doctrine. In an article on the ethics of Jesus, Emil G. Hirsch explained that an examination of Jesus' doctrine in the light of the historical setting of first century Palestinian life could account for the instances in which Jesus differed from Jewish ethical norms. Thus, standards preached by Jesus that called for giving all of one's possessions to the poor, abandoning one's family to follow him, and passive submission to evil resulted from his messianism. The messianic ideal of the suffering humble Isaianic servant of God motivated Jesus, and he felt that by exemplifying this ideal he would disarm the wicked. Moreover, Jesus believed that he was living during the time of suffering and social injustice which, according to Jewish tradition, was to precede the redemption. In the new redeemed world, private possessions would be unknown for God would provide for all, and family relationships would blend away into a broader fellowship. These teachings, therefore, were perfectly understandable within the context of Jewish apocalyptic messianism. However, detached from their historical context and vested with absolute authority, they were harmful to society.[21]

A more usual method used by the Reformers to deal with the preachments of Jesus that did not conform to those of the Judaism of his day was to critique them and to try to demonstrate their inferiority to Jewish ethical ideals. A good example of the Jewish critique is found in Kaufmann Kohler's contrast of Jewish and Christian ethics. Kohler explained that the basis of Jewish ethics was their concept of God. The Old Testament presented a holy God who was "the consuming fire to purge the world of sin and wrong-doing, falsehood and impurity." He was a jealous God whose anger was a manifestation of His moral nature. It was kindled in order to establish justice and truth in human society. The goal of Judaism, declared Kohler, was the moral uplifting of man individually and socially. Judaism was the only religion that had this as its aim. Christianity's great failure was that it adopted a pessimistic and despairing view of man:

> Denying man the crown of divinity, in order to place it solely upon the head of one man, it learned to distrust humanity's power of recuperation, and, in despair of this world became all 'other-worldliness,' preaching a love which disregards justice and all the claims of human society.

The results of this on one hand, have been an altruistic socialism which negates the claims of the self, and on the other, an extreme individualism such as that preached by Nietzsche, which ignores the claims of society. Kohler contended that modern ethics, with its emphasis on meliorism and its assumption of man's essential goodness represented a return to the basics of the Jewish ethical outlook.[22]

According to Kohler, Jewish ethics were based on truth, justice and holiness. Whereas Christianity proclaimed love to be the greatest virtue, Kohler pointed out that love untempered by a passion for truth had led Christianity to emphasize doctrinal creed. This, in turn, had resulted in persecution. Love was not a proper foundation upon which a workable structure for social relations could be built. It was subjective, for no man could love all men alike, and it overlooked faults and thus condoned wrongdoing. Justice, not love, was an assertion of the worth and innate dignity of every human being. Moreover, the Jewish principle of justice incorporated love and elevated it beyond condescending charity or sentimental sympathy by insisting that maltreatment of the poor and weak was an affront to God. Christian philanthropy and love were inadequate to meet the needs of contemporary society which was torn by social and economic injustice. The poor would not be satisfied by a few crumbs from the tables of the rich. Only the demands of justice could set society aright.[23]

A major point of contention in the argument over ethics between Jewish and Christian liberals was the Christian assertion that Christianity was universalistic while Judaism was narrow and particularistic. The Reformers responded to this claim by trying to show that Jewish ethics were more universalistic than Christian ethics. Emil G. Hirsch countered the charge that Jews were hostile to Christianity by citing medieval Jewish sources that portrayed Christianity as a monotheistic religion, and by pointing to the fact that it was not the Jews who had persecuted Christians during the Middle Ages but rather Christians who had persecuted Jews. Far from being hostile to non-Jews, Judaism, according to Hirsch, manifested its greatest genius in its universalism. He pointed to the prophetic writings and the Psalms as examples of Jewish religious literature containing universalistic sentiments. On the other hand, charged Hirsch, the gospels presented Jesus as a nationalist Jew who had come to preach only to the Jews, and who on occasion, showed marked dislike of non-Jews. The claim by Christian liberals that Judaism was inferior to Christianity because it had never taught the ethic of "love your enemies" was misleading. In practice, wrote Hirsch, Jews had lived up to this ideal far more than had Christians, and he cited as an example the fact that Jewish hospitals served Christian patients as well as Jews. Christians, on the other hand, had displayed little love for their Christian opponents and none at all for the Jews.[24] Kohler, in his response to the charge of Jewish particularism, alluded to the intricate, although seemingly paradoxical, link between Jewish universalism and particularism. He declared that Jewish ethics were universalistic because they were based on the belief that all men were created in the image of God. However, although Jewish ethics were universalistic, the world had not yet accepted them, and until it did, the Jews had to maintain their own separate existence. Kohler explained that the Jewish vision of justice and holiness had been so antagonistic to the prevailing ethical notions in ancient times that a special law of seclusion for the Jews had to be created in order to preserve it. A people whose function was to live a life of disciplined self control was needed to direct mankind onto a better path. This people, "a kingdom of priests and a holy nation," was to teach mankind by example. Today, when vice was still rampant in society, mankind continued to need the vision and the example of the Jewish people, and therefore, the Jews had to continue to exist as a separate group. Thus Kohler attempted to resolve the tension between the universalistic and particularistic aspects of Judaism by maintaining the superiority and universal application of Jewish ethics while at the same time insisting upon the continuing Jewish mission to teach those ethics to mankind.[25]

V

All of the Reform writers portrayed Jesus as a loyal Jew who loved his people and was at one with them in their aspirations and doctrines. In this way, the Reformers denied the liberal Protestant claim of spiritual uniqueness for Jesus. The Reformers, however differed over whether or not there wasn't some way in which Jesus was special. There were those who agreed with Emanuel Schreiber, who said that Jesus was not at all exceptional. For him, "Jesus was a star among stars, the light of which mingles with the brilliancy of the others so much as scarcely to be distinct from it."[26] Others, however, did perceive something exceptional in Jesus. Emil G. Hirsch wrote that Jesus perfected the rabbinic method of teaching by parable and that he became the outstanding example of the rabbinic teacher.[27] Kohler stated that Jesus' willing fellowship with the poor and the outcasts of society set him apart from the other Jewish religious leaders of his time.[28] These distinctions, however, implied no departure from Judaism. Where Jesus differed was in emphasis and tone, but not in content. Indeed, for the Reformers, those characteristics that distinguished Jesus did not separate him from the Judaism of his day. They were, on the contrary, an illustration of the great spiritual vitality that informed first century Palestinian Judaism. Rabbi Hyman G. Enelow's understanding of Jesus is a good example of this approach. According to Enelow, Jesus was a supreme individualist who was able to give "a fresh message concerning the meaning and the purpose of religion, a new illumination of the sense and the object of the old law and of the old prophetic utterances." While the content of his message was not new, Jesus did teach the essential truths and beauties of religion in his own way and by means of his own personal experience. Jewish teachers generally taught through impersonal principles and doctrines. Jesus, on the other hand, taught personally, pointing to himself as an incarnation of his teaching. Thus,

> when Moses addressed the Israelites, and wished to bring the thought of God home to them, he said: 'The God of your fathers has sent me unto you.' Jesus, on the other hand, always spoke of his own God, his own Father. It was not a different idea; it was a change of emphasis, and the change was toward the accentuation of the personal element, Jesus' own interfusion with his teaching.[29]

Neither the Essenes nor any other group shaped Jesus' personality and spirituality. He belonged to no group although he was closest to the Pharisees. Enelow attributed his outstanding traits to his Galilean origin. Like his Galilean brethren, Jesus possessed a mercurial temperament and this explained some of his contradictory actions and statements.

> He is capable of love and hate, of devotion and of detachment a man of fervid friendship and of solitude. His mood is not always the same. He is lyrical rather than legalistic. He does not set out to break the laws, but he knows that character is greater than conformity. He is loyal and devout, true to the past, but also to himself. He is now tolerant and now contemptuous of the Gentiles. A true Galilean![30]

Enelow's description of Jesus contained another important element. Like most of the Reformers, Enelow distinguished between the cultic and the prophetic strains in Judaism. Jesus was an exemplar of the prophetic strain, emphasizing the spirit of the law over its letter. By describing Jesus as a Jew who had been energized by the prophetic spirit, Enelow, in effect, was characterizing him as a proto Reform Jew. Since the Reformers argued that the driving force in Reform Judaism was the prophetic spirit, and since Jesus' spiritual greatness lay in his individualistic articulation of that spirit, the identification of Jesus with the ideals of Reform was clear. With this, the Reformers' appropriation of Jesus from Christianity was now complete.[31]

VI

Having described Jesus as Jewish in thought and deed and having attributed to him nothing that would distance him either from the Jews or the Judaism of his time, the Reformers had to account for the divergence of Christianity from Judaism in a way that eliminated Jesus as a factor. They did this by stressing the role of Paul as the founder of Christianity.

Reform statements about Paul have to be understood within the context of two separate but contemporaneous polemics, one internal and the other external. The internal polemic focussed on the Reformers' answer to the charge levelled by the traditionalists that Reform's rejection of the mandatory nature of the Law was Paulinian. The external polemic was a response to liberal Protestants who had rejected the Paulinian scheme of salvation and who claimed that elements of that scheme had their basis in Judaism.

The latter decades of the nineteenth century were marked by a growing tension between Reformers and traditionalists in the American Jewish community. This tension reached a peak in the wake of the 1885 Pittsburgh Platform, a declaration of principles defining Reform Judaism in America. This far-reaching statement that denied the religious authority of the Mosaic law, except for those laws that conformed to the spirit of the age, and rejected the traditional Jewish hope for the restoration of the Jews to the land of Israel, angered the traditionalist camp and was a major contributing factor leading to the establishment of a traditionalist rabbinical school, the Jewish Theological Seminary of America, which was to rival the Reform dominated Hebrew Union College in Cincinnati. In the contention between the two sides, the traditionalists charged that the Reform position on the nonbinding nature of the ceremonial law was Paulinian, and that Reform, therefore, represented a step towards Christianity. Since some Christians also interpreted the Reform position in the same way, there was a clear need for a Reform response on the issue.[32]

Reformers met the charge of Paulinianism in a number of ways. Emil B. Hirsch sought to turn the tables on the traditionalists by alleging certain affinities between orthodoxy and Paul. Since orthodox Judaism was legalistic, he asserted, the orthodox Jew feels himself to be a sinner, at least to some extent, because he cannot fulfill all of the commandments. Unlike Paul, however, the orthodox Jew cannot abrogate the Law and is, therefore, trapped in his sense of guilt. Reform Judaism, which does not accept the Law as binding, averts this trap. An added problem was that the legal emphasis of orthodoxy and the sense of guilt that this engendered might make orthodox Jews more vulnerable to missionary appeals. Hirsch admitted, however, that he had no evidence that this was happening.[33] On another occasion, Hirsch charged that by reducing Judaism to law, orthodoxy was giving ammunition to Christians who contrasted legalistic Judaism with the nobler religion of Jesus.[34]

Aside from his critique of orthodoxy's emphasis on law, Hirsch sought to deflect the traditionalist equation of Reform with Paulinianism by pointing to what he alleged were borrowings from Christianity that had been absorbed into contemporary orthodox practice. Hirsch, the sober rationalist, decried the emotional piety that the recently arrived east-European immigrants were injecting into the traditional synagogue. "The influence of Christianity," he declared, "where unction and its expressions are legitimate" has become part of American orthodoxy. He lashed out at the "wearisome prayerfulness of the men of the new piety" and ridiculed the traditional rabbis as a "hymn-singing and eye-shutting set of reverends." Hirsch also perceived Christian influence in the area of Sabbath observance. He claimed that "Puritanical idiosyncracies" had developed among the traditionalists and that as a result they were transforming the Sabbath into an austere and mournful day. In addition, he blamed the traditionalists for transforming the customary role of the rabbi as teacher and scholar into that of pastor. The scholarly Hirsch declared that: "In radical temples the rabbi is known to have other and more useful obligations than to be an appendix to the apron of some 'sister' and an adornment to the parlors of some newly-ennobled baron by the grace of a plethoric purse." He criticized this "pastoral humbug" as a borrowing from the Christian ministry for which the orthodox were responsible, and asserted that in contrast to the orthodox, "The radicals have refused to be Christianized in this as in everything else."[35]

In addition to the claim that it was orthodoxy and not Reform that had been influenced by Paul and by Christianity, the Reformers also presented a sharp critique of Paul's theology. This was meant to prove that the ideas of Paul were incompatible with Judaism in general and with Reform Judaism in particular. Disassociating Reform Judaism from Paul would not only answer the orthodox charge of Reform Paulinianism but would also serve as a response to liberal Protestant writers who claimed that Paul's theory of salvation was rooted in Jewish ideas. Many nineteenth century liberal Protestants who considered the unique personality and ethical teachings of Jesus to be the essence of Christianity, sought to divest Christianity of its Paulinian dogmas which they viewed as a deterioration from the religion of Jesus. They identified Judaism as the core source of Paul's ideas. The Reformers denied this link. They agreed with the liberal Protestants that Paul's ideas represented a setback in the progress of religious development. However, for them, neither Jesus nor his ethical teachings were unique. Both Jesus and his teachings were part and parcel of first century Palestinian Judaism. That being the case, in the words of rabbi Bernhard Felsenthal: "The religion of Christ and the Christian religion are not identical."[36] It was Paul who founded Christianity. Now, when many enlightened Christians were ridding themselves of Paulinian theology, they were, in effect, disassociating themselves from Christianity and thus proving the truth and superiority of Judaism. For Christians to understand this, however, it was necessary to show that Paulinian theology was not a product of Judaism.

Two outstanding examples of Reform's distancing Paul from Judaism were Kaufmann Kohler and Emil G. Hirsch. Kohler, like all of the Reformers, considered Paul to be the founder of Christianity. His writings, according to Kohler, contained no trace of rabbinic teaching and only those unfamiliar with rabbinic writings and theology could base Paul's doctrines on Jewish ideas. Paul was a Hellenistic Jew who had been influenced by Gnostic ideas and probably by the pagan Hermes literature as well. Kohler wrote that Paul's harshly negative attitude towards the Law was the clearest example of his antagonism towards Judaism, while, his entire theology of redemption centered on Jesus' atoning death was alien to the Jewish mind. To be sure, Kohler's negative attitude towards Paul was mitigated to some extent by an appreciation of Paul's universalism. Kohler described him as "an instrument in the hands of Divine Providence to win the heathen nations for Israel's God of righteousness." However, while Paul succeeded in turning the heathens away from idolatry to the worship of God and provided them with a higher ethical standard, his unviersalism was flawed. Instead of dividing mankind into Jews and Gentiles, Paul's system made a division between those who were saved and those who were damned.[37]

In a sermon delivered in 1894 entitled "Paul, the Apostle of Heathen Judaism or Christianity," subsequently published in his *Reform Advocate,* Emil G. Hirsch tried to demonstrate how the basic assumptions upon which Paul's system rested were antagonistic to Judaism. While granting that Paul borrowed the concept of a mediator between God and man from Alexandrian Hellenistic Judaism, Hirsch maintained that the fundamental element in Paul's system was Greek and not Jewish. Paul's starting point was the sinful nature of man, an idea alien to Judaism. He mistakenly equated man's feeling of imperfection with sin, and then attached to this the Greek belief in the transmission of sin from generation to generation until expiation was made. Against this Greek belief, Hirsch pointed to the Bible's limitation of inherited evil to four generations and to Ezekiel's declaration that the sons shall not die for the sins of the fathers. Paul's next step was to provide a framework of substitute atonement through which man could overcome the consequences of his sinful nature. Hirsch asserted that this concept of vicarious atonement was Semitic, not Jewish. It was based on the ancient tribal custom of blood vengeance in which the life of one of the tribe answers for the life of another. Moreover, insisted Hirsch, the belief in vicarious atonement also diverged from Judaism because it was based on the concept of a wrathful rather than a loving God.

> As in the anti and ante prophetic religions, sin is an offense against God and may and must be compensated by gifts, that is sacrifices; so in the system of Paul, sin is an outrage perpetrated upon God who in consequence is bound to punish and must be placated by the one great and mysterious sacrificial death of the substituted lamb. Christianity proclaims the wrathful God, who dooms and damns all men because one man disobeyed, as did paganism the capricious God.

In contrast, Judaism maintained "that love, not sacrifice, knowledge, not holocaust open the gateway of mercy and bring peace to man." Hirsch did concede that there were statements in rabbinic literature that seemed to indicate belief in transmitted sin or vicarious atonement. These however, he dismissed as merely "poetic" expressions that were not meant as statements of dogma.

One more important way in which Paul differed from Judaism was his rejection of the law. While Hirsch, like Kohler, conceded that this had the beneficial effect of making it possible for Judaic monotheism to spread to the Gentiles, it also had an important negative consequence. It led Paul to place an exaggerated stress on faith. Prophetic Judaism too, declared Hirsch, had broken with legalism, however, it did not do so at the expense of ethical action. Paul's emphasis on faith was foreign to Judaism for Judaism taught that proper action rather than correct belief led to salvation.[38]

While Kohler and Hirsch reflect the Reform attempt to claim Jesus and to disassociate Paul from Judaism, both of these Reform leaders found one positive element in Paul—his universalism. Other Reform writers, notably Isaac M. Wise and Joseph Krauskopf, showed an even greater appreciation of this and manifested less of an attempt to sever Paul from Judaism.

Isaac M. Wise identified Paul with Elisha ben Abbuya, the famous Talmudic scholar who became a sectarian after undergoing a mystical experience. According to Wise, Paul was a loyal Jew, an "Orthodox Pharisee," who sought to spread Jesus' teaching of the coming of the kingdom of heaven to the Gentiles. He believed in neither a triune God nor the divinity of Jesus. Wise described Paul as a mystic, an apocalyptic who believed in the imminent end of the world which would be accompanied by the last judgment of all men. He sought to provide a means through which the Gentiles could be saved from the effects of their sinfulness when the judgment came. He did so by transferring the rabbinic belief in the angel Metatron to Jesus, calling him the Son of God and transforming him into a nondivine intermediary between man and God. Faith in Jesus and his atoning death and resurrection would save man from punishment in the coming judgment. Paul, however, did not really believe this salvation myth that he had created. He intended it to frighten the Gentiles and to bring them to a belief in God. The problem arose when the end did not come, and Paul's later followers misunderstood his intention and continued to adhere to his ideas, thereby extending them into absurdities. Wise described Paul as a great man who had a broad vision of universal salvation and whose goal was to destroy heathenism. To be sure, Paul had committed a grave mistake when he resorted to "fictions" and these fictions were the root of the distortions that led Christianity to diverge from Judaism. However, it was never Paul's intention to depart from Judaism, and for Wise, Paul was a spiritual hero because of his broad universalistic vision of a Judaized world.[39]

Joseph Krauskopf also presented a sympathetic treatment of Paul in his *A Rabbi's Impressions of the Oberammergau Passion Play.* Largely ignoring Paul's theology, Krauskopf instead dwelled on his universalism. When Paul became the apostle to the Gentiles:

> the Nazarenes ceased to be a sect and Judaism a tribal religion. In that moment a cosmopolitan religion was born. In that moment the ethical teachings of Judaism crossed the border of their birthplace, under the spiritual leadership of Jesus, the Jew, in the guise of a mystical Christ. In that moment a spiritual alliance was formed between Jew and Gentile that has endured to this day. That moment opened a new epoch in the world's history.[40]

It was a great tragedy of history, wrote Krauskopf, that a compromise was not effected between Paul and the Nazarene followers of Jesus who continued to observe the Biblical commandments. Such a compromise, under which the Nazarenes would have yielded their fondness for ceremonialism and their spirit of exclusiveness, and Paul his mythical and mystical Christology, would have given birth to a purified ethical Judaism that would have spread throughout the world. Krauskopf declared that it was the appeal of Jewish ethics rather than the attraction of the mythical Jesus that drew heathens to the new religion. Judaism had been a successful missionary religion even when it was burdened with ceremonialism. It would have achieved far greater success had it dropped its ceremonialism; and with a man of Paul's dynamism to preach the ethics of Moses, the prophets, and the rabbis, while holding up Jesus as an exemplar of those ethics, it would have conquered the world. The fact that in the development of Christianity, the mythical Jesus prevailed over Jewish ethics was a tragedy that resulted in great harm to both Christianity and the Jews. The Jews, however, were grateful to Paul, declared Krauskopf, for showing them how Judaism could become a world conquering religion by ridding itself of useless and repellent ceremonials. Krauskopf looked forward optimistically to the coming day when Christianity, shorn of its dogmas, and Judaism, rid of its ceremonials, would see a new religion in which "Jew and Gentile will be one."[41] Thus, for Wise and even more so for Krauskopf, the inadequacies of Paul's theology are overshadowed by his universalistic vision, a vision rooted in prophetic Judaism. This universalistic element in Paul was fully consonant with their own anticipations and hopes for a future universalistic religion, a religion that they equated with Reform Judaism.[42] Paul, the founder of Christianity, created a religion that was an extension of Judaism. His theology was a necessary expedient to make it possible for the heathens to accept Jewish monotheism more easily. In this, Wise and Krauskopf were following in the footsteps of those medieval Jewish authorities who viewed Christianity and Islam as means of spreading Judaism. The writings of Wise and Krauskopf on Paul are another example of appropriating from Christianity its positive aspects and claiming them for Judaism. This emphasis on Jewish–Christian commonalities left Christianity without any inherent positive religious contribution of its own. The assertion that true Christianity (non–Paulinian) was identical with true Judaism (nonceremonial) was the heart of the insidership claim of American Jews that Judaism and Americanism were the same. Kohler and Hirsch, who took a critical attitude towards Paul based on his theology, were making the same argument for insidership. In their responses to both traditional Jews and liberal Protestants, they identified Christianity with Paulinian theology. By denying altogether or at least minimizing the Jewish roots of Paul's thought, they were pointing to the dissimilarities between Judaism and Christianity, and to the superiority of Judaism. However, at a time when Christianity was shedding its Paulinian cover, the gap between the two religions was narrowing and eventually all that would be left of Christianity would be Jesus and his teachings, which, if understood correctly, would be recognized as Judaism.

VII

American liberal Christianity posed a significant challenge to the Reformers who had discarded so much of the traditional religious life style on the grounds that it did not conform to modern taste. A Judaism shorn of its historically distinctive way of life and its hope for national restoration appeared to some (both Christians and Jews) to be barely distinguishable from contemporary liberal Christianity with its rejection of the Calvinist framework and its reevaluation of the nature of Jesus. Moreover, some Christian liberals were espousing a more appreciative view of Judaism, especially Reform Judaism. The Biblical scholar Crawford Howell Toy expressed admiration for Jewish spirituality and perseverance in the face of adversity. He criticized Christian maltreatment of the Jews and considered Christian prejudice to be the cause of the Jewish problem in the modern world. Similarly, the liberal theologian Lyman Abbott pointed out Christianity's debt to Judaism and wrote movingly of Jewish suffering at the hands of Christians. Nevertheless, neither Toy nor Abbott was willing to concede that Judaism was the equal of Christianity or that it had a future. Both viewed Judaism as a precursor to Christianity which had superseded it, and both anticipated that the Jews would ultimately accept Christianity.[43]

The hope of Jewish conversion seems to have been widespread among Christian liberals at this time. In an article entitled "Can Jews be Christians?", Washington Gladden described his impressions of the Jewish ghetto of the lower east side of New York. He noted approvingly the industriousness, close family life, and remarkable efforts at self help that characterized the immigrant community. He lashed out at past Christian persecution of the Jews and expressed the hope that in free America Christian and Jew would live together in peace. The point of Gladding's article, however, was to show that since the Jews did possess positive character traits, they could become Christians. Contemporary trends in both Christianity and Judaism, according to Gladden, seemed to be pointing in that direction. The liberalization of theology in Christianity, and the progress of reform which had discarded the "merely formal and technical" aspects of Judaism, boded well for the reconciliation of the two faiths. However, that reconciliation would have to be on Christian terms, as Gladding made clear when he concluded his article by inviting the Jews to "join with us in honoring and following your kinsman and our Master, Jesus Christ of Nazareth."[44]

It was in this atmosphere of hope for Christian-Jewish reconciliation that suggestions were made that the Jews merge with the Unitarians. Several such proposals came in the wake of the promulgation of the Pittsburgh platform. One originated with Felix Adler, founder of

the Ethical Culture movement. Another came in a letter from Lewis
Godlove to Rabbi Solomon H. Sonneschein of St. Louis. The Reformers quickly and categorically rejected these proposals. Responding to
Adler, Rabbi Gustav Gottheil argued that if a union were to be effected, the Unitarians should join the Jews because Judaism was the
older religion. Gottheil, however, did not argue strongly that Judaism
and Unitarianism were incompatible.[45]

Other Reformers, however, did point to the incompatibility of the
two religions. Maurice Harris, rabbi of New York's Temple Israel, explained the impossibility of a Unitarian-Jewish merger by citing the
difficulties posed in overcoming the differences created by the past histories of the two groups. He believed that Unitarianism represented a
Christian return to Judaism, and, like Gottheil, felt that the Unitarians
should seek a merger with Judaism rather than vice versa. Asking Jews
to become Unitarians was like "asking the ocean to flow back into its
tributaries." The real problem in effecting a merger, however, was not
a dispute over who was the progenitor. It lay instead in overcoming the
force of "sentimental association and historic background in religious
life." A religion, argued Harris, consists of more than beliefs and ceremonies. It also contains essential symbols that go back to its earliest
stage of development. While within each religious group, radicals and
traditionalists might disagree over the interpretation of these symbols,
all were united in the need to retain the symbols as vital and defining
forces for the religion. Neither Jews nor Unitarians could escape their
histories. Even though Unitarians accepted biblical criticism and modern science, and despite their rejection of the concepts of the trinity,
original sin, vicarious atonement, and the divinity of Jesus, they still
retained the central religious symbol of Christianity—Jesus—and insisted that he was in some way unique. This was something that they
could never surrender. "The divine man in some sense he will always
be to them, for this is their inheritance from Christianity that has become part of their very being. He is still the Master with a capital M.
Even with those Unitarians who doubt God, who are agnostic—the
worship of Jesus abides." As Harris saw it, the issue separating liberal
Jews from liberal Christians was the same issue that had always separated Jews from Christians—Jesus. Jews in the past had never accepted
the worship of Jesus as a divine figure, and while Jews in the present
could appreciate the value of Jesus the man, they could not accept his
veneration as someone unique who had surpassed the Judaism of his
day. Harris felt that Unitarianism had nothing to offer to the Jews. Its
value was in holding up a more rational and liberal ideal to orthodox
Christianity.[46]

Harris' pessimistic analysis clearly took account of contemporary trends in Unitarianism. The latter part of the nineteenth century was a period of controversy during which the denomination was split over how to define its relationship to Christianity. At one pole stood the evangelicals who felt an affinity for more traditional modes of Christianity, and some of whom left Unitarianism to join traditional Christian denominations. At the other pole were the radicals, the most extreme of whom, like Francis E. Abbot, rejected Christianity entirely and went over into free religion. However, the main thrust of Unitarian development was represented by a centrist group known as the Broad Church. Their position entailed a primary commitment to Christianity; an assertion of the importance of the Church as an institution; and an insistence on historical continuities in religion. The Broad Church men claimed a uniqueness for Christianity, but they eschewed the evidence of miracles. Instead, they believed that Christianity not only contained the truth that all other religions taught, but in addition, supplied what they lacked. Even without its supernatural origins, Christianity "would still be the indispensable medium through which men and women could best find expression for their religious sentiments and satisfaction for their religious longings."[47] The Unitarian commitment to Christianity and belief in its superiority clearly demonstrate that even when dogmatic considerations were removed, emotional and sentimental commitments rendered impossible a Jewish-Unitarian merger.

Emil G. Hirsch also reacted to the suggestions that the Jews join the Unitarians and added other reasons why this was impossible. Like Harris, Hirsch maintained that the critical issue between Jews and Unitarians was Jesus. However, there were other factors as well that prevented the coming together of Jews and Unitarians. He was angry and frustrated at liberal Protestants for not acknowledging that Judaism had created enduring religious and spiritual values. Repeatedly, Hirsch expressed his deep resentment at liberal Protestants for their assertion that Christianity had a broader and nobler spirit than Judaism and that it had surpassed it. Addressing the World Parliament of Religions in Chicago in 1893, Hirsch complained that Christian speakers, even liberal ones, always proclaimed that Christianity was the religion of absolute good. If virtue were seen in a Jew, it was not because of, but despite, his religion. "It is always Christian sweetness and Christian love that acts like oil on troubled waters. Jews are admitted to the circle of the elect, but their function is always that of a peg where on others may hang their tolerance and liberalism."[48] As long as Christians refused to admit that Judaism contained enduring religious values,

Jews could not give up the name of Jew. Hirsch expressed his defiance in an editorial in the *Reform Advocate:*

> Shall we then give up our name as long as it is a by-word among the nations; as long as it is held that it covers either stubbornness, obstinacy, blindness or downright wickedness? He is a coward who would take to his heels in days of danger. Shall we be cowards? They must first give up the name Christian as qualification for all that is noble or good, or true, before we will consider the proposition to sink our historic designation. We may make ready to give up our livery, when they abandon theirs.[49]

For eighteen centuries the world had equated Judaism with evil. To abandon Judaism now in the face of Christian self-righteousness and condescension would be a dishonorable act of treason against the Jewish past. "The fathers," declared Hirsch, "call upon us from their graves to defend their memory from this opprobrious, this unjust imputation," and, he continued, "I as one of their sons cannot be deaf to the call, I must defend this sacred memory as long as it is aspersed and attacked; in this sense we are Jews." There was, however, another sense in which Hirsch felt the need for continued Jewish existence. While his anger at the perverse intellectual anti-Jewish prejudice that prevented liberal Christians from granting Judaism its due, and his recoil from the thought of betraying the Jewish past, may be viewed as responses that are largely emotional in character, Hirsch also presented an argument against a Jewish-Unitarian merger that was not essentially emotional. The argument was Reform's mission theory. Judaism was contributing something unique and necessary to the world in its active social-oriented ethical system, and this would be lost if the Jews were to disappear. Religious mergers were not a simple matter. Religions were not all alike; they were separated by essential differences. "Judaism is not the equivalent of other religions merely; it is more than the equivalent, and you cannot substitute one religion for another. You cannot make a new religion by taking in five drops of Judaism and eight drops of Christianity, and five drops of Buddhism and then the whole to be well shaken before taken." Judaism was different from all other religions because it alone "stands for every positive conception of the world and of life."[50] In an article entitled "Are the Jews the Chosen People?" Hirsch explained that God was using the Jewish people in an experiment to see how far the principle of social cooperation could be actualized. Conceding that Unitarianism and Ethical Culture had messages that were "substantially identical" with that of Judaism, Hirsch insisted that the Jews had "the historic duty to show what it essentially means; ours it is to prove that cooperation translated into action is highest law." This was Israel's mission, and until the day came when "monotheism will be incorporated in all the social institutions of humanity" that mission would not be fulfilled.[51]

VIII

Liberal Protestant assertions of the ethical superiority of Christianity and hopes for a Jewish merger into Christianity were not the only threat that the late nineteenth century Reformers faced. Their claims of Jewish uniqueness based on the Jewish mission theory and Jewish ethics also had to contend with a number of liberal Jewish challenges. The most cogent challenge came from Felix Adler who founded the Ethical Culture Society in 1876. Adler, son of the famous Reform rabbi, Samuel Adler, formulated a denationalized, nondenominational form of religion based on a humanistic ethic lacking a belief in God. Like the Reformers, Adler emphasized ethics as the core of religion. However, he differed from them in that he believed that modern scientific knowledge had rendered unfeasible the basic Reform religious beliefs in monotheism and the mission of the Jewish people. He also rejected the absolute superiority of Biblical prophetic ethics because they rested on a belief in God and on the concept of Jewish mission. He even expressed a preference for the Christian emphasis on love over the Jewish stress on justice, believing it better suited to address the social needs of man. Adler's ideas, therefore, present a total negation of the Reform position in their denial of God, of Jewish mission, and of the superiority of Jewish ethics. They left no rationale for continued Jewish group existence.[52]

The Reformers' response to Adler was one of anger and frustration; anger because this keen Jewish intellect and son of a prominent rabbi had left the fold, and frustration because his public lectures drew significant numbers of Jewish listeners. Nevertheless, the Reform rabbinic response to Adler was muted. This may have been due in part to friendship, as in the case of Emil G. Hirsch, or a desire to convince Adler to proclaim some formal adherence to Judaism, as in the case of Bernhard Felsenthal. It has also been suggested that the rabbis did not want to alienate their congregants who attended Adler's lectures and who paid their salaries. Some of them recognized that Adler possessed a superior intellect and, therefore, did not want to lock horns with him. In any event, among the Reformers, only Kohler issued a sharp attack against Adler calling him an atheist, and, by virtue of this, someone who had left the bounds of Judaism.[53]

The Reformers may have been hesitant to take on Adler, but they manifested no similar reluctance in responding to the challenge posed by Josephine Lazarus. In a series of articles in the Jewish press which

she later published in book form under the title *The Spirit of Judaism,*
Lazarus, the sister of the poetess Emma Lazarus, declared that Judaism
no longer had any spiritual value and therefore had no reason to continue to exist.[54] She advocated a new universalistic religion into which
both Judaism and Christianity would merge, but in which the Christian element would predominate. Duty, the basic ingredient of Judaism, would join with love, the essential ingredient of Christianity, to
form the basis of the new religion; but Christian love, which both incorporated and went beyond Jewish duty, would be its dominant
feature.[55] Lazarus agreed with the Reformers that the essence of Judaism was its moral code which had reached its highest expression in the
Biblical prophets. Prophecy, however, had died and its moral emphasis
had failed to become the religion of the masses. Instead, the people
needed a more concrete means to bring the Deity to life, and they
found it in the regimen of the law. When the Jews lost their state and
the external trappings of a nation, it was the law that held them together. At the same time, however, it made them turn inwards and, as
a result, Judaism lost the universalistic spirit that had been characteristic of its moral outlook.[56] If Judaism was to have any spiritual relevance today, it had to move beyond its particularism. Judaism could
not be saved, she wrote, "in any narrow, in any broad sense even, unless we lose it, by merging and adding to it that which will make it no
longer Judaism, because it is something that the whole world claims,
and therefore cannot be the exclusive prerogative of Judaism. . . . "
Both orthodoxy and Reform were inadequate expressions of Judaism
because both concerned themselves primarily with Jewish self-
preservation. In a stinging attack on what she perceived to be the shal-
lowness and lack of spirituality of contemporary Jewish religiosity,
Lazarus declared:

> In a word, we are still Pharisees and Sadducees, rival sects, intent upon
> our own salvation, and divided among ourselves: those of us who would
> keep the Law to the letter in order to survive, and those of us who would
> break it and still survive—the worldly-wise in our own generation,
> who would relax and infringe for worldly purpose and convenience, while
> still keeping sacred and intact the distinction and prerogative of race. We
> have not changed our point of view in any direction . . . our spiritual ho-
> rizon has not widened. The banner that we hold aloft is "Self": self-
> defense, self-preservation are our watchwords always.[57]

The time had come for the Jews to search within themselves in order
to attain a new religious understanding, to grasp "a truth larger and
deeper than sect or race, binding together even as one sect and race all
who may hold it in common, God's chosen people everywhere." The

time was ripe for this because Christianity was ridding itself of its dog-matism. She urged Jews to abandon their traditional hostile attitude towards Christianity and to open their minds to the possibility that Christianity might contain some religious truth. Declaring that the best of Christianity today was "for the most part, outside the churches and entirely outside of doctrine," Lazarus appealed to the Jews to judge Christianity on the basis of Jesus' message of love, and to see in it a spiritual ideal that surpassed Judaism's emphasis on justice. Christians, too, had their part to play in bringing about the reconciliation between Jews and Christians that would lead the way to the new religion of the future. In the epilogue to her book, Lazarus addressed herself to Chris-tians and appealed to them to live up to Jesus' ideal of love in their treatment of the Jews. Antisemitism was a blot on the Christian char-acter and it reinforced Jewish feelings of antagonism towards Christi-anity. If Christians would exemplify Christian love, and if Jews would move beyond particularism and narrow concern for self-preservation, the major obstacles to the realization of the new universalistic religion would be removed.[58]

Lazarus' book evoked a number of responses from the Reformers. In a review published in the *Reform Advocate,* Kaufmann Kohler con-trasted Lazarus' book with one that had the same title written fifty years earlier by the English Jewish writer Grace Aguilar. While Aguilar was a faithful Jewess who had acted as a spokeswoman for Judaism, Josephine Lazarus called to mind the tragic figures of Uriel Da Costa and Dorothea Mendelssohn, Jews who had wandered from one religion to another in an unsuccessful search for spiritual peace.[59] Kohler, how-ever, did agree with at least part of her critique of contemporary Jew-ish life. He conceded that Reform Judaism had failed to regenerate Jewish spirituality. It had modified the outer form without bringing about either a rebirth of the Jew or of Judaism. Himself one of Re-form's outstanding intellects, Kohler criticized Reform for being too intellectual and for aiming at "an ethical theism with a growing ten-dency to mere humanitarianism." While agreeing that contemporary Jewish life lacked spirituality, Kohler nonetheless argued that Lazarus' argument was seriously flawed. He accused her of being more at home in the New Testament than the Old, and of reading the latter through the eyes of the former. Her basic mistake was that she accepted Paul's dichotomy between Jewish law and Christian love. It was simply un-true to say that Judaism did not stress love. Furthermore, Christian history, replete with its many bloody persecutions, proved that it was impossible to base a social ethic solely on love. Kohler also argued that although contemporary Jewish life might be lacking in spirituality, Ju-daism was not. Lazarus had misunderstood the nature of Jewish spiri-

tuality, and how it differed from Christian spirituality. Whereas
Christian spirituality derived its strength from an emphasis on other-
worldliness, Jewish spirituality was not "mystical or visionary," but
instead, hallowed this life, seeking to enlist man in the service of God,
striving always for truth and righteousness. Moreover, in her discussion of Jewish spirituality, Lazarus had failed to understand the contemporary meaning of the messianic concept. She did not realize,
asserted Kohler, that the idea of a personal messiah had been replaced
by the concept of the Jewish people as the messiah people. Kohler
agreed with Lazarus that contemporary Jewry was too materialistic.
He acknowledged that few Jews were imbued with the messianic spirit,
"this true 'Spirit of Judaism' which demands an humble 'Christ-like'
life to accomplish the priest-mission, the Messianic task of God's chosen ones." Nevertheless, despite the failure of contemporary Jewry to
draw sufficiently from the wells of Jewish messianic spirituality, those
wells contained the nourishment that would regenerate Jewry and
bring redemption to mankind.

Several weeks after the appearance of Kohler's review, Emil G.
Hirsch added his criticism of *The Spirit of Judaism*. Lazarus, he
charged, was typical of many modern Jews who, out of ignorance of
Jewish history and literature, concluded that Judaism was nothing
more than an anachronism. Their primary concern was antisemitism,
and they believed that the Jews could end it by eliminating those things
that differentiated them from the Christians. Since antisemitism was
Lazarus' main concern, she was no more in favor of Reform Judaism
than of orthodoxy. For Jews like Lazarus, wrote Hirsch, "Judaism
must consistently commit harikari, slowly but surely, that there be no
further provocation for non-Jews to complain of the presence on earth
of Jews." On the other hand, the loyal Jew who understood his Judaism "has other ideals to uphold than admission to the hotels and clubs
of descendants of fur trappers and oyster peddlers, of the sons and
daughters of successful railroad wreckers and stock waterers." Hirsch
correctly pronounced Lazarus a Unitarian in everything but name.
Like the unitarians, she accepted the Christian antithesis between love
and law, and like them, she misunderstood law to mean obedience resulting from outward compulsion combined with a hope for reward
and a fear of punishment. She, like the Unitarians, failed to understand
ethical law which was, in fact, the highest form of love. Rather than
lacking spirituality, ethical law spiritualized the law of conduct into
personal sanctity and social justice, and thus manifested its love "not as
an hysterical sentiment but a helpful sense of the solidarity, the brotherly bond between man and man."[60]

From the viewpoint of Kohler and Hirsch, Lazarus had, to all intents and purposes, removed herself from the bounds of Judaism. She neither understood the value of Jewish ethics nor saw the need for continued separate Jewish existence. Josephine Lazarus typified a deeply troubling phenomenon for the Reformers—intelligent but Jewishly ignorant American Jews who had accepted the liberal Protestant assessment of Judaism.

Yet another, although different, kind of liberal Jewish challenge confronted the Reformers when in 1900 the California Jewish businessmen and communal leader, Harris Weinstock, submitted a proposal to the Central Conference of American Rabbis suggesting that the life and teaching of Jesus be included in the curriculum of Jewish religious schools.[61] Weinstock thus challenged the Reformers to put into effective practice their view that Jesus was nothing more nor less than an outstanding Jewish religious teacher. He presented a detailed explanation of his position in a book published two years later entitled *Jesus the Jew.*[62] In it, Weinstock emphasized the complementary nature of the relationship between Judaism and Christianity and the indispensability of the one for the other. Jewish ethics, he wrote, were the basis of Christianity. Judaism, however, was incapable of spreading its ethics to the world because it had turned inward. It was Christianity and especially Paul, who realized that the ceremonials of Judaism hindered its spread among the Gentiles, and who communicated the message of Judaism to mankind. "Had there been no Judaism, there could have been no Christianity. Had there been no Christianity, the message of Judaism could not have become so speedily universalized."[63] Unlike Josephine Lazarus, Weinstock maintained that neither religion should give up its identity to merge into the other or into some new universalistic religion. Both should continue to exist alongside each other. Each, however, should become aware of the essential service that the other was performing for it. This required that Jews adopt a new attitude towards Jesus the man. Following the standard Reform view of Jesus, Weinstock asserted that a careful study of the New Testament, aided by the results of modern scholarship, showed that Jesus "was simply striving to practice and to preach the great moral code established by Moses and the prophets, and to put into practice literally in his daily life the great lawgiver's precept of 'love thy neighbor as thyself.' " The life and teachings of Jesus manifest a simple love of Judaism "which he tried to keep pure and undefiled."[64]

Weinstock's position on Jesus did not go beyond what most Reformers were saying. To be sure, his assertion of the indispensability of Christianity for the world wide dispersal of Jewish ethics was some-

thing that would give the Reformers trouble. While it was true that
Christianity had performed this service in the past, when Judaism was
still encrusted with ceremonialism and parochialism, it was no longer
true today when Reform Judaism, unhindered by ceremonialism and
energized by its mission theory was fully capable of presenting prophetic ethics to the world. Nevertheless, what Weinstock had to say
about Jesus was neither new nor different for the Reformers. Therefore, it is perhaps surprising that the rabbinical organization turned
down Weinstock's proposal. In a carefully worded statement, the committee that had been selected to report on the matter declared that the
historical Jesus, his role in the development of religion, and the Jewish
character of many of his ethical teachings were all matters of "individual view and conviction." However, none of this could "form part
of nor be incorporated in any official statement or declaration of Jewish belief."[65] Clearly there were limits to how far the Reformers were
willing to go even with a human and thoroughly Jewish Jesus. To be
sure, some rabbis did admit to teaching about Jesus in their religious
schools when the occasion called for it.[66] However, the Central Conference was not willing to grant official sanction to this. It is certain
that there must have been a deep seated emotional bias to this reluctance. Despite new intellectual formulations it was impossible to ignore centuries of past history. In all likelihood, an equal if not more
weighty consideration in the decision was the fear that the teaching of
Jesus would cause confusion. It was one thing to preach in sermons
and to write in magazine articles that Jesus was a good and faithful
Jew, who taught nothing contradictory to Jewish doctrine, but it was
another matter to take the next step and incorporate Jesus into formal
Jewish teaching. Without a Christian acknowledgement that Judaism
possessed lasting religious value, and that it was a full partner with
Christianity in bringing redemption to the world, formal Jewish recognition of Jesus by placing him in the Jewish religious school curriculum would be misunderstood by both Christians and Jews alike.
Christians would view it as a step towards Jewish acquiescence with
Christian claims for Jesus.[67] Worse still, the blurring of the lines between Christianity and Judaism could lead to a situation in which not
only liberal Protestants but Jewish youth, too, would ask why Judaism
did not merge with Christianity.

The rabbis' reaction to Weinstock's proposal also raises the question of how broad was the support for the liberal attitude towards
Jesus within the Jewish community at large. It is clear that among the
intellectual elite of American Reform, the Reform rabbinate, the reevaluation of Jesus as an answer to liberal Protestantism was widely
accepted. However, within the wider nonreform community, and even

among the Reform laity, there is little evidence to indicate that the new views enjoyed much support. Indeed, at the very time that the rabbis were promulgating their ideas, an American edition of the medieval Jewish pseudo-history of the life of Jesus, *Toledoth Jeshu*, was published with an English translation accompanying the Hebrew text.[68] Despite Emil G. Hirsch's denunciation of the *Toledoth Jeshu* as "a cesspool of all nastiness, of fabrications out of the whole cloth," and his assertion that Judaism should not be held responsible for it because Jews never shared its sentiments, its publication demonstrates that the old negative views were still current.[69] It may not be too far from the mark to suggest that the Reformers' writings and statements on Jesus were directed more towards liberal Christians than towards Jews.[70]

Jewish writers, of course, failed to convince Christians that Christianity purified of its creedal accretions was little more than Judaism minus its ceremonials, and they failed to convince Christians that Judaism was the equal of, let alone superior to, Christianity. Nevertheless, their writings on Jesus and Christianity served an important purpose. The stress on the Jewish nature of Jesus and on his ethical message was the means by which the Reformers undermined the liberal Protestant claim for the uniqueness and superiority of Christianity. This allowed the Reformers to define for themselves a rationale for continued Jewish group existence and to demonstrate that Jewish ethical ideals were best suited to meet the needs of contemporary society. By identifying pure Christianity with Judaism, the Reformers presented an argument that not only would disarm antisemites, but would also emphasize the consonance, indeed the equivalence of Judaism with Americanism. While Isaac Mayer Wise's expressed belief that Judaism would soon become the religion of America may be an extreme example of Reform hopes, it is an accurate expression of the sentiment that underlies the Reform statements that we have surveyed. The message that the Reformers were delivering in their anti-Christian polemics was that the Jews were the Americans par excellence.

5   Conclusions

Throughout their long Diaspora history, Jews have had to devise strategies of survival in a world that was largely hostile to them. American freedom posed unusual challenges for a people used to facing persecution. Their situation in America required the Jews to formulate new definitions of their relationship to the outside culture and society. As we have seen, American Jewish writings on Christianity and Jesus provide us with a useful window onto the different definitions that American Jews formulated.

Jews, whether traditionalists or Reformers, contested the claim, put forth by a variety of nineteenth century Protestant spokesmen, that America was a Christian country and they fought vigorously against measures such as the Sunday laws that reinforced that claim with the authority of law. In addition, Jews had to contend with the threat posed by missionaries of a militant and triumphalistic nineteenth century Protestantism. On a practical level, Jews developed a variety of methods to fight the missionaries. They defended the Jewish religion and employed traditional as well as some new polemical arguments against Christianity; they forged temporary alliances of convenience with Christian or free thinking opponents of the missionaries; and they argued that missionary activity violated the constitutional guarantee of religious liberty. However, confronting the claims of a Christian America and the missionaries presented more than just practical problems for the Jews. They recognized that America was de facto a Christian country. The challenge for them was to be able to enjoy the benefits of freedom while insuring group survival in a Christian environment. This required clarifying the relationship of the Jews to America society and of Judaism to Christianity.

Ambiguity characterized the most important Jewish responses. The traditionalist Isaac Lesser sought to assure the security of American Jews by fighting against the notion that America was a Christian country, and by constantly reminding his fellow citizens—Jew and Christian alike—of the basic principles upon which the Republic stood. While grateful for the freedoms that Jews possessed in religiously tolerant and pluralistic America, Leeser was ever aware of their vulnerability as a religiously deviant minority whose past history was marked by persecution at the hands of Christians. This undoubtedly strengthened his traditionalist yearning for a revived Jewish state in the land of Israel, where Jews would not have to worry about ill treatment at the hands of non-Jews. Most important for Leeser, American Jews had to maintain the traditional Jewish life style in order to assure their separate group existence. This meant that Jews had to distance themselves, to some extent, from American culture and society. In order for Jews to assume this outsider stance in the open and inviting atmosphere of America, it was necessary that they understand the differences between Judaism and Christianity, and appreciate the religious superiority of the former over the latter. Hence, Leeser's writings on Christianity do not stress its commonalities with Judaism, but emphasize, instead, the differences between the two religions.

In contrast to Leeser's outsider stance, nineteenth century Reform writings on Christianity and Jesus reflect a strong Jewish claim for insidership in America. Like Leeser, the Reformers understood the potential threats to Jewish security posed by assertions of a Christian America and by a missionizing Protestantism, and they were well aware of the dangers of assimilation in a free America. Their strategy, however, was not to dwell on the differences between Judaism and Christianity in order to bolster a sense of Jewish identification. Indeed, their denial of authority to the system of Jewish law, whose multitude of regulations defined the life style of its practitioners and which clearly set them apart from the Christians, would have made such an approach quite difficult. Instead, they pointed out the commonalities between Judaism and liberal Christianity and tried to prove the identification of Jewish with American ideals. The personality and teachings of Jesus were crucial to the Reform argument. Finding a useful tool in contemporary scholarly trends, the Reformers attempted to reconstruct a demythologized historical Jesus. The result was a portrayal of Jesus as a Jew who was loyal to his faith and his people; a teacher of Jewish doctrine, unoriginal in the content of his message, but inspiring in his personality and method of instruction. This view of Jesus allowed the Reformers to proclaim that the best in Christianity—Jesus and his teachings—were Jewish to the core. Those characteristics of Christianity that differentiated it from Judaism were attributed not to Jesus but to Paul or to later Christian development. With the identification of the highest ideals of both Christianity and America with Judaism, there could be no question about the place of Jews in American life.

The Reform strategy in America is similar to that in nineteenth century Germany. There, Samuel Hirsch, Abraham Geiger, and other

Jewish writers stressed the Jewish nature of Jesus and his teachings in order to counter the position of those like the theologian Bruno Bauer who argued that the Jews should not be emancipated because Judaism was an inferior religion. The situation in America, however, was quite different. The Jews there were citizens and they enjoyed equal rights, and no one seriously questioned the propriety of this. To be sure, antisemitism existed in America and it was on the rise in the late nineteenth century. However, the Reformers did not emphasize the Jewishness of Jesus and argue for the religious superiority of Judaism over Christianity merely to counter antisemitism. Instead, we may conclude that they argued that Jewish and American ideals were identical and that the best of Christianity (i.e. the Jewish Jesus) differed little if at all from Judaism, not only to prove their worthiness in the eyes of their Christian fellow countrymen, but as an expression of their belief that in America, the Jews and the Jewish spirit had found more than in any other community in Diaspora history, a congenial environment in which they could flourish.

PART TWO

Sources

6 A Missionary Attacks the Jewish Religion

Joseph Samuel C. F. Frey was born in Maynstockeim, Franconia, on September 21, 1771. He converted to Christianity in 1798, and four years later he began to missionize the Jews of London under the sponsorship of the London Missionary Society. In 1809, he helped to found the London Society for Promoting Christianity among the Jews. The London Society terminated Frey's employment in 1816 for reasons that are not entirely clear and sent him, at its own expense, to New York. There, Frey became the missionary of the American Society for Evangelizing the Jews. Later (1820), when this organization became the American Society for Meliorating the Condition of the Jews, Frey continued as its missionary.

In the following extract from The Converted Jew, *Frey, like other missionaries, tried to arouse Christian support for missionary work among the Jews by showing their spiritual poverty.*

AN ADDRESS TO CHRISTIANS OF ALL DENOMINATIONS, IN BEHALF OF THE DESCENDANTS OF ABRAHAM.

God is good, and does good, his tender mercies are over all his creatures, yet, he is especially good to them that are of the household of faith. It is a faithful saying, and worthy of all acceptation, that Christ Jesus came into the world to save sinners, yet it is not less true, that he came not but to seek the lost sheep of the house of Israel. To preach the Gospel among the Gentiles, was the express commission of the Apostle Paul, and among them he labored more abundantly! yet, for his brethren and kinsmen after the flesh, only, do we hear him say, I could wish myself accursed from Christ. Soon after my conversion I felt a great desire to promote the salvation of all men, yet my most frequent and fervent prayer to God was, that Israel might be saved. By the kind providence of God I was brought to this country, where for more than six years I have had the honor and pleasure of being employed in endeavoring to promote the salvation of my beloved brethren the Jews, by declaring unto them the unsearchable riches of glory by Christ Jesus. Considering the peculiar nature and difficulties of this work, I may well say, much has been done in a short time, much more, however, may, and must be done, before all Israel can be saved. The object is noble, and the success, sooner or later, is certain. The harvest is great, but, alas! the laborers are few. Permit me, therefore, Christian reader, to invite you to come over and help us. In the following address I shall call your attention to,

1. The deplorable state of the Jews:
2. The chief difficulties in the way of their conversion:
3. The obligations of Christians to promote this object: and,
4. The means by which it may be assisted.

In the first place we shall contemplate the present deplorable state of the Jews. 1. Let us take a short survey of their temporal, moral, and religious state. From profane, as well as from sacred history, we learn that the children of Israel were for successive ages, the light of the world, and the glory of the whole earth; but, alas! what has been their condition for centuries past, even to the present day! "The crown is fallen from their head; the gold is become dim, the most fine gold is changed, the nation, once exalted to the pinnacle of honor, has, for more than seventeen hundred years, been a hissing and a proverb amongst the people; hated and persecuted, scattered, and peeled by every nation; strangers and sojourners in every country, without the liberty of purchasing or possessing an inheritance or enjoying the privileges of citizens!—Notwithstanding all this, confiding in their natural descent from Abraham, and viewing themselves still as God's ancient people, they are puffed up with pride, imagining themselves to be "rich and increased with goods, and to have need of nothing, not knowing that they are wretched, and miserable, and poor, and blind, and naked."

Besides this, the glory of the Lord is departed from the house of Israel, and the wrath of God is come upon them to the uttermost. The spirit of grace and supplication, has been withdrawn from the sons and daughters of Abraham, and blindness in part (alas, how great a part!) hath happened unto Israel. How lax their moral principles, how degraded their conduct, how much is it to be lamented, that few amongst them either fear God or regard man. The golden rule—thou shalt love thy neighbor, as thyself, is still in their Bible, and acknowledged by their Rabbies as the great universal precept of the law. But "who is my neighbor," is a question which receives a very different explanation from the Christian and the Jew. The former is taught by Jesus Christ to extend it to every one of the human race; whilst the latter, according to the tradition of the Rabbies, applies the term "neighbor," to his Jewish brother only, and to the proselyte who embraces the law of Moses. It is not, therefore, to be wondered at, should a Jew at any time be found guilty of defrauding a Christian, especially as the rabbies themselves are not agreed whether to defraud a stranger, is lawful or not. . . .

Though exceedingly painful to my feelings, thus to lay open the blindness, guilt, and misery, of a people so dear to me, yet to obtain the desired end of this Address, I must proceed at least one step farther, and notice the carnality and irreverence of their religious worship. From the days of Abraham to those of Christ, true religion was only to be found in the tabernacle of Jacob. Whilst all nations had sunk into ignorance, idolatry, and misery, the posterity of Abraham was a chosen generation, a royal priesthood, a holy nation; but from the period when the tribe of Judah was prevented, by the destruction of the holy city and temple by Titus, from going up to Jerusalem at the solemn feasts, it seems that holy dispositions and spirituality of worship also fled from their hearts.

At that time the branches were cut off from the true olive tree, and O! how barren and unfruitful have they been for nearly 1800 years. Where are the fruits of the spirit, such as love, joy, peace, long-suffering, gentleness, goodness, faith, meekness, and temperance? Christians know, and the Jews should learn that I am here speaking of these qualifications as the genuine fruits and effects of religion, a right faith and the fear of God. There are, no doubt to be found amongst the Jews, as well as the Heathens, Mahometans, and nominal Christians instances of natural good dispositions and moral feelings, but these have nothing to do with genuine religion, see Matt. xix, 16. Are there any of Abraham's children who possess the holy, gracious, and heavenly dispositions of Abraham? Do they, like him, declare by their conduct, that they have here no continuing city, but that they seek one to come?

We shall meet with equal and painful disappointment if we expect to find a Jew engaged at the family altar, or in secret devotion. How different was the worship of believers under the Old Testament. The voice of religion and salvation was in the tabernacle of the righteous. Abraham, Isaac, and Jacob, wherever they pitched their tents, built an altar for family worship. Joshua and his own household served the Lord.—Daniel prayed upon his knees three times a day, and from the book of Psalms it is evident, that David the king of Israel, must have spent much time and found great delight in private meditation and fervent prayer; nor does he deserve the name of an Israelite, who wrestles not with God by prayer and supplication like Jacob our father.

The Jews, indeed, go frequently to the synagogue to perform public worship; but can that service be pleasing to God or profitable to man, which is generally performed without reverence or godly fear? It was not beside the mark when a late author observed; that "a modern synagogue exhibits an appearance of very little more devotion, than the Stock Exchange, or the public streets of the Metropolis at noonday!!" Nor is it very surprising, considering that few, very few indeed, understand the literal meaning of their prayers in the language in which they are read. . . .

2. The lamentable condition of the Jews, may also be deduced by contrasting their present state with the scriptural account of real happiness, of which the unbelieving Jew is wholly destitute. Both in the Old and New Testament, that people and those individuals only, were counted happy and blessed who knew the way of salvation, whose sins were forgiven, who lived in communion with God, and enjoyed the light of his countenance.

The true Christian is convinced of the reality of these assertions, for he has more or less experienced them himself, and the New Testament abounds with passages in confirmation of the same truth. How often have our blessed Redeemer and his apostles assured us, that without believing in him, as the Messiah, and without the influence of the Holy Spirit upon the heart of the sinner, there is no deliverance from spiritual misery, no title to eternal life, no fitness for the service and enjoyment of God in the life which now is, or in that which is to come. If these declarations be true, (and who can deny them?) how miserable must the poor Jew be, who rejects the salvation of our God, and trusts in his own righteousness . . .

I cannot conclude this part of the address, without observing, that having been myself born a Jew, having lived amongst that people for more than twenty years, and having had opportunities of seeing and knowing Jews in different countries, and in different circumstances, I can assure the reader, that I scarcely met with any walking with God, like Enoch; patient in tribulation, like Job, or saying, as he did, "I know that my Redeemer liveth;" panting after communion with God, as holy David, or as Paul the apostle, and like genuine Christians in all ages, desirous to depart and be with God, as far better.—"What shall we eat? what shall we drink? and wherewithal shall we be clothed?" is the only anxiety of the Jew, as well as the heathen. The awful description which the apostle gave of the condition of the Ephesians, before their conversion, is too applicable to my brethren and kinsmen after the flesh; "They are without Christ, without hope, and without God in the world.". . . .

From this belief statement of the deplorable condition of the Jews, considered in a temporal, moral, and religious view, with a scriptural account of real happiness, of which the unbelieving Jew must be destitute; may I not hope, Christian reader, that you will "come over and help us," in promoting their conversion, by which alone they can be delivered from present and eternal misery. Should any inquire what particular need there is of help? may they not attend on the preaching of the Gospel as well as others? I answer in the negative, and proceed,

Secondly, To point out the chief difficulties which encounter a Jew, who seeks to know the way of salvation.

The first and chief difficulty which claims our attention, is their ignorance of God's method of salvation; this is owing to their defective education, their neglect of the Bible, and the infrequency of preaching among them. God, in infinite mercy, has revealed, how a sinner may be justified, sanctified, and eternally glorified. This revelation was made to the Jews first; but how different are their circumstances now! blindness indeed has happened unto Israel; few of them have any knowledge whatever of the Messiah. How can it be expected otherwise, when we see the rising generation neglected? The children of both sexes, instead of being educated in religious knowledge, and useful employments, are driven into the streets, at the tender age of nine or ten years, (a time of life which peculiarly needs restraint and instruction,) to provide for themselves, or to assist in the maintenance of the family. It is most melancholy to find that very few of them can read any language but Hebrew, and fewer still who understand the meaning when they can read it! so that, if they had the whole of the Old Testament in Hebrew, of what benefit would it be to the generality of them? for the mind will be no more instructed by reading, than the heart can be edified by praying in an unknown tongue. It must also be acknowledged, that though the way of salvation was revealed in the Old Testament, yet few, if any, can see the substance through the types and shadows without the New Testament; or human aid, or the immediate teaching of the Holy Spirit. Besides this, it has already been observed, that those parts of the Old Testament which contain the clearest revelations of the Messiah, are withheld from the generality of the Jews. Add to this, there is no preaching in Synagogues from the beginning to the end of the year, except a few occasional exhortations, enforcing the strict observance of Judaism, with all its superstitions, and renewing the threatenings against those who are, in the least degree, even suspected of inquiring into the truth of Christianity. We need not be surprised then, to find that the descendants of Abraham are ignorant of that Messiah, in whom he believed, and to whom therefore it was counted for righteousness. . . .

3d. The early prejudices of the Jews against the Christian religion, is another difficulty in the way of their conversion. Perhaps no difficulty is harder to be removed than early prejudices in matters of religion. The Jew takes care, as soon as possible, to instil prejudices into the minds of his children, against the name, religion, and followers of Christ. As a general outline of this has been given in chap. i, I shall merely state, in this place, that when the blessed name of Jesus is mentioned, they are taught to spit upon the ground, as expressive of their hatred! For the same reason they have given names peculiarly reproachful to the Redeemer himself, to the New Testament, to the Christian places of worship, to the holy religion of Christ, to his sacred ordinances, and to his humble followers! These things have such an effect upon many, that they consider the mere repetition of the name of Jesus, or the least discussion with his followers, in matters of religion, to be of a more defiling nature than the eating of swine's flesh, which is well known to be held in the utmost abhorrence by the Jews.

The 4th and last difficulty in the way of the conversion of the Jews, which I shall notice, is, the false methods which they are taught to use in order to obtain salvation. Notwithstanding all that has been said, many of the Jews would, doubtless, listen to the word of salvation, were it not for the refuges of lies in which they shelter themselves from the wrath to come. These delusions are so numerous, that it is difficult to know where to begin. As the Jews in the days of the Apostles had confidence in the flesh, because they had Abraham for their father, and were circumcised on the eighth day, so do they now hope for salvation upon the same ground.

7 A Christian Defense of the Jews

Frey's missionary activities and his negative statements about Jews and Judaism evoked the critical response of a non-Jew who wrote under the pen name "Tobit". In the following extract from Tobit's Letters to Levi, the author defends the Jews against Frey's charges of immorality. He dismisses Frey's contention that the Jewish religion instills unethical character traits in the Jews, and argues that where Jews have manifested hostility towards Christians, it was the result of Christian mistreatment of them. This was one of the arguments used by eighteenth and nineteenth-century advocates of Jewish emancipation in Europe. Tobit states that in America, where the Jews enjoy full citizenship rights, "you find them good citizens, and with full as much morality as any other sect of believers."

LETTERS TO LEVI

In pages 9 and 10 of your Narrative, you inform your readers, you became instructed in using the knife, for killing fowls or beasts, and that these ceremonies are difficult to be acquired. You state that in the use of these observances, you were very strict, but deny that "any one of them is to be found in the Book of God;" and then say "these are only a few of the innumerable vain and extremely burdensome traditions, received of the fathers." In this place you exclaim, "O, blessed Jesus, thy yoke is easy, and thy burden light. Happy, thrice happy those, who are brought into the *holy liberty* of thy glorious and everlasting gospel." Here it is, Mr. Levi, that you display the cloven foot, which induced you to become a Christian; it was not from a reverence of the doctrine of Christianity, but, as I have before stated, to cast off the burdens and the restraint which a strict performance of the Jewish ceremonies, imposed upon your naturally loose disposition, and to enjoy this *"holy liberty,"* which you most wistfully sighed for, and which *"liberty,"* you understood, was embraced in the title of Christian. That you should complain against these ceremonies is quite natural to my opinion of you, and quite in character with the rest of the book. "Vain" and burdensome as you thought them, however, these very ceremonies are thought highly of by Christians who consider, that as they are intended to give the animal, to be slain for our wants the least possible pain, that they are entitled to respect and applause; and as a proof of their respect for them, the Jew beef is often bought by Christians at a higher price, knowing, as they do, that the animal killed for Jews must be perfect and sound, and that great attention is paid, by a person appointed to perform and superintend the operation, in examining the lungs, &c. of the animal killed, which, if found defective, is rejected.

You who are well acquainted with these ceremonies, and who tell your readers you devoted a year to perfect yourself in the use of the knife, sneer at them as *"vain and burdensome,"* taking good care, at the same time, not to inform them of the humanity which they inculcate, and the advantage they are of in providing wholesome food, and avoiding that which is considered otherwise. Since your conversion, you no doubt would prefer to eat of an ox which, on being killed, displayed but half his lungs, or the whole of them in an impure and corrupt state, or a limb in gangrene condition. For my part, although not a Jew, I must say, if the choice of the animal were offered for my table I should prefer the other.

To follow you, word for word, in your accusations, against the Jews and their religion, I should have to quote one third of your *"Narrative."* This would not be convenient for me, neither have I room for it in the compass to which I mean to confine this letter. I shall, therefore, merely make a few more remarks on the slander you cast on them, &c. In general terms you say, that the Jews confine the golden rule of "love thy neighbour as thyself, merely to their Jewish brethren;" that therefore it is not surprising, that Jews are found at any time defrauding Christians. With regard to the first accusation I reply, that such is not the construction of the "golden rule" in this country. Were it necessary, I could cite instances of many good actions performed by Jews to Christians, and even where they have returned them *good for evil;* but among nations where, in your own words but the page antecedent, you state them to have been "for more than seventeen hundred years a hissing and a proverb, hated and persecuted, scattered and peeled, strangers, without the liberty of purchasing or possessing an inheritance, or enjoying the privileges of citizens." Under such unmerited, such blasphemous, such ungenerous persecution, is it to be supposed that suffering humanity would turn to kiss the sandal which trampled it in the dust? Who were they who thus hissed, hated, peeled and persecuted these people? Was it Christianity? and if so, was it likely these people, driven by anguish and despair, would embrace a religion which admitted of such infernal cruelties and injustice, and call the perpetrators of them holy men, and the "elect of God?" Turn to Fox's Book of Martyrs, and view the abominations which the Inquisitions of Spain and of Portugal, of Germany, your own country, have inflicted on these people—Look to the history of England; which you quote yourself, and then, if you have *common sense,* do interrogate it and say, have these enormities, committed under the mantle of Christ, been the means to convert Jews to Christianity, or to confirm them in their own belief? But, according to your argument, it is because they have been insulted, spit upon, and treated with more indignity than the negroes of Africa in slavery, that you would invite them to embrace the religion of their persecutors! Indeed, Mr. Levi, you have a quaint method of maintaining and proving the orthodoxy of your own conversion; but suffer me to tell you, that the arguments you use in this your literary production, are more calculated to make Jews of Christians, than to convert one of the seed of Abraham from the faith of his ancestors. Indeed, believing you still to be a Jew, which, notwithstanding all you may say to the contrary, I am still at liberty to believe, I should not be surprized that your perigrinations and adventures ended in uniting more closely the Jews of every place, who read your book, and hear your name, and on this score you may hereafter claim even honour in the synagogue which you now desert.

It is in America, alone, that the Jewish nation have been treated with the characteristic humanity of the Christian religion; and here it is you find them good citizens, and with full as much morality as any other sect of believers. You state, as a reproach against them, that it is not uncommon to see a Jew defraud a Christian in Europe. Let me tell you, it is not uncommon, in Europe, to see a Christian cheat a Jew; neither is it in this country, to see the Christians of all sects commit frauds upon each other, and if a Jew comes in their way, they are not likely to spare him for his gabardine. There are bad men, and impostors, and cheats, among all nations and all sects, whether Jew, Turk, or Christian; whether Catholic or Protestant; whether of the Church of England or the dissenters therefrom; be they Presbyterian, Quaker, Methodist, or any other tribe: but because there are bad men in each, it is not a reason to condemn, *en masse,* their creed, their doctrine, and their congregations.

You are not content with any one or two crimes to lay against those brethren of your desertion. You seem anxious to muster up the whole catalogue of human enormities and frailties. In the 71st and 72d pages of your narrative, you accuse even their Rabbis of fornication, and glorying in the commission of it. It is a very true remark, that when a man attempts to prove too much, he even disproves the testimony that might have passed current. Thus it is with you, Mr. Levi; you forget when you are attempting to prove the Jews unchaste, and fornicators, and their Rabbis glorying in it . . . you forget, I say, that in casting such a slander on the Jews you are reproaching Christians with enormities of which there are many millions on record, if they were to be sought after, which would call down shame upon them. . . . Let a view be taken of the horrid lusts committed in Rome, and in Spain, and in Portugal, &c. by the religious of all denominations from the Pontiff, to the Inquisition; from the Inquisition to the Monks; from the Monks, to the lowest order of Laymen.—Look at the clergy of France previous to the revolution—even an Abbé without an intrigue was as rare as the black swan of Virgil . . .

You continue in your abuse of the customs and manners, &c. of the Jews. And after stating you yourself had been a Jew, and had lived among them for twenty years, that you seldom met any walking with GOD like ENOCH; that is to say, that you rarely met a pious man. Again, "what shall we eat, what shall we drink, and wherewithal shall we be clothed," is the only anxiety of the Jew, as well as the Heathen. Again, "the Jew takes care to instil prejudices in the minds of his children; when the blessed name of Jesus is mentioned they are taught to spit upon the ground." I shall merely notice these three accusations, and pass over the various other reproaches you make, with equal regard to the correctness of your report and the character of the people you presume to convert.

If you walked for twenty years in the society of Jews, and seldom met a pious man, it is rather a proof that you did not keep the best company, than that there are no pious men among them! You walked some years with christians, played cards, and danced away your Sunday. It is presumable (though I do not make the accusation,) that you had some lasses to help you lead down the ball, for a set of clumsy-heeled shoemakers, as were your companions, to pretend to make a dance by themselves would have been worse than the *pas de deux* of the bear and the monkey. For my own part, I must say I would much rather have been a spectator of the dancing dogs of Paris, than one in such a merry set of *wax-ends* as you must have been, unless you had female partners. Your accusation, therefore, of there being but few pious men in your walks among Jews will not go far to convince the world of its truth, as regards the Jewish people, especially when we read the narrative of a man who says he had been but lately a *pharisee* in the Jewish faith, yet neglectful of every moral regulation of the sabbath of the new religion he had assumed.

"What shall we eat, what shall we drink, and wherewithal shall we be clothed," are three very important considerations to poor Christians, as well as poor Jews; yet, that it is not *the only* anxiety of Jews, is not only well known to the christians who read your book, but to you yourself. They have an anxiety to maintain all their forms and articles of religion, even at the expense of hunger and of thirst. Their fasts are rigid and severe, yet they as rigidly keep them. Why did you not attend the fast of the day of atonement lately held in this city, and you would there have seen, whether Jews have no other anxiety than their appetites, and whether the religion you pretend to despise has not some qualities about it which even the proudest christian must admire, rather than condemn? You yourself state the rigid care of your mother, and your own despair in having broken the Sabbath; and I should rather say, the inquiry "of what shall we eat, and what shall we drink," more properly belonged to a Jew who renounced his faith, than one who maintained it.

As regards spitting out at the mention of the name of Jesus, I ask any christian to converse with a Jew on the divinity of Christ; I have frequently done so; and have never noticed a custom, which I certainly should have done, from its being a disgusting one. The spitting out of the Jew, on hearing of the name of Jesus, I therefore class with many other of your assertions.

I shall now only mention one egregious contradiction among numbers with which your book abounds, and if you can reconcile it to yourself, I will own you a *"miracle"* of a man, but I fear it will be a hard task to bring your readers to the same opinion.—I quote your words:

"Looking upon all nations, except themselves, as idolators, they believe that he who with his dying breath repeats the sentence, *Hear, O Israel* the Lord thy God is our Lord, is sure of going to Heaven, whatever *may have been his past conduct.*" FREY, p. 85.

In page 86. you say "Many times I have witnessed the miserable and despairing condition of dying Jews, which no tongue can express, or pen describe." You then paint your own apprehensions of death of former days, and add, "This fear of death is still increased, by the superstitious rabbinical doctrine of purgatory, for *every soul,* they say, must go into *Gay* Hinnom, i.e. a *place of misery,* to endure the most horrible sufferings, as an atonement for his sins."

This contradiction is so palpable and ridiculous here, that I shall not throw away a comment. I feel, indeed, some regret, that I have neither time nor room, (for I confined myself to limits before I began) to expose your book, even to the full scope which it invites. I think,

however, that I have succeeded in displaying, *by your own words,* that
you are the very opposite of the character who is capable of interesting
a Jew, so far as to forsake his religion, and that the very means you use
are calculated rather to inspire him with disgust, than with esteem or
reverence, for your character. I shall, therefore, take my leave of you,
Mr. Levi, after having devoted a few hours, perhaps, in your service;
for if the present pages do not excite you to the folly of a reply, they
will have one effect, that of furthering the sale of your frontispiece—I
mean your portrait, with your Narrative stitched thereto. I remain, sir
without malice or esteem, your's as before,   TOBIT.

8 Reversing the Christian Charge of Jewish Spiritual Blindness

Solomon Jackson's periodical, The Jew, *was the first major Jewish attempt to confront the missionaries.* The Jew *was primarily concerned with answering the misstatements about Jews and Judaism published in* Israel's Advocate, *the periodical of the American Society for Meliorating the Condition of the Jews. The following selection from* The Jew *contains an exegesis of Isaiah 29, which Christian tradition, based on Mark 6:7, has interpreted as referring to the spiritual blindness of the Jews. The author tries to show that the reverse is the case and that the chapter is really alluding to Christian spiritual blindness, and especially to the American Society for Meliorating the Condition of the Jews. The author is unknown and signed the article "C".*

THE JEW

It is about fourteen centuries since the Gentiles have undertaken to convert the Jews to . . . ianity; and which they have continued to the present day without success. No possible method however cruel, impolitic, or destructive to morality, has been neglected; all means, however wicked and impious, have been resorted to, to produce the nefarious purpose. Mulks, robberies, assassinations, persecutions, massacres, martyrdoms, exilings, alienations, inquisitions, tortures, flatteries, persuasions, and bribes, have been used at various times, without producing the desired effect. Arguments have always been resorted to as an assistant mean of conviction, and invariably addressed conjointly with some of the above enumerated methods; but then these arguments have invariably been addressed to the Jews, they being first bound not to answer under the penalty of being accounted guilty of blasphemy.

The Jews, on the other hand, thus cruelly treated, have never gainsayed their opposers and persecutors, although their mouths were stopped from defending either themselves, or the cause of truth, for which they were suffering; they still treasured up their arguments, and whenever they perceived the least enlargement from oppression, have invariably answered their persecutors, who as invariably condemned and consigned those answers, as well as the writers (when they could lay hands on them) to the flames. . . .

This then is the state of the question between the . . . ians and the Jews at this day. On the one hand the arguments are published in all the living and polite languages, encouraged and sought after, they meeting and fitting the prejudices of the world. On the other, published principally in the learned languages, and only sought after by the Gentiles, to be deposited in secret places, or destroyed, . . . It is no wonder then that . . . ians have accused the Jews of being stubborn, stiff-necked, hardened, and blinded to the light of truth; and have followed the writer of St. Mark by applying to them the 13th verse of the 29th chapter of Isaiah—"This people honoureth me with their lips, but their hearts are far from me. Howbeit in vain do they honour me, teaching for doctrine the commandments of men." With all the above considered, it is no wonder that they charge the Jews with being judicially blinded; that whenever Moses and the Prophets are read, they (the Jews) have a veil before their eyes, as Moses had over his face, that the children of Israel should not see the glory of his countenance; . . . That there is blindness somewhere, is acknowledged by both parties; each accusing the other of mental darkness; . . . but who is the party blinded is the question we shall now examine; in doing which, we shall take the text as it stands, . . . and explain it literally, according to the context of the whole prophecy, of which it only is a part. . . .

Verse 7.—"And the multitude of all the nations that war against Ariel, even all that fight against her and her munitions, and that distress her, shall be as a dream of a night vision."

In a dream and night vision men are persuaded they see plain, when there is nothing in reality.

Verse 8.—"It shall even be as when an hungry man dreameth, and behold, (he conceits) he eateth, but he awaketh, and his soul is empty; or as when a thirsty man dreameth, and behold he drinketh, (he thinks he drinks,) but he awaketh, and behold, he is faint, and his soul hath appetite; so shall the multitude of all the nations be that fight against Mount Zion."

In the last two verses, those nations who have fought against Jerusalem are, and have the denunciation of judicial blindness pronounced on them; they think they possess and enjoy what they have not in reality got. But the Prophet will best explain his meaning.

Verse 9.—"Stay yourselves, and wonder; cry ye out, and cry: they are drunken, but not with wine; they stagger, but not with strong drink.

Verse 10.—"For the Lord hath poured out upon you the spirit of deep sleep, and hath closed your eyes: the prophets and your rulers, the seers hath he covered."

Thus we see that it is judicial blindness that is here spoken of; they have become as drunken, staggering, sleepy, dreaming people, for the crime of fighting against Mount Zion. All the Roman empire, all the Europeans particularly, are here spoken of; the veil is over the whole of them, people, prophets, rulers, and seers.

Verse 11.—"And the vision of all is become unto you as the words of a book that is sealed, which men deliver to one that is learned, saying, Read this, I pray thee: and he saith, I cannot, for it is sealed.

Verse 12.—"And the book is delivered to him that is not learned, saying, Read this, I pray thee: and he saith, I am not learned."

Here we see wherein their blindness was to consist; they would not understand the book of all vision, they cannot comprehend it, because they are judicially blinded; and we might as well expect of a blind man to distinguish colours, as a . . . ian divine, a learned D.D. a prophet or seer, for in truth they are so, to explain or read what they call the Old Testament; the book of the vision of all; it is a sealed book to them, the veil is on their hearts, they dream, they are drunken, they are covered of heart; they think they preach truth, and hold with vanity, and expect salvation, and grasp vexation of spirit. Truly the spiritual man is a fool.

Verse 13.—"Wherefore the Lord said. For as much as this people draw near me with their mouth, and with their lips do honour me, and their fear towards me is taught by the precepts of men."

We do not deny but . . . ians (this people) draw near, or wish to draw near to God; but we say they do not do it acceptably.—Their fear of God is the precepts of taught and learned men; from their youth they are taught in the precepts of men, Matthew, Mark, Luke, John, &c.; these are the precepts of men, not the command of God.

Verse 14.—"Therefore behold I will proceed to do a marvellous work among this people, even a marvellous work and a wonder: for the wisdom of their wise men shall perish, and the understanding of their prudent men shall be hid."

Truly is the wisdom and understanding of the wise and prudent men among . . . ians lost and perished as regards religious affairs. Again I must cry, O, that they were wise; O, that they understood this; O, that they would consider their latter end. Is it a wonder that judicially blinded they say others cannot see? Truly with a beam in their eye, they are for plucking out the mote from the Jew's eye, which they conceit they see there.

Thus I have shown that this quotation, so far from meaning what the writer of St. Mark would have it to intend, the Jews in the days of Jesus, is in truth spoken of the . . . ians, the descendants of the Romans, who fought against, and destroyed Zion and her munitions. This religion of theirs, the . . . ian religion, is the drawing near to God with the lips, and honouring him with the mouth, while in truth the heart is removed far from God, being that the fear of God is taught by the New Testament, the precepts of men, and that the inward spirit, which . . . ians pretend bears witness within them, is the spirit which benumbs the intellectual faculties, called the spirit of deep sleep, causing them to dream of happiness and felicity they will never enjoy. They thirst, and conceit they swallow copious draughts of spiritual love, but when they awake it will be to real hunger and thirst. Horrid, horrid infatuation!

And now, gentlemen of the American Society for Meliorating the Condition of the Jews, what can you answer to this prophecy? Is it not perfectly fulfilled in you, as we see at this day? Your ostensible purpose is to convert Jews to . . . ianity. You wish them to drink of the cup you drink of, and be drunk as you are, to stagger as you do, to dream away their existence and accept the visitation of the spirit that possesses you, the spirit of deep sleep. Are you not descended from that people who have distressed Ariel? Have not your fathers, from that period to this our day, slain the children of Ariel? Your present feelings toward them . . . we have every reason to believe is philanthropic. You no doubt really mean well, but are you not yourselves under a strong delusion? If . . . ianity is not this deep sleep; if you are not the people who have distressed Ariel; if I have not given a true explanation of the prophecy; say ye, what it does signify, what the prophet or holy spirit did mean. I call on you collectively and individually; remember, a bribe is no argument—that you will find wretches enough willing to accept of the price of iniquity no one doubts; and when you have them, poor miserable creatures, they can give you no further assurance of their spiritual standing than yourselves. Are you not each of you answerable to God for seeking the destruction of his peculiar people? If you do not answer, how is your own standing? Can you, who have brought me to defense, answer to other well-intended and good . . . ians for the destruction you are bringing on the . . . ian religion? Do you not see the props are falling one at a time from under the building, and that you will finally lose more members by this foolish society of yours, than is gained by all your foreign Missionaries?

But you cannot answer; there is no answer that can be given to controvert any position I have taken; and you well know that to answer will only hasten your fall, as it will show the world your weakness, the weakness of the position you are obliged to hold. However, by your silence you virtually acknowledge your errors, and the frivolity of your pretensions. I must close with the words of the Prophet— "On whom do ye depend? against whom make ye a wide mouth, and draw out the tongue? are ye not children of transgression, the seed of falsehood?"—Isaiah lvii. 4. C.

9 An Appeal to the Jews to Convert

In October, 1849, the New York Synod of the Presbyterian Church addressed an appeal to the Jews of New York to convert. Isaac Leeser published the appeal in the January, 1850, issue of the Occident *along with his response as well as the response of Rabbi W. Schlessinger. Schlessinger wrote under the pseudonym Israel Philalethes.*

THE ADDRESS OF THE SYNOD OF NEW YORK TO THE ISRAELITES WITHIN THEIR DISTRICT

Brethren, "beloved for the fathers' sakes:"— In taking the unusual step of presenting a formal address to you, we introduce ourselves as an ecclesiastical body, embracing nine Presbyteries, six of which are in New York City and the vicinity, and two in China. The ordained ministers of these Presbyteries, who, for the most part, are pastors settled in churches, and the lay delegates from our church sessions, are, according to our constitution, the members of our body. We come together annually as a Synod, and our chief object is to devise and carry out the best plans for the edification of our churches. We are aware of the fact, that you have an immense and increasing influence among our churches and in our country: hence we have resolved as a body to acknowledge your presence and influence, and to send you an address on our common relations and interests.

In respect to both our faith and our spiritual offices, we feel ourselves united to you by strong and pleasant ties. The history of our officers of pastor and ruling elder runs back into the history of your synagogues. It is our own history which we are endeavoring to trace to its fountain head, when we examine how it was the ancient custom in Israel to convene, on sacred days, in the houses of the prophets, for religious exercises; and how, after the Babylonish captivity, synagogues were erected in nearly all the villages of the Jews, for the reading of the law, for the exposition of the Scriptures, and for prayer. According to our view, the local service of the temple, with its bloody offerings, its altars, its priesthood, and its mysterious ceremonies, was never designed for all the nations of the earth; was very inconvenient for even the Jews themselves, and was unquestionably destined to accomplish its restricted and preparatory work in a few centuries, and then entirely cease; but the synagogue was the institution which God raised up, during the gradual decline of the glory of the temple, that it might carry, simply and yet effectually, all the essential truths, and all the essential benefits of the temple to every city, to every village, and to the door of every family. The temple, with all its awful grandeur and dark ceremonies, was to be dissolved, and everything in it worth preservation was to be committed to the simple reading, exposition, and prayer of the synagogue. God was carrying out gloriously his own plans for the spread of his truth, and the promotion of his glory, in all the earth, when he moved the Jews to multiply synagogues in Jerusalem, and throughout Palestine, in Alexandria, and in Rome. We look back on Jerusalem, before the final destruction by the Romans, with her four hundred and eighty synagogues, and acknowledge that there is the mother of us all! We see, in your present synagogues, the clearest proofs that we both have the same origin; and we find a special proof of our oneness with the ancient synagogue, in the attestation of history, that in the synagogues of the Hellenist Jews the law was read in the Alexandrian, or Greek, version. The Christian church was the baptized synagogue. Our pastor is your *Sheliah Zibbur,* angel of the church, or *Hazan,* and it is a Presbyterian peculiarity to acknowledge no office higher than this. Our elders have their origin from the rulers in your synagogues. The different services in our churches likewise run back, in their descent, to the synagogue. And if the great end of God, in the establishment of the synagogue, was to spread the truth and worship of the God of Israel among all nations, we humbly claim that we are, to some extent, advancing this object, and that the true spirit of the synagogue is among us. All the oracles of God that were ever read in the ancient synagogue, are read and expounded in our churches. Men go out from us to establish Christian synagogues in the worst regions of ignorant and depraved population in our country, and there to distribute, from house to house, your own Scriptures. You observe that two of our Presbyteries are in China; and some of our most promising and beloved members have gone far hence, to the most unpromising and dangerous fields, not for the purpose of obtaining either the riches or pleasures of this world, but, if we know our own hearts, from love to the God of Israel, and the perishing souls of men.

Now, brethren, we earnestly appeal to you, are we accomplishing the word of God, or are we not? Mention to us any imaginable way in which we may accomplish more for the fulfillment of the promise that all the earth shall be filled with the glory of God, than by the distribution of Bibles, in every family, and the establishment of our synagogues in every neighborhood. It grieves us deeply that you take no part with us; that you even look on us with suspicion. We are convinced that you ought to be by our side; that you ought to be among the leaders in this work. Many among us severely accuse our indifference to the melancholy fact, that the great body of the house of Israel stand aloof from us. We believe that the day of prophetic promise will never be revealed in its glory while you stand at this awful distance from us. And why this separation? Where lies the fault? The standard of Judah ought to be in the front of the armies of the living God, as they go forward to invade the kingdom of darkness. Why, then, do you not unite with us, and carry on triumphantly the standard of Judah in our front?

There appears to be a complete exhibition of the original design of the synagogue, in the history recorded in the 7th chapter of Nehemiah. The people, men and women, collected together in the street of Jerusalem before the water-gate in a great multitude; Ezra, with several others, stood upon a pulpit above the people, and read in the law from morning till noon; and as they read, they interpreted in the language most intelligible to the people, and explained the meaning fully. This was accompanied with blessings, lifting of the hands and bowing to the ground; and all the people attended to the reading and explanations, with silent captivated attention and deep emotion. Another historical fact serves equally to throw light on the original design of the synagogue. Two strangers once appeared in the synagogue in Antioch of Pisidin, and after the reading of the law and prophets, the rulers invited them to speak, if they had anything which they desired to communicate. One of them then delivered a discourse on the history of the Jews, and the consummation to which the history was designed to lead, which awakened an intense interest, and drew a multitude of inquirers to the strangers. It is an important question, whether our synagogues have at present the same liberal, enlightening, sanctifying, and awakening influence in society. It is necessary that we understand well those principles or influences which, so far as they prevail in any synagogue, whether of the circumcised or of the baptized, necessarily render it apostate, and turn it, from being a blessing to society, into a curse. On this subject we ask your attention to a few suggestions, which may be equally profitable to ourselves, and which must commend themselves to every enlightened reader.

It is a fearful sign of prevailing degeneracy in the synagogue, when the Scriptures and prayers are read in an ancient language, and the words are not understood, and those who read without understanding, think that they have been really worshiping. We hold to the principle, as of vital importance, that there is no true worship of God in any instance where the understanding is not enlightened, and where the heart is not affected with the truth. It makes no difference how sacred the portion of Scripture, or of prayer, may be, which we read, it is useless and profane to us, unless we understand it. It is an equally fearful proof that the synagogue is far gone in apostacy, when it has ceremonies, of the existence of which, among the ancient people of God, the Scriptures do not furnish the least intimation, and of the propriety of which they furnish no evidence. For instance, your prayers in behalf of the dead, have not even the slightest foundation in the Word of God.

Let the religious duties and religious distinctions of the members of a certain synagogue consist chiefly in peculiarities of food, of dress, of festivals, and such outward things, and here we can infallibly identify an apostate synagogue. How plain and important, and reasonable the principle laid down in the New Testament.—"For the kingdom of God is not meat and drink; but righteousness and peace and joy in the Holy Ghost." The prophet Isaiah, in severely reproving his people for their hypocrisy, introduces his strongest charge against them in these words: "And their fear toward me is taught by the precept of men." The meaning is, that their fear of God, or piety, had become little more than implicit obedience to arbitrary human precepts. This reproof comes to us in all its severity, if we are governed by human precepts and traditions in our most solemn religious duties; us, for instance, in the solemn duty of sanctifying the Sabbath; when, before sunset, we must commence? how we may then read, by a lamp or fire? what we may permit another to do with a lamp? what prayers we must say in the morning? in what way we must put on the shawl, and handle the fringes? how we must make an offering for the privilege of taking out the scroll from the ark, and for the honour of returning it, and for the inspection of the seven portions in the passage for the day? what gestures we must make in the service before the ark? how many meals we must have in the day? and how we must go through the afternoon and evening services? All this looks very like a fear of God that is a senseless precept of men.

It appears to us very clear, that the great object of the synagogue among us ought to be to do good spiritually to all men—to enlighten, sanctify, and save all men. The temple itself, with all its restrictions, was to become a blessing to all nations, and God raised up the synagogue out of its ruins to fulfill this purpose. How sadly, then, does the synagogue forget its origin and its commission, when its instructions and prayers are for none but Jews? The consciousness that we are debtors to all men, Jews and Gentiles, Greeks and barbarians, bond and free, is one of the most essential and powerful sentiments in the bosom of every worthy member of the synagogue. And when this consciousness ceases, spiritual life ceases. The synagogue on earth should be as open to all men, and its richest spiritual privileges should be as freely and earnestly pressed on the acceptance of all men, as the privileges of the heavenly temple are freely offered to all men. If you believe that the gentiles will as certainly enter Heaven, without coming to the light of your synagogue—without embracing your faith and reading your Scriptures, as otherwise; you cannot, in the nature of things, be prompted by any potent conviction of duty, or any sentiment of benevolence, to make sacrifices for their spiritual interests. It is the love of immortal souls, and the fear that they will perish, and the conviction of the obligation and privilege to labour for their salvation, that carry the worthy missionaries of the synagogue, with the Word of life, to the ends of the earth. And where these powerful motives are not felt, it is easy to account for the want of a missionary spirit.

We anticipate that the most weighty reply which you will make to our address, is this—that you have no faith in many of our leading doctrines, and that, therefore, you cannot form any union with us. You will admit at once, that there are some probabilities in favour of our doctrines. Jesus Christ and his apostles certainly stand, in history, as worthy of credit, as the rabbis of the Talmud. There is as great a probability that Paul understood the original Judaism, and explained it honestly in his epistle to the Hebrews, as that the writer of the Mishna understood it some hundreds of years afterwards. Permit us to inquire whether you have thoroughly and candidly examined our doctrines? We are afraid that many of you have never read the New Testament. We hope to be able to supply all of you, who are willing to read, with Bibles containing both Testaments; and we press it upon you to examine the subject more thoroughly and prayerfully. If Christianity is true, it is your highest interest to embrace it.

Have you ever examined the argument in the epistle to the Romans? Have you never felt the force of the proofs presented there, that the gentiles are ruined in sin, and that the Jews themselves never can stand justified before God, in their own righteousness? Is not all this sufficiently proved by the few quotations from the Old Testament, placed together in the 3d chapter? If the sinner is thus, on his own account, under the deadly condemnation of the law of God, is it not clear that the righteousness of Jesus Christ, if he is the person whom we hold him to be, is perfect, and sufficient for the most unworthy?

How do you account for the origin of our doctrine of justification, if it is a fable? Do you see nothing grand and attractive in the doctrine, that God has entered into different covenants with man; and that, as in the first covenant, all have fallen into sin and condemnation through the sin of the first man, so we must be restored and justified through, the obedience of the head of the second covenant? But our request is that you examine the whole epistle for yourselves . . .

Brethren, your history, for fifteen hundred years before Christ, is distinguished by your special favour with God, and, particularly, by the familiarity of your prophets with the mind of God; for the last eighteen hundred years you have suffered the most cruel persecutions; your synagogue has, in all probability, been standing immovably on ground foreign to its original purpose; and you have, apparently, been spared only to show the fulfillment of the threatenings of your law. Your people were almost crushed through your own violent rebellions, and the revenge of the Romans; you have experienced, most bitterly, the deceit of the first friendship of Mohammedanism, and we are sorry to add, that Christendom, itself, in direct opposition to the teaching of our Saviour, has set itself in the most deadly opposition to you. It humbles us to know what you have suffered from the crusades, and in Spain, France, and other countries; and we, as Christians, certainly ought to have less sympathy with your persecutors than you have. In all this bloody history, there is nothing which, properly understood, should prejudice you against us. The spirit of persecution is as little chargeable to the Presbyterian church as to yourselves. We most ardently desire that the God of providence may never employ our beloved country to punish any people for their sins; we especially deprecate being employed to bring new chastisements of persecution on the sons of Abraham; we would have our country exclusively consecrated to the diffusion of the peace of the gospel. Far be it from us to do anything to revive old prejudices against you. We come to you, not as the friends of war—not with clamorous accusations—not in concealed deceit, but in honesty and love. We come to you not in the storm of opposition, but with "a still, small voice," a voice that speaks of the remission of sin, and everlasting peace,—a voice of heavenly, touching invitation—the same voice that was once heard at your temple and in your solemn assemblies. Horrible will that day be when this voice ceases to be heard in our country. Consider anxiously whether God does not come to you in this small voice, "Come unto me, all ye that labour and are heavy laden, and I will give you rest." "I am the way, and the truth, and the life; no man cometh unto the Father but by me." "Ought not Christ to have suffered these things, and to enter into his glory?" It remains now to be seen if, in the old spirit of the Pharisees, you will still cast the believers in Jesus out of the synagogue, and meet our address either with aroused opposition or with silent indifference. In any event, as to the reception of our address, we will still continue to feel a deep interest in your welfare. Signed by order of the Synod,   JOHN H. LEGGET, Moderator.

E. D. BRYAN,

E. B. EDGAR, Temporary Clerks.

JOHN M. KREBS, Stated Clerk.

Goshen, Oct. 17th, 1849.

THE PRESBYTERIAN SYNOD OF NEW YORK AND THE JEWS

The public was lately somewhat taken by surprise, at the appearance of an address emanating from the highest authority of the Presbyterian society of the state of New York, being no less than a polite invitation to forsake our religion, and to join ourselves to them. They call themselves the true and legitimate successors of the Synagogue, as constituted at the time of Ezra, and assert that the Jews have ceased to represent the true and ancient order of things. Hence they call upon us to examine the claims of their Messiah, and to adopt him as the great sacrifice made for all men; through whose death, moreover, atonement was made once and for all, thereby securing salvation to mankind in general. It may readily be believed that this singular address caused some remark among our people into whose hands it fell, not because it contains anything new, or remarkably well placed in words and supported by weighty argument;—far from it, since the sentiments have been uttered before; the language employed contains enough to afford a strong handle for a counter appeal, and then the arguments barely deserve the name; they are in fact unworthy of the great theme proposed, that is, the conversion of the Jewish world to Christian Presbyterianism. What caused then the remarks we speak of? Simply that an address should be sent to us at all through the public press, from so dignified a body as the Presbyterian Synod of New York, among the members of which are men, we will gladly concede, eminent for learning and piety. But their addressing us is a step neither warranted by propriety nor common sense, unless they can bring forward some new motives and some new arguments, both stronger than ever were offered to us for a change of religion. Do our Presbyterian friends think that it is with us a quarrel about church government—whether the one party represents an image of the Synagogue more than the other, or not—which has caused us to maintain our separate organization as Jews? If so, they err greatly. Much as we love the independent, republican constitution of the Synagogue, in which each congregation is perfectly independent in its civil government of any other, in which the minister, the *Sheliach Zibbur,* that is, not as the address translates it, "the angel of the church," but "the messenger of the community," (though perhaps they understand by angel, from the Greek word *angelos,* a simpler messenger or a delegate, and by *church* "the assembled people,") is the delegated speaker to the Throne of Grace for those who send him, in which the civil rule is placed in the hands of trusty persons, chosen by the people from among themselves; in which all power is derived from the governed, to be exercised only for their spiritual, and often, too, for their temporal benefit,—notwithstanding all this, we say, we consider the whole church system as quite subordinate to the great end of our religion; the church with us is but the servant of the people, to lead them to God, the One, the Great, the Mighty, the Tremendous, the Creator of all things; and apart from this, we know of no church, no ministers or elders. This is bold language, and will sound strangely in the ears of those who think but superficially; but it is sound and wholesome truth, and we assert without equivocation, that church going, public prayers, and preaching are nothing, if they lead not to the great result desired,—the upholding of the unity of God. We will therefore neither deny nor affirm that the Presbyterian form of government is nearer to ours than any other Christian church. But we ask of the learned gentlemen who have fixed their signatures to the paper before us, whether they believe, knowing the Jews as they must do, that we can at all value their organization, seeing that it is not its business, as it is that of the Jewish Synagogue, to uphold the unity of God, but to propagate the doctrine of a trinity, against which we have always contended, and against which we have borne our public testimony amidst those trials and barbarities endured at the hands of Christian men, Christian rulers, Christian divines, Christian pontiffs, Christian nations, of which the address itself speaks in terms of condemnation.

Do you think, Christian friends, that the Jew cares the least about the form of ecclesiastical law of those who tortured him in times gone by?—that we will take the trouble to consider whether the priest claimed his power as a right derived from the founder of his church, or from the imposition of hands of one who was an ecclesiastic before him? No, we tell you; we look to the doctrines which the church preaches, whether Roman, Greek, Anglican, Gallican, Arian, Calvinistic, Lutheran, Friend, Baptist, Millerite, Mormon, Wesleyan, Puseyite, Swedenborgian, Shaker, Moravian, or whatever shade or shadow of complexion it may assume; and we will withstand the priest who teaches us what we call error, whether he wear a pontiff's triple crown, a cardinal's cloak, a bishop's broidered robe, a vicar's white surplice, or a cannon's black gown; whether he cover his head with the broad brimmed hat of a Quaker exhorter, or appear with the shaven crown of a servant of the Romish hierarchy; whether he have a peculiar church dress in any shape, or merely come before us with a white cravat as the badge of his office. We tell you we will have none of them; we will argue with them, if they will hear us; we will weigh the reasons which they address us; but they must not expect that the Epistle of Paul to the Hebrews shall convert us at this day, when it failed to have the least effect on the Jews of his time. We assert that the Jew wars against the very ideas Paul puts forth, and to enforce which oceans of blood have been shed; and that it matters not by whom they are broached, for we will resist them as we have done hitherto.

We may rejoice, as rejoice we do, that a large, virtuous, and intelligent portion of Christians have sought and found a model in our Synagogues to govern themselves by; that they have cut loose their connexion with tyranny and misrule, (for there is no greater tyrant than an inflated churchman, who thinks the world made for him to govern, and not that he is there for its benefit,) and adopted in its stead the simple system that the people and their teachers have the same rights, and are responsible to each other for the manner in which they act their respective parts; but this is no reason why we should abandon our position, and renounce the object for which we have been so long united in opposition to nearly all mankind; and it would indeed be a woful consummation of a long and bitter struggle, to retire from the scene of history, and become lost amidst our ancient oppressors, simply because a number not half as large as ours has partially adopted our church government. And it is at best but partial; because our ministers are not like theirs, peculiarly hedged in with privileges and duties; for they are only delegates of the people, chosen when they are wanted, and from among those their electors please; and when they retire from their position, they are free to enter into the active walks of life, without any discredit or hindrance from their brothers. They are not, therefore, angels of the church at large, but messengers from each particular body of Israelites; and whoever is called upon to officiate, if it be even for once, he becomes a Sheliach Zibbur for the time being, and has the same privileges, that is to say, none at all, which a regular minister has. To be sure, we endeavour to elect worthy men, those who will properly represent the people; we place, or ought to place them on a permanent footing, so that they may devote their time and talents to the service of God in properly serving the people. We do this that we shall not be dependent upon voluntary offers to perform the necessary services of the Synagogue; but having done this, we consider it no wrong on the part of another, whether he be a mere private man or a minister of another place, to officiate with the consent of the people; and without their assent, the greatest and the highest in dignity among us would be a usurper, and not permitted to address the public or to offer up prayers in their behalf. We do not now speak of Rabbis, or those who have made the law of God their especial study, and who are therefore authorized to be consulted on all matters touching the prohibited and permitted things; but even these are not selected clergymen, in the sense they are among the Christians. Still, with all this freedom of election and liberty of retiring into private life, we may challenge the world to show men more devoted to their calling, and less tainted with crime than the Jewish ministry can show. They are faulty, like all mortals; but it says but truth of them, to assert that their moral and religious character will suffer nothing in comparing them with the large body of Christian theologians, who are educated from the cradle for their calling, and always so trained that they may bring the largest amount of efficiency and peculiar learning to the business for which they are destined.

We acknowledge, then, that we rejoice that some light has broken in upon our Presbyterian friends; and we only hope that, as they have proceeded thus far, they will examine into the subject more closely, and then be led to embrace the full effulgence of light which is with Israel. They—the younger in age—invite us to join them: we will in our turn ask them to join us; to call their attention to the ten commandments; to the Deuteronomy of Moses; to the last address of Joshua; to the prophecies of Isaiah, especially from chapter 1x. to end of his book; to Zechariah xiv., and many other passages innumerable; and if they read them prayerfully and devoutly, they must cease to believe in a crucified god, and adhere, as do the Jews, to the Lord Eternal, the Creator and Savior, who slayeth and bringeth to life, who woundeth and whose hands alone can heal. Let us enlarge the place of our tents; let us increase the dimensions of the true Synagogue; let all come who now stand aloof; and they will find that Judaism is no failure. . . . We say this in sober seriousness—we never jest on sacred subjects—and we mean what we say, that the world will be ultimately converted to our doctrines, and to the law in the manner the Lord will clearly reveal it for the gentiles, in which the glorious prophecies of the 54th of Isaiah will be accomplished; and it will be by a spirit of inquiry gradually awakened and carried forward *through* the doubts and misgivings of the force of ancient and preconceived prejudices, that the truth will triumph; and who knows but it may be by such friendly encounters as the New York Synod proposes, that the great accomplishment may ultimately be witnessed?. . . .

A RABBI'S REPLY TO THE ADDRESS OF
THE SYNOD OF NEW YORK

Brethren, "Beloved for our Father's Sake"—Were we to meet your address without, at least, some acknowledgment, we might not only be accused of indifference and want of respect towards you and towards the holy cause in which your labours are engaged, but we might also appear in the unenviable light of not comprehending or appreciating the exalted position allotted by your enlightened body to the remnants of Israel. With sorrow, we must confess that we have to present ourselves to you, beloved brethren, without the authority of any particular established association or ecclesiastical body of our co-religionists, but humbly venture to assert, that in the general purport of our sentiments and opinions, we are supported by the pure and lofty-minded of our brethren in both hemispheres.

The joyful evidence of an expiring prejudice, wherewith for centuries the human intellect has been darkened; the sentiments of philanthropy and kindness expressed in your message to us, have not failed to conquer our hearts, and to fill them with lively sympathy, admiration, and heart-felt gratitude towards you.

We admire your generous and noble motive in the wish to draw closer the ties of our spiritual relations and interests, for the amelioration of our spiritual welfare, and would be wanting in candour and self-respect were we unwilling to acknowledge it. Our hearts are gladdened to see the high import of Judaism recognized in this country, and the sacred veneration you bestow on that source whence we jointly draw our most important religious and moral doctrines; that you are conscious of the vast and beneficial influence of the synagogue on the improvement of the human race; that you consider it an honourable privilege to prove an analogy between our religious tenets and ceremonies, and in your candour not even deny that you are indebted to us for the same.

Most particularly, however, do we rejoice that the barbarities of by-gone ages, the useless and cruel persecutions during the crusades, the pillages, banishments, and massacres to a pretended glory of God, are at last viewed in the genuine light by our Christian brethren, and meet with their just condemnation and abhorrence.

We also regard the founder of your religion in a different light from that by which our ancestors viewed him, whose opinions were necessarily influenced by the horrible treatment they received at the hands of his worshipers, and it is with pride that we contemplate that the man, who for nearly two thousand years has been the object of divine adoration of a great portion of the human race, was a scion of the house of Judah. Cheerfully do we also admit the great beneficial influence of Christianity; and its moral doctrines, on the advancement of civilization; but we do not hesitate to give it as our decided opinion, that Christianity inadequately, and in part only, developed the truth which constitutes Judaism, and that, as yet, only part of that truth has been imparted to mankind.

It appears to us that an inscrutable, mysterious Providence has wisely decreed that the deliverance of mankind from deep-rooted polytheism should not suddenly be accomplished, but that the illusion and error should gradually vanish before the splendour and truth of a sublime divinity; and we discern, in the mysterious doctrine of the Trinity and Redeemer, the intervening incident—the connecting link—by which, hereafter, to a more perfect human race, the sublime truth will be unveiled. By the abandonment of the adoration of the Virgin Mary, and the refutation of the belief in her immaculate virginity, by Protestantism, a very important point has already been gained.

An adequate and full reply to your address would demand from us arguments too voluminous for our present epistle, and we have, therefore, to restrict and compress our remarks and opinions to your most important questions only.

We perfectly coincide with you, that there is no true worship of God, where the heart is not understanding, and the mind enlightened with the truth of the prayer; but in order that those of our brethren in faith who come to us from all parts of the globe, may have an opportunity to participate in our worship, we wish that, in our prayers, the sacred language of the prophets may be retained. By the instruction of the greater number of our youth in the Hebrew language, and by using prayer-books with a translation in the vernacular, the principal objection is obviated. Besides, considerable attention has already been devoted to the subject, and several synagogues have not only abolished many prayers adapted to the spirit of past centuries, but have also substituted others, and hymns in modern languages, and the most essential and instructive part of worship, the sermon, is nearly always delivered in the country's language.

We also do not hesitate in saying, that the blood-offerings in the temple are considered by all contemporary Israelites, who have found the subject of their religion worthy of an examination, as inadmissible, and unworthy to be retained in our present era; but that, in former times, according to the doctrines of the illustrious Maimonides, they were a necessary preservative against idolatry.

Although the Scriptures do not furnish a distinct intimation of the propriety of prayers in behalf of the dead, there is still a strong resemblance to prayer in the Lamentations of David, at the death of his son Absalom.

Supposing even that these prayers are of no essential advantage to those slumbering in death—which no human being can positively assert—the idea that, by such religious performance our dear departed might be benefited, cannot but produce a salutary and soothing sensation in the mind of the survivor.

We confess that frequently by our brethren in faith, as also by mankind in general, an undue and extravagant homage is rendered to outward appearances; but this even was the work formerly assigned to our prophets, and now to our ministers and preachers, to admonish and instruct the people how the Lord requires of them to be righteous, to exercise virtue, and to walk before him in humility. "Ye shall be holy, for I am holy."

Proselytism, either for effect or for emulation, was never attempted by us; we grant to every one the privilege to attain salvation "agreeably to his own fashion;" neither do we close our synagogues, our religious works or prayer books, against the believers of a different faith from ours. To whatever church or sect a man may belong, if he only has the fear of God before him, and exerts himself in the advancement of his fellow-beings' welfare, the path to salvation, according to the doctrines of our religion, is unobstructed.

You see, therefore, beloved brethren, that our opinions on several subjects agree, but that on others again, they widely differ. To us it remains inconceivable, how any one can earnestly believe that by the death of one man, the sins of his whole race are remitted, particularly when we see that a lapse of near two thousand years has worked no beneficial change in sinful man, and the laws of God are violated now as then; or how the advent of God's dominion—according to the predictions of the prophets, a reign of universal peace—can be credited, when, after the death of Christ, wars, persecution, and fanaticism rather increased than diminished.

Is the supposition, that by the virtuous life and fervent prayer of a pious son, a departed father's soul might be rescued from everlasting punishment, not by far more probable and acceptable than the presumption, that by the shedding of the blood of a single human being innumerable millions of his race should acquire salvation?

By numerous Christian scholars, amongst them the learned, far-famed Gesenius, the attempt to prove the divinity of Christ by the prophecies in the Old Testament has long ago been abandoned; and we only wish to convince you that all those who have acquired implicit faith in God, and the modesty to acknowledge how presumptuous it would be in mortal man to endeavour to explain the manner of his being—"for there shall no man see me and live"—will never bend their knees, or render divine honours to any other being, but to the invisible, living God alone. It is our firm belief, that, sooner or later, you and all mankind will agree with us, that it is blasphemous and sinful in the extreme to render divine reverence to woman-born mortal.

Till the advent of that happy epoch, when from world's end to world's end God shall be one and His name one, we will endeavour to entertain brotherly feelings towards each other, and continue, not in words only, but by deeds of kindness and philanthropy, to perform the works of love to all. And the God of love and mercy will judge and reward all men according to their actions. He, who is capable to penetrate the inmost recesses of the human heart—He, alone, sees, who in truth and sincerity walks before Him! He will not leave unrewarded Israel's faith and firmness, in the hardest trials and strongest temptations.

No mortal, not even the noblest, is free from faults and errors! Let us, therefore, be indulgent to each other, as is our Father in heaven, who to all of us is indulgent and merciful.

ISRAEL PHILALETHES.

New York, Nov. 5, 1849.

10   A Response to
A Radical Jewess

The belief that Judaism stressed duty and justice to the neglect of love and spirituality was propounded not only by Christian spokesmen but also by the Jewish writer Josephine Lazarus in her book, The Spirit of Judaism. *Lazarus proposed that Judaism could be enriched by borrowing the Christian emphasis on love and merging it with its own emphasis on duty. For this to happen, however, the Jews would have to overcome their narrow and parochial interests and step out into the broader humanity that surrounded them. Lazarus' book elicited a number of Jewish responses. Below is Maurice Harris' review of* The Spirit of Judaism.

THE SPIRIT OF JUDAISM.

"The Spirit of Judaism" is the name of a work written by Miss Josephine Lazarus. Its views have been brought to notice largely from the fact of the author being the sister of Emma Lazarus, the gifted poetess, and also, too, let it be justly said, for the thought contained in the book itself. For Miss Lazarus writes with fervor and power. This little book voices the need of a Jewish woman who feels the insufficiencies of Judaism and would suggest a remedy.

Miss Lazarus turns to Orthodoxy first, and condemns its ceremonialism, its worship of the letter, and its ignoring of the spirit. In it she sees nothing but a narrow adherence to a multitude of mechanical precepts, that shut out the larger view of spiritual religion. With her arraignment of Orthodoxy we have nothing to do, for the very attitude of Reform implies that it, too, rejects this phase of Judaism; it, too, has found it insufficient. The censure of the formalism of Orthodoxy is rather old. It seems, in fact, late in the day for Miss Lazarus to present it at all. If anything, we think that too much has been said on that subject, and the tendency of the latest critics is to conclude that it has been overdone, and that, in declaring that Orthodoxy is all ceremony and no spirit, we are doing it in injustice . . .

But with Reform she is equally dissatisfied. It has dropped the ceremonial code—at least it has been given a subordinate place—and the essential truths of the religion, chiefly as embodied in the teachings of the Prophets, have been brought strongly to the fore. And yet, while the purpose of Reform may have been to get nearer the heart of Judaism, to reach the central spring of the living faith, which had been obscured from view by the legalism of the Shulchan Aruch, it has not, so far, succeeded. It has dropped the ceremonial side of Judaism; it has not, however, reached its spiritual side. The Reform Jew is more rational and his creed more simple, but he is not necessarily more religious.

There is yet a third class, who have gone beyond the bounds of Judaism, who have lost the old faith, who have drifted into agnosticism. They may be attached to the creed of their ancestors by race, nationality, but hardly by positive faith. Altogether, the tendency of the modern Jew of all shades of belief is towards the material. He is a man of this world; he does not yearn for the spiritual; he is moral, he is ethical; but religion is a lessening factor in his life.

Her arraignment of the modern Jew is strong and just. She re-echoes the reproach of many a modern pulpit. We feel that we are losing ground, we feel that Judaism has not the old hold upon its mechanical followers. We find them keen, intellectual, ambitious, successful, but they are doing nothing in the world of religion. They are no longer a "kingdom of priests." They have given up that field to others, they have sold their religious birthright for a mess of pottage.

But when Miss Lazarus attempts to offer an explanation and a remedy for this evil we can follow her no longer. Her next step is both surprising and disappointing. The causes of our condition lie largely in the limitations of our creed. Even the Prophets felt there was a something more not yet attained. She, therefore, bids the Jew "cross the Rubicon, the fly-leaf behind the Old and the New Testament, read the story of Jesus of Nazareth with fresh eyes," and give to Judaism the one great needful factor that the teaching and practice of Jesus of Nazareth supply. She is deeply read in the New Testament. She has become so strongly imbued with the Christian atmosphere that, even when she reads the Old Testament, she reads it from the New Testament point of view. Her definition of Judaism is Paul's definition; her contrast between the two faiths is his contrast. She tells us that Judaism stands for justice, Christianity for love, that love is larger than justice and includes it. Let us see in how far this definition is true.

I need not attempt to detail all the passages throughout our Scriptures that dwell on the love of God and the love of man, in the Law, in the Psalms, in the Prophets, familiar to all. I will but passingly say that the cardinal teaching of Jesus within the New Testament, his summary of the law, are but two famous quotations from the Old Testament: "Thou shalt love the Eternal, thy God, with all thy heart, with all thy soul, and with all thy might," and, "Thou shalt love thy neighbor as thyself." If one prophet happens to dwell, for instance, upon the stern side of our faith and another upon its tender side, the divergence is due to the disposition of the individual preacher. Elijah and more particularly Amos, uncompromisingly severe, hold up the moral code to the people, and tell of the punishment of the evil doer. Elisha and, later, Hosea, men of deep tenderness reveal to an erring generation the love and forgiveness of a merciful Father. Jesus no more teaches love as a new principle than does Hosea; both men reveal their sympathetic natures.

But if we wish to find out whether justice really expresses the spirit of Judaism and love the spirit of Christianity, it is not sufficient to look through the writings of both and decide by majority of texts. We must look into the actual doings of the respective followers of these religions. We must look up their historical reputation and see in how far their practical life has revealed the spirit of their faith. We need not rehearse the story of Christianity from the time when it attained its mature growth, under the Emperor Constantine, down to our own days. It is a monotonous story of war, of bloodshed, of persecution. Can it be honestly said that the love taught by Jesus or practiced by him was the ruling spirit of the religious life of a creed founded in his name, *though without his knowledge or consent?* Was not that utterance of his, "I bring not peace, but the sword," rather its watchword in all the dark past? Let us hope that we Jews have long since forgiven our expulsion from Spain, from France, from England. Let us hope that the massacre of St. Bartholomew's Day history will never repeat, and that the Thirty Years' War between Catholicism and Protestantism was the outcome of mediaeval barbarism. Although so much of what we know of Christianity is but the persecution of Jews and Moors, and the persecution of other Christians who differed from them on theological niceties, we would still not have the right of inferring that the spirit of love did not sometimes exercise its influence with many a softening touch in many of the lives of the people of the olden time. Let us hope that it did. Tragedies more easily lend themselves to historical record and tend to dominate the pages of the chronicler. But, certainly as far as the growth of Christianity is revealed up till about the last century, we are compelled to say it is largely a story of violence and war. Not till almost our own time has a kinder, a tenderer spirit pervaded the faith of our neighbors; and not till they began to feel a regard for their fellow-men in their own hearts, did they first begin to seek it in the character they were taught to make their type and master. For the character of Jesus of Nazareth, of which we have so few actual details, is largely an imaginary creation and, therefore, can easily lend itself to the conceptions of every age. Therefore, the cruel tendency of mediae-valism knew no loving Jesus, and only the modern Christian—upon whom the modern spirit of sweetness and light has shone, the out-growth of our civilization—begins to discover that the central charac-teristic of Jesus of Nazareth is love.

If, on the other hand, we look to the doctrinal growth of Christi-anity, we find at least one great denomination, known as Calvinists, that, under the name of Puritans, played a large part in the early his-tory of this country and, under the name of Presbyterians, survives as a powerful sect to-day, hardly demonstrating the dominance of divine love. Of all religions Calvinism is the severest, the saddest. Its heaven is small, open to a select few; its hell is large, and burns fiercely for all *predestined* to its flames, and even the innocent but unbaptized babe goes to feed its fires. Its morality is stern, rigid and severe. Its life is gloomy, hard; its doctrine narrow and repellent.

Turning now to Judaism, that period of our history, immediately subsequent to the Exile, when Ezra and Nehemiah were the leaders, is more nearly akin to Puritanism than any period in our history before or after. As we get into rabbinism proper, we find a milder spirit, and it is significant that Hillel, the gentle, and not Shammai, the severe, becomes the typical sage. The ceremonialism of rabbinism has been perseveringly dinned into the ear of the public, but they have been told nothing of its *softening* spirit that is quite as characteristic. For we find that, great as was the reverence of the rabbins for the Biblical law, they dared to modify many of its severe injunctions. The "lex talionis," "an eye for an eye," was softened in their legislation to the payment of the damage done. The Biblical law that permitted a parent to bring to the tribunal a hopelessly wicked son, asking that he be put to death, was hedged round by rabbinical law with so many restrictions as to make any such case practically impossible. The horror of the rabbins for capital punishment urged them to make the death penalty so very difficult that it created the proverb "A Sanhedrin that puts to death one in seventy years is a bloody Sanhedrin."

As we enter into the spirit of the Talmud, we find that the relation of the Jew to his Maker is not that of the cowed child before a severe parent; there is a familiarity with which the Deity is spoken of that is hardly even dignified. The Jew seems so at home with his Almighty Father, that he feels permitted to approach Him with easy deference. And even in the old synagogue, the absence of strict decorum is largely due to that same spirit, that sense of nearness the Jew felt to God, the perfect assurance of his Father's indulgence and love. In how far that

spirit is left in the Jew to-day, we would say that among those who
criticize and ostracise our generation are many who say that our manners are not refined, but our hearts are warm—not a cultured people
but a charitable, loving people. It is, then, not true that our religion
lacks the element of love, that stern justice is characteristic of the Jew,
past or present. Nor can we honestly say that this spirit is so strongly
present in the faith of our neighbor. Not that we agree with our author
either that love is larger than justice, but justice is hardly our ethical
watch-word; rather righteousness. Righteousness is more comprehensive than both justice and love, it includes them. That is, we believe in
God and in God working through righteousness. We accept this excel-
lent definition of the spirit of our faith from a Gentile critic. That,
if any, is its fundamental statement, and on that dogma will we stand
or fall.

When Miss Lazarus would say that morality alone will not bring
us to God, certainly is she correct. But that is hardly the message that
she need bring to the Jew; let her take that message to the ethical-
culturist. Love, also, is not sufficient and will not bring us to God,
though she would infer otherwise. Yet, Miss Lazarus would ask of us
that we lose ourselves in the world about us, that we should yield up
our individual faith, give up our distinction, not only of race, but also
of creed, lose all our distinct identity, and let our lessons and our message be absorbed in the culture of humanity at large. Now, if she had
said that it is our duty to take the great religious truths for which we
stand and preach them to Gentile as well as to Jew; that we should
open the doors of our synagogue more widely and hospitably, and invite all to come and drink from the living waters of our faith; if she
had said that we should not exclusively keep our great lessons for ourselves only, but endeavor to make all our disciples—heartily would we
endorse her. I have already expressed that duty in the sermon: "Is Proselytism the duty of Judaism?" answering it in the affirmative. But she
does not ask us simply to preach our faith to a larger world, to give a
closer regard to the religious welfare of our Gentile neighbor. She tells
us to mingle it with the faith of Christianity, to save it by losing it, to
encourage its absorption.

If she really believed in Christianity rather than in Judaism, we
could understand her asking us to lose ourselves in the dominant faith.
But she does not accept Christianity as the full statement of her belief.
If she has been severe in pointing out the shortcomings of Judaism, she
has been almost as severe in pointing out the shortcomings of Christianity. She clearly states that we cannot become converts. She acknowledges that the spirit of Jesus, as she depicts his character, is as lacking
in the popular Christian life as in the Jewish; she acknowledges the

narrowness of the dogmatism of Christianity. She would ask for a union of the best elements of both these faiths, and bids the Jew lead the way by losing himself in the larger humanity about him.

Now, if we believe in the preciousness of our message and our mission to the world; if we are really convinced that we have a great truth to teach—and she believes it as sincerely as we do—we know no other way of perpetuating these lessons than by preserving them through the preservation of our distinct identity; to live up to this great faith, to hold it thereby in trust for mankind. Indeed, we know no other means of teaching it to the world than by living it ourselves. There is no better way of letting the world know what is Judaism than by preaching it week after week in the thousands of synagogues throughout the world, by publishing and spreading its lessons in the current literature, and by practicing its teachings in our daily doings. In this way, we have preserved the Bible for man. In this way the world is learning from us that which it lacks, but which we possess, just as we are learning from the example of Christianity about us some of its lessons that we may lack, and that may enrich our religious life. We do not hold an exclusive copyright over our beliefs. They are the world's if the world will have them. As a matter of fat, the world is absorbing Jewish teachings; Judaism is absorbing Christian teachings; every day the mutual debt is growing, yet, without either renouncing the religion that it loves and believes. For, granted that we broke down the barriers as she would suggest and all the distinctions that maintain our individuality, that we encourage indiscriminate intermarriage, that we renounce our distinct observances and all forms and institutions that single out Judaism as a distinct faith, permitting ourselves to be gradually absorbed in the life about us,—what would be the practical result? For a generation we would hear much edifying talk about the liberal spirit of the modern man and of the coming together of the faiths. In the next generation, the religious civilization would be identically the same, with but one factor, the Jewish factor, missing. Judaism would be sacrificed while Christianity would gain nothing. Christians are so many, Jews are so few—but a drop in the bucket of the nations—that the latter would be absorbed by the former without any perceptible difference in its religious life. We can exercise our influence only by preserving our distinct identity. In this way only can we make our faith felt by the great world.

What is the religious creed that she would hold up to us as an ideal? Sometimes we infer from her pages that it is Unitarianism. Is this the high water mark of religious life? Is this the eventual dogma? We are not drawn towards it, we do not find it particularly rich in that spirituality which she so often demands, and which she finds in us so

woefully lacking. If anything, we see more spirituality in the orthodox
Christian than in the Unitarian. He is thoroughly scientific, he is rational, the incidents in the life of Jesus may be used by him for edifying
sermons; we do not see that in any other respect the Unitarian endeavors to conform his life to this, the acknowledged master. Should Judaism give itself up to modern Unitarianism, this creation of yesterday?
Let us wait and see how it will bear the wear and tear of centuries. It
certainly has not earned the confidence of the Christian. Why should
it invite the Jew?

Our sister would have a universal religion. It is the popular cry
to-day. We hear it here and there from the pulpits of the sensational
and the superficial, not that she is either. It is a chimera, a will-o-the-
wisp. While men have individual minds and individual opinions, and
different ways of looking at life and the universe about them, will
there be different religions. Christianity in theory was to be a universal
religion, a faith catholic-universal. We find it split up into many denominations, which are to all intents and purposes separate religions.
The gap between, let us say, the Baptist and the follower of the Greek
church, is wider than the gap between many a Jew and Christian.
There are no religious boundaries separating man from his fellow, except the boundaries of belief, and they create themselves. The faith that
is to ignore all differences of creed, all differences of historic background, of time-honored observance, of sentimental association, it
would seem to us loses all characteristics and forfeits all value. We have
always been previously taught that it is a virtue to suffer for our convictions, to die for them if necessary, that to let them go for the sake
of peace and harmony is ignoble—it is peace bought at the price of
honor. When man has learnt to be truly tolerant he will not make the
renouncing of his neighbor's faith the condition of his love. A true
union of man with his fellow, a true sympathy with our neighbors, a
true regard for every race of men is yet possible, even though our religious faiths may differ. The Jew can feel sincere affection toward the
Christian, each loving and believing his own faith, while history has
too often shown the picture of men under the one banner of the one
creed, hating and fighting each other and condemning each other to
death. *Union of creeds does not imply union of hearts, nor does distinction of
creeds exclude it.*

We, then, cannot accept the panacea that Miss Lazarus would offer
for our religious problem to-day. And yet, we need not despair. Religious indifference and doubt are but the natural consequences of an age
of criticism, rationalism and unrest. This wave of skepticism is not
confined to ourselves. We recognize it in our brother Christian, too.
Nor do the shortcomings of Reformed Judaism make us despair of its

rejuvenating power. It has but entered its first phase, which is always destructive. The upbuilding phase of Reform is yet to come. Already the re-action has set in, already our people are earnestly asking to be taught the lessons of the faith. We want no new creed. We need infuse in Judaism no new elements, we need borrow theories from no other faith. We must breathe the old spirit into the children of Israel. We must echo with a revivifying power the old message of the Prophets. We must deepen that trust in God that our fathers held, and that we may yet hold again. Not love is the message we need most now, but duty; a keener sense of our obligation, a more earnest realization of our responsibility to the past and to the future, to ourselves and to the Gentiles. "Ye are my witnesses, saith the Lord, the servants whom I have chosen." Let us realize that we still have a mission for our fellow-man, that we should stand distinct, though not apart, from the world, while trying to interpret our obligations and the solemn meaning of our almost miraculous survival through the ages. Our religious inheritance, our glorious past, our unique place among the nations and our diverse influences upon them, all urge us to the conviction that the Law will again come from Zion and the Word of God from Jerusalem.

11   Comparing Moses and Jesus

"... comparing a sweet flower to a mighty oak ... "

Nineteenth-century Christian liberals pointed to the personality and to the ethical teachings of Jesus to demonstrate the superiority of Christianity. In "Moses and Jesus", Kaufmann Kohler compares the personalities and teachings of Moses and Jesus and concludes that Moses' message of duty and justice is better suited to the realities of life than is Jesus' message of love and nonresistance.

MOSES AND JESUS

When Moses prayed to God to show him His ways, the Lord said: "I will make my glory pass, and thou shalt behold me, after I have passed by thee, but my face shall not be seen." All beginnings of things are hidden from mortal eyes. No eye ever saw the grass grow. Nor did any one ever observe the awakening of self-consciousness in a child. The origin of physical and mental life is veiled. God says: Let there be light! and behold, there is light. However much light modern investigation has thrown upon the process of evolution of matter and mind, creation and revelation remain mysteries. As it was two thousand years ago, so science is still puzzled by the question: What came first? The egg or the hen? The acorn or the oak? The grain of sand or the hill? Science, in order to operate, must separate cause and effect, while actually they form one organic whole. In history, too, the problem vexes us: Are the great men, the master-minds of the centuries, the products or the builders of the ages? Is the genius the child or the father of the idea or the movement, he represents? Is music the creation or the creator of Bach and Beethoven? Did poetry produce Shakespeare or Shakespeare his poetry? Did art make a Phidias, a Michael Angelo and a Raphael, or the men these arts?

There was a time when religion was looked upon as the invention of priestcraft, and the great religious leaders and law-givers as a sort of impostors. We know better now. We have learned to recognize religion as the strongest and deepest of all human forces, as the one that cradled laws, arts and sciences, as the guardian of morality and the chief factor of civilization. But the prevailing tendency to skepticism and criticism has, on the other hand, led us to attribute everything to the successive work of ages, and to underrate individual power. We are inclined to reduce the lives of Moses and Jesus, not to speak of the founders of other religious systems, to mere myths and fables, because they are wrapt in legend. Yet is the great drama in which a powerful nation here, and a world conquering sect there, is ushered into existence really cleared and brightened up by the mere striking off of such names as Moses and Jesus from the pages of history? Is the great historical fact of the appearance of a power like Judaism and like Christianity better accounted for by unknown impersonal factors than by known personal forces? The more I ponder on the history of Moses and Jesus in connection with the two great religions of which each forms the central figure, the more does the conviction take hold of me that the life and teaching of each not only reflected but actually determined and embodied the character, the aims and ideals of their followers to an eminent degree. Their own principles became characteristic types of the religions they represent, and because these principles run in convergent lines, they could not avoid colliding with one another, while, in fact, they must merge into one another and complete each other, as they have grown from one and the same root. And only in the same measure as a mutual understanding is reached between them, are mutual recognition and respect and a final reconciliation between Jew and Christian made possible.

I

Who is Moses, around whose banner we, the progressive sons of the nineteenth century, are still to rally, and whose law we must, under a thousandfold martyrdom, if it needs be in the midst of a hostile world, forever uphold? Egypt's unlocked hieroglyphical treasures furnish no glimpse of him and his doings. The monuments of King Rameses II. and Menephtha, his contemporaries, show no trace of the Hebrew exodus with its miraculous events. The annalists are perfectly silent concerning Jehovah and his servants. And yet no surer did the law of gravitation by which Earth and Neptune are bound to the solar orb and this again to a larger system of stars flash upon the mind of Isaac Newton to enlighten for him the universe, than did the law in the wilderness of Sinai beam upon the mind of the Hebrew shepherd by which nations are freed from thraldom and the eternal right of man is established. Explain it as you may, a spark of the divine fire of righteousness fell upon the soul of Moses to dispel for him the world's darkness. The Decalogue may be the successive work of generations;

Moses was the first to give voice to the call: "I am the Lord who leadeth out of the house of bondage."

Did he, then, steal the name of Jehovah out of the mysteries of the Egyptian priesthood, as has been claimed? Or was it transferred from some obscure corner of Syria by some unknown seer to Israel's sanctuaries, as recent critics maintain? The idea is so preposterous, that one wonders how wise men could seriously express it. On the contrary, if anything, Jehovah, the God of Abraham, of Moses and of Elijah, strikes us as being rather too realistic, too natural a power. Dwelling on the heights of Sinai, enwrapt in pillars of fire and smoke, sending forth hail and storm wind to shake the earth, the air and the water with the powers of His awful majesty, He still had in those days all the qualities of a Bedouin Deity ruling the vast desert. However, the spiritual insight of Moses lifted Sinai to sublimer heights. His religious genius invested the thunder, the lightning and whirlwind of Jehovah with the sacred purpose of purging the world of its wrong in order to establish righteousness. Earth assumed a new aspect when the frown or smile of heaven betokened the wrath or the pleasure of a God of Justice. The wisdom and skill of the priests on the Nile were set to naught by the plain shepherd of Midian who, without title and mandate from their schools, brought a new message from the great Ruler of heaven. How did all the gods of proud Egypt crouch and tremble before the great Jehovah, whose shield was righteousness, whose seal truth, whose essence the all-devouring fire of holiness! All their gigantic temples, obelisks and pyramids, all the colossal structures of art and science dotting Egypt from sea to cataract, totter and tumble as His hand touches, as His eye scans them, since they are built on injustice, on oppression.

Yes, there is a deep inward relationship, a great moral affinity between Jehovah and His prophet. There is a fire in Moses bosom, mighty and deep as in a glowing yet slumbering volcano, the top of which is all serene and bright with smiling landscapes, while suddenly it pours forth its devouring streams of lava to spread terror round about. Moses soul is set ablaze with the holy wrath of justice at the sight of violence and innocent suffering to avenge the wrong on the evil-doer, while his heart reaches forth in tender compassionate love to vindicate the right of the oppressed. Thus is Jehovah a jealous God, who tolerates no wrong. His fire consumes injustice and falsehood, while righteousness is at the core. Sure enough, there is something hard as a rock and unyielding like granite in the character of Moses, yet only he who says: "Let the heavens fall but justice prevail!" is the man to unhinge a world of cruel wickedness and folly and rebuildt on the adamantine foundations of the right and the good.

There is a sternness and rigidity in the Old Testament, that often startles and scares the soft-hearted, yet this was the forge in which the Jewish character was to be formed and the laws made that were to outlast the ages. This was the quarry out of which "pyramids of men" were built; this the chisel with which men were carved, endowed with a heroism that defies death.

In the plain of Babylonia palaces have been unearthed, each brick of which has the name of King Nebucadnezar, its builder, engraved on it. So does every single law in the Mosaic books, no matter when they were written, bear the stamp of that mind which liberated the Hebrew slaves by the principle of justice, saying: "Yield not! Swerve not! Right must triumph over every wrong!" Hearken to the awe-inspiring threats of the Pentateuch! Read the fulminant and fury-lashed appeals of the prophets! Or peruse the minute statutes of Talmudical casuistry. They are all born of the same spirit of unbending righteousness, of unflinching truth. The sum and substance of Judaism is: As God's eyes cannot behold evil, so banish all injustice from His sight. Stand up in defense of the right, be it that of the high or the low-born, of the rich or the poor, the free or the slave, the native or the stranger! Yield not for justice is God's. Brook no sin. Bad means can never be justified by good ends. There is forgiveness and repentance for sinners, but not until the wrong has been undone; for the fruit of sin is death and Jehovah is the God of life.

And behold the people moulded by the great law-giver. What are the classic people of Hellas with their master-works of art and science, the Roman with his law, the Chaldean with his astronomy, and all the great nations of history with their glorious achievements compared with the insignificant, the despised and persecuted yet unyielding Jew? Indestructible like Sinai, he seems to be hewn out of the rock. While the rest furnished the framework, the modes of culture, the followers of Moses offered the basis, the essence, the law of conduct. Men can live without letters, without art and science, without comfort and beauty, but not as men without justice and goodness. And what is the secret of this wonderful endurance of the Jew, this marvelous power of resistance? The souls of all coming generations partook in the oath of the convenant of Sinai, say the rabbis. Indeed, there is a spark of that fire of Moses in every Jew, to make him defy the persecutor and brave the enticer. The baptismal fount only worked, according to Leroy Beaulieu, by the law of natural selection to make the rest of the Jews the firmer and more steadfast. Sneer as much as you may at those sharply cut features of the Hebrew, they betoken resistance to the last. Light-hearted audiences may applaud Portia and vilify Shylock. If, however, heroic wrestling with injustice deserves the prize, Shylock must receive our homage. The laws of Venice are wrong, and the Jew is right. Nor is the Jew satisfied with a bill drawn on the world beyond the grave. This life of man here on earth must turn out right. Justice must hold sway first, then love and peace can reign—not before. From Isaiah to Cremieux and Lasker the Jews have been God's champions of Justice and Truth.

And glance over the march of centuries. Watch the path of history. The trumpet blasts of Sinai, announcing Jehovah's Day of Judgment, sounded the dirge over antiquity's fall and rung in the era of Christianity. Only by an appeal from the New Testament to the Old, from Jesus to Moses, did Luther, Calvin and Cromwell succeed in combatting and defeating Papal tyranny. The tempests and thunders of Mount Horeb ushered in the Reformation, the Revolution, the American Declaration of Independence, the modern era of liberty.

There is a majestic grandeur in the statue of Moses created by the chisel of Michael Angelo. His every muscle and nerve from head to foot betray a resolute firmness of will and clearness of purpose which seem to inspire us with confidence, telling us to safely commit the destinies of mankind to these arms, that carry the tablets of the law, to those shoulders that bear that lofty head protuberant with light. And yet Moses died with the land of promise unreached before him. He claimed no perfection, no infallibilty, no goodness nor holiness. He was but the servant of the Most High, and died, leaving his work to be continued and finished by all the coming generations.

II

Who on the other hand is Jesus, the central figure of the New Testament, the divine ideal of the Christian? We shall leave aside the story of the crucifixion, the tragic end of Jesus, with which Christianity began its course. Never would the name of Jesus have been uttered by the Jews with any but reverential admiration, had the guilt and the curse of his murder not been flung upon them, his own kinsmen, at a time when it was deemed wise policy to exonerate the Roman prefect and his soldiers from the crime. We shudder at the thought of the millions that fell as victims to this slanderous charge; but we do not blame Jesus for the cruelties perpetrated in His name. Neither shall we consider Jesus as a performer of miracles in which quality alone, to judge from Rabbinical tradition, he left a lasting impression on the generality of Jews. These wondrous cures formed the specialty of the entire class of Essenes, a sect of saintly hermits practicing baptism and invocations of the Holy Ghost, from whom the carpenter's son of Nazareth emanated.

We are exclusively concerned here with the great popular teacher of Galilee, the preacher of the Sermon on the Mount, the promulgator of a new covenant, of a new law of love, as is the Christian claim. And there behold the sweet silver-tongued prophet of the people, as he walks among the untaught and forsaken, attracting the crowds by his exquisite parables and bringing them the cheering message of the All-loving Father in heaven. He moves among sinners saying, "I am the Good Shepherd who leaves the ninety-nine sheep in the fold to seek the one that has gone astray in order to lead it back." He takes his seat among the forlorn and outcasts saying, "Not the healthy need the physician, but the sick." Listen to him as he teaches, "Be not angry with thy brother! Resist not evil! Hate not! Love your enemies; bless them that curse you, and do good to them that hate you." Or watch him, as he takes a little child and, putting it in the midst of the crowd, says, "Be like little children and you are not far from the kingdom of heaven." Seeing a woman dragged along to meet her punishment on the charge of adultery, he cries out, "Let him that is without guilt cast the first stone!" and then tells the fallen one, "Go thou and sin no more!" There is a wonderful music in that voice, an undefinable grace about the serene face. There is a fascinating charm about every word that drops from those benign lips.

And again how bold and crushing does his language become when, turning to the haughty aristocracy, he exclaims, "It is easier for a camel to go through the eye of a needle than for a rich man to enter the kingdom of heaven," or when speaking of unlawful desires of the flesh, he says, "If thy eye offend thee, pluck it out! If thy hand offend thee, cut if off. It is better for thee that one part of thy body should perish than that thy whole body should be cast into hell."

There is a ring of true greatness in all these words. We need not wonder if the multitude followed with ardor and admiration the young master who spoke thus differently from all the rest, eager to offer him the highest crown within the gift of the Jew, the diadem of Messiahship which he bought at the price of his life.

Yet does this holy man with all his heart-winning persuasiveness and touching humanity really surpass the imposing nature of Moses? Does the prophet of the New Testament eclipse the creative genius of the Old? It is like comparing a sweet flower to a mighty oak, the slender steeple to the massive structure upon which it is reared.

Naturally enough did the twelve centuries which elapsed after Moses elevate the moral status of the people ennoble their ethical and spiritualize their religious views. Most of the teachings ascribed to Jesus by the New Testament writers were current among the Essenes and in the Pharisean schools. The Golden Rule, the so-called Lord's

Prayer, the greater part of the Sermon on the Mount are derived from other sources. In fact, half of what is attributed to Jesus contradicts the other half of what he is reported to have said. For if he really placed himself on the shoulders of Moses, saying, "I have not come to change one iota of the law; I am not come to destroy but to fulfill," he could not well have dreamt of antagonizing either the Sabbath or the temple. And if he dared refuse to cure a heathen woman, saying, "It is not meet to cast the bread to the dogs," his was not even the broad-heartedness of a Hillel and Philo whose religion of love knew no confines of race or sect.

The greatness of Jesus lay in that he lent new grandeur to humility, in that he broke down the barriers of the school and brought the wisdom of life from the learned home to the lowliest, thus striking the keynote of humanity. He actually became the redeemer of the poor, the friend of the cheerless, the comforter of the woe-stricken. He lent both through his life and through his death as the Man of Sorrow, a deeper meaning, a more solemn pathos to suffering, sickness and sin. Life received from him a new holiness, a greater inspiration. And as he went forth to seek and provide for the lost sheep in Israel, so did the Church founded on his name go forth to redeem the poverty-stricken, the ignorant and the neglected, all the lower classes of society. Christianity was the gospel for the poor and the despised. Hence all the works of love, of charity and philanthropy, fostered among the Jews, found under the cross a new powerful impetus, a larger, world-wide scope.

But the very virtue of the teaching, of the character and life of Jesus was also his weakness. He was of that type of idealists that appeal to the sentiments, but overlook the demands of real life. Considering the terrible catastrophe that soon afterwards befell Judea and was already fast approaching, we are amazed at the almost idyllic life the Nazarene saint passes in the midst of his followers on the beautiful lake of Genezareth, perfectly listless and unconcerned, while a world around him sinks into ruin. The sentiments expressed by him remind us of a recluse waiting and praying for the millennium of peace, while the shocks and earthquakes of war resound in the distance. It is the political apathy of the Essene, which, in the face of the boiling wrath of the patriots, prompts the cool advice: "Render under Caesar what is Caesar's, and unto God what is God's. *'Resist not the Evil One!'* for the Kingdom of God is at hand!" This is the substance of the entire New Testament. "Yield, rather than assert your right! Swear not! Struggle not! Abandon all worldly care and ambition. Renounce all possession and domestic bliss. The God who clothes the lilies in the field will also provide for you!" This was the road straightway to the cloister and the nunnery, to world-contempt, to misanthropy and asceticism, to a double code of ethics, one for the layman and another for the monk.

This principle of non-resistance influenced and determined the entire course of Christianity. While the Christ was, after the visions of his resurrection, expected to come down from the clouds with his angelic host to redeem his saints, the new sect surrendered the world to the Evil One. "Resist not!" being the maxim, passion, vice and ignorance speedily took hold of the Church, and the sword in the hands of the former persecuted made them persecutors. Resist not! was the principle, and consequently justice had to yield to violence, and truth to pagan falsehood and folly. Error and wickedness forced their way into the council and up to the throne, and the mild figure of Jesus was transferred to ideal heights beyond the reach of worldly pursuit. He assumed now the face of a Syrian, then of a Greek, and later on that of a barbarian god, and his name shielded all possible wrong.

Justice and Truth are the foundations of Jehovah's throne: Christ's—the Christian god's, is love, yet lacking justice and truth. Jesus' strong side was the heart, the sentiment. And so did Christianity deepen the pathos, enrich the emotional side of life. By her care for the sick and the suffering, by her cultivation of art, of music, of painting, the entire soul-life of man was unfolded and refined by the church as by no other sect. Yet when, after the centuries of mediaeval barbarism and depotism, freedom of thought and action was to be regained for Europe, when the State, when science and industrial independence, had to be built up, Sinai with its Decalogue offered a safer basis than did Calvary with its beatitudes. The idealism of Jesus was, like any other Utopian system, like communism and mysticism, the vision of a time when the wolf and the lamb would pasture together in peace, not the programme for a life of struggle and strife, full of contrasts such as ours is.

Moses, too, spent forty days on the heights of Sinai immersed in contemplation, but he stepped down with his law to elevate and educate his people for their high mission of righteousness and truth. For religion is not a dreamland, a mere realm of vision, a hope for a world to come. It is the up-building of divine life in all its realities here on earth. It is the indwelling of God in man. Jesus represents the highest ideal of the Christian. Moses points to a higher type of manhood. Neither Sinai nor Golgotha, but Zion is the focus and goal of united humanity. Did Christianity indeed enshrine and embody love, the feminine element of the world? Judaism insists first on, and battles for, righteousness and truth. Duty, the sterner part of life, is also the stron-

ger and more indispensable one. Still we believe that, as has recently
been so well said, the two together yield the perfect ideal; their unity
will make humanity whole and free.

12 A Jewish View of the Teachings of Jesus

One of the most important ways in which Reform Jewish leaders contested the Christian claim to religious superiority was to argue that Jesus' religious message was not original. Instead, they emphasized the Jewish nature of Jesus and his teachings. In analyzing Jesus' teachings, the Reformers found parallels in contemporary Jewish sources. In those few instances where Jesus differed from Jewish doctrine, the Reformers explained how the Jewish teaching was preferable. Emil Hirsch's "Doctrines of Jesus" is a sermon that typifies the Reform argument concerning the unoriginality of Jesus.

THE DOCTRINES OF JESUS

Well-nigh universal is the contention that Christianity, especially as represented in the gospels, marks a decided, if not a distinct advance in spirituality and morality beyond the height reached by Judaism. In this claim, all differences of sect, or even of philosophical party shibboleths, are forgotten. The orthodox Christian is joined in this by the most liberal, yea, the very atheistic pupil of the latest German rationalistic school. The orthodox Christian, of course, beholds in the religion of Jesus the promised fulfillment of which that of the Old Testament was merely the suggested coming. He is, therefore, free of all admixture of contempt for the religious views presented in the Old Testament. Perhaps there lodges pity, deep pity, in his heart for those who will still cling to the old when the new light has risen above the horizon. The new is the fully unfolded flower, the old but the imperfect bud; the new is the completed structure, the old but the scaffolding: and with compassion, pathetic and touching alike, he regards us who will still cling to the scaffolding though the edifice is completely erected. There be some among these churchmen who insist that the Jew must cling to the scaffolding in order that the beauty of the building behind may by contrast all the more potently be revealed. In this opinion, the thought is fundamental that the Jew witnesses . . . to the

higher truth of Christianity; and must, therefore, crushed under the
load of the curse, walk dreary earth in order that the freedom of Christ
be all the more gloriously exemplified. The liberal German atheist fel-
lowships the most thorough churchman in holding with him that
Christianity is a higher development out of Judaism. Christianity does
not appeal to him; why, then, should Judaism? And in these queer days
of sad confusion, there be Jews pretending to be educated, who are
never so glib as when, with assumed philosophical profundity, they
stilt the same argument. Christianity has been recognized as out of
keeping with the rhythm of modern days. Judaism is older than Christianity; if the daughter more beautiful than the mother is now out of
touch with the onward sweep of modern religious ideas, is it at all
rational to suppose that the less agile parent should be able to keep step
to the steady march of victory, of light and of truth but lately found?
By this argument they would excuse their cowardice, which at any
cost would be rid of their Jewish patrimony. But do they succeed in
covering their total ignorance? Verily, they neither studied Christianity
nor Judaism. Of Christianity they know but what is to be found in the
common and vulgar attacks. They have read somewhere about the inquisition, and now confound the inquisition with Christianity; they
have been told somewhere about certain ridiculous, if not low and im-
moral stories of the Bible, and they confound these Biblical accounts,
which they misconstrue, with Judaism; and thus in their supreme conceit of liberalism they will have none of either Christianity or Judaism.

I have said advisedly, the claim is made that the New Testament is
a decided advance beyond *Judaism;* even our friends the Unitarians are
loud in their protestations to this effect, and the offshoot of Unitarianism, ethical culture, if represented by one who erst was a Presbyterian
or Christian minister, will be glad to echo the accusation. In Unitarian
literature we run at times across the words, "the great refusal." This
phrase, as there used, stands to cover the conduct of the Jews at the
time when Jesus appeared among them; the light had risen, the Jews
were blind to its radiancy; they refused to acknowledge that the full-
ness of time had come, and their later history, even by Unitarian writers, is represented as the primitive drama consequential upon this great
"refusal." The cruse fell upon the Jews, and they are doomed forever,
until they turn to the fuller light, to carry this divinely pronounced
malediction. But *Judaism* must not be confounded with Old Testa-
mentism. The Old Testament is very frequently read under a mistaken
notion which, present at the elbow of the reader, leads him into fatal
error. That it dropped from the clouds complete; that at a certain hour
of time God gave unto Moses this book—or at least that part of the
book which marks the high tide of its spiritual rise—is the common

prejudice, wedded to the other that beyond that point in morals and religion Judaism could never have grown and never did grow. This view, very popular though it be, is the turbid source of a thousand and one misjudgments—errors that cling to life with a tenacity which truth often lacks. Judaism is not identical with the Old Testament, and in the Old Testament the law doth not mark the high water notch. The prophets occupy a by far higher altitude than is represented in the Pentateuch, a compromise as it is between priest and prophet. Fifteen hundred years lie between the first word of Biblical literature and its last broken echo; during fifteen centuries, we may suppose that morals and thought developed. And, in truth, they have developed. Foolish are they who in the name of Judaism, protest against the introduction of critical methods in the reading of our ancient literature. Judaism has naught to fear from however bold a critical analysis; for the critical school has shown more clearly than aught else, that Judaism is a tendency and a movement, historically developing, pushing on and on to its latest destiny. Judaism is not a stake driven into the glacier, so that, the stake remaining to mark the position of the icy field when measured by the investigator, when the glacier moves on from the point so indicated, the stake is left a sad and solitary monument to its own inability to keep pace with its neighbors. No; Judaism is the very glacier that moves on and on, and is glad that the sun's rays kiss into life its sacred truth, so that it may trickle down the slope a limpid rill and gather into a river and then sweep on, urged by its own yearning to meet its own death in the wide ocean of humanity, in the mean time irrigating barren tracts and charming into flowery smiles pouting deserts.

Judaism is distinct from certain parts of the Old Testament. If the contention be raised that certain portions of the New Testament represent a broader level of spiritual outlook and of moral uplook than do certain parts of the Old Testament, I agree, and every unbiased scholar will agree; but whenever the insistence is pointed that Judaism represents a lower phase, and Christianity, as such, a higher attitude and altitude, not in the name of my religion, but in the name of scholarly truth, must I demur. Judaism at the time of Jesus had risen to the same level as is represented by the words of the great teacher. We cannot properly understand the New Testament unless we are thoroughly acquainted with the methods of applying the Biblical texts, and of presenting the thoughts and the ideas and ideals, current among the Jews, in vogue in the synagogue and in the schools at the period when the New Testament was compiled, or when Jesus lived and taught and instructed among his people. The New Testament may properly be designated as a Jewish Midrash. Those who are acquainted with the

architecture of the Midrash, those who know the homiletic methods of
the Jewish preachers of that time, find themselves at once at home in
the New Testament atmosphere. The synoptic gospels are not an ex-
otic plant by some miracle dropped from the clouds or carried from a
distant zone to the hills of Palestine; but they are indigenous to the soil
which grows the cedars of Lebanon. They are rooted in the Jordan,
and their crown courts no other sky but the one that arched itself o'er
the academies under the very shadow of the Temple in Jerusalem. The
New Testament is flesh of our flesh and bone of our bone. As Jesus
quoted Old Testament verses, so did the rabbis apply the texts of the
law and prophets; as Jesus teaches by parable, so do the Talmudic doctors impart instruction by means of simile and story (Mashal). Some of
the words of Jesus at once awaken a response in the memory of him
who is read in the Jewish literature of that period. Strike a key on one
instrument, another attuned alike will vibrate in answer. So it is with
the New Testament sayings; they all are vibrations in a key that can
awake at once into harmonious response the strings on the harp of
Jewish literature. Many of the sayings of Jesus can be duplicated almost
verbatim from Talmudic writings; others are but slight variations of a
favorite theme. The method, the language, the way of presentation,
recall those of the rabbis in the "houses of instruction" (Battei-
Hamiddrash) that then dotted the whole land and could be found in
every town of Palestine.

If not the method, is perhaps the matter new? This is often held to
be the case, and not merely by Christian orthodoxy. Christian orthodoxy is entitled to its insistence, for Christian orthodoxy is not supposed—as orthodoxy, in fact, never is,—to harmonize its statements
with historical or critical methods. Orthodoxy starts with a dogma; it
begins the discussion with the question answered beforehand. For
Christian orthodoxy, Jesus is the fulfillment of the law, and therefore
the fulfillment must be fuller at least than the empty measure to be
fulfilled. But rationalism, Unitarianism, ethical culture even, have forgotten their very ground principles, in dealing with the phenomena of
the moral or religious life of Judaism. Whenever the equivalents of Judaism and Christianity are to be weighed one against the other in the
balances, the operations is conducted with malice and prepense. Judaism is a thorn in the flesh of these would-be Liberals. Judaism without
compunction may therefore be represented, or rather misrepresented as
being the lower of the two; for if the assumedly higher be proven out
of rhyme and reason with modern needs, it stands to reason that the
less valuable loses all title to respect. This trick, often resorted to accounts for the strange readiness and unanimity with which from Unitarian pulpits and from ethical culture platforms the orthodox refrain is

taken up—that Jesus in his doctrines, in his outlook, in his uplook, stands on a pedestal on which the feet of Jew never did rest or could have rested; that he saw the Heavens open and beheld the vision of the prospective union of all men, while Jew never could have had in possession the key wherewith to unlock the gates of that paradise to be, of humanity denationalized but united in the grand service of the highest love. Is this true? I am not approaching the question, believe me, with prejudice; for all my Judaism would suffer, for all your Judaism would weaken, it may and it might be shown that Jesus, eighteen centuries ago, preached something broader and taught something nobler than did the rabbis of the synagogue. The rabbinical religion in its restricted sense is neither mine, nor, at least I trust, is it yours; our Judaism is ours, and we might take light from whatever lamp, and we might take waters of life from whatever bubbling spring; if it were true that the rabbinical well had been exhausted, that at the time of Jesus the waters had run dry, I should not hesitate to say so; but historical truth forbids, and the liberal as little as the illiberal, has the right to be disloyal to one that should, above all, be his beloved, the genius of truth.

Did Jesus teach new ideas; did he raise new ideals? He teaches, it is said, the Kingdom of Heaven—world to come. These phrases cannot be understood unless they be translated into the Hebrew of those times. Kingdom of Heaven, world to come: What did these two terms connote in the minds of the Jews of that day? Was Kingdom of Heaven a kingdom beyond the clouds? Was it a Heaven to welcome the weary wanderer after life had bidden him farewell? The Jew never did believe in life to come in this sense. Even rabbinical Judaism expresses life to come, if taken in that sense, by the term the garden of Eden, and its contrast by the valley of Hinnom. The phrase "Kingdom of Heaven" is not in the mind and in the mouth of the Jew a synonym for "life to come;" 'Olam Habba, the world to come, or as it is in the Aramaic of those days—for the Jews then spoke Aramaic and no longer Hebrew— Olmā de-Athe, the world which is to come, does not signify life to come. Both of these terms have naught in common with the doctrine, either affirmative or negative, of the immortality of the soul. The word 'Olam, in Hebrew, means a cycle of world years. According to their peculiar construction of the sweep of universal time, the Jews believed this vast ocean of life and of events passing before us gradually with the years circling in the circling sun, to be divided into sections, as it were, of a certain length, and such section was an 'Olam, a world, a cycle of years. And at this time the Jews were convinced that again they were approaching the end of such a cycle. The new "age" about to dawn was the 'Olam Habba. At the end of the present they were confident would open a new period, the Messianic time. The

"Kingdom of Heaven" was a clear paraphase for the Kingdom of God. Under God's scepter the new age was to be a contrast to the one now hastening to its appointed termination. If this was under riot, the new will be under righteousness. If now violence prevailed, in the new order of things justice will predominate. Heaven is a well-known equivalent in the Hebrew of those days for God. In preaching the approach of the Kingdom of Heaven, Jesus had in mind no other concept. He foretold the Messianic time here on earth, here under the moon, not in another sphere nor in another life. If Jesus taught, as he did, the doctrine of the world to come, he taught it in no other sense than did the rabbis; it was his firm belief that this present world or order of things, this world of riotous evil and vice, would come to an end, and with its end the new cycle would unroll itself, the world to come of righteousness. The "Kingdom of Heaven" meant the reign of righteousness instead of as now the scepter of violence; the triumph of justice instead of the ascendancy of injustice. This the prophets had prophesied before. Every prophet of old had rhapsodized about the coming day when justice would flow like water, when Zion would be redeemed by righteousness, when violence would pass away from earth, when peace would reign everywhere. In the theology of the synagogue, however, the establishment of this triumphant rulership of righteousness could not take place as long as Israel was under foreign yoke. The expulsion of the Romans from the sacred territory of Israel was the prelude necessary for the dawning of the Kingdom of Heaven. Hence, among the Jews of that time, resistance to Rome, rebellion against Roman dominion, was a precondition to the ushering in of Kingdom of Heaven. Kingdom of Heaven, then, was treason in the ears of the Romans; he that preached that doctrine was an anarchist, the distruber of existing political relations; he was a traitor, he was an outlaw. And another feature of "kingdom to be" was a new social order. Rich shall no longer lord it over the poor. Do you believe that only in these latter days of ours have men risen to protest that riches entail obligations corresponding to the advantages which they command? Do you believe that only within the last five hundred years, or perhaps only in the last one hundred years, the cry of the down-trodden has gone up to the sky, pleading for a better life than such as human selfishness assigns to brother man? The hills of Palestine have echoed the outcry of agonized humanity ever since the prophets found their voice of thunder. The prophets were the first socialists; they were the first to teach that the rich does not own his own wealth except as a trust to be administered for all. Read the old prophets with open and unbiased mind, and you will find page after page the demand for social justice. And the establishment of this social justice was one of the concomitants in the coming of the Kingdom of Heaven. If Jesus taught the doctrine of the Kingdom of Heaven, as he did, he taught it as the Jews then believed it: A new order of things for *this* earth, which implied the expulsion of the Romans from Palestine and the reorganization of society on the basis of love and of common humanity. "Repentance" was the preparation demanded of every one that would become a citizen of the new kingdom.

It is, however, at this point that our would-be liberal friend and his orthodox preceptor takes an exception: In this kingdom to be, say they, according to Jesus, all men are to be citizens. For Jesus certainly refused to recognize the national bounds of Israel; he called himself the son of man, not the son of Israel: his sympathies spanned the world; he was not satisfied with hugging to his bosom the fellow of his race. For him, humanity marked the bounds and the limits of love and of affection; this no Jew ever felt—and ethical culture liberal will add: This no Jew today will feel. Is this true? Let me leave, for the moment, out of question the consideration of this part of the argument, which assumes that Judaism has never flooded beyond the narrow fastnesses of its nationality; let me, for argument's sake, grant that the Jews of that period were the haters of humanity and the lovers, if at all, merely of Israel; let me even own that you and I, because we are Jews, cannot love humanity, though the welcome over our gateway greets the visitor with the assurance that "My house shall be called a house of prayer for all nations;" a quotation from an old Jew, Isaiah of Babylon, who lived about twenty-one hundred and fifty years before, in America, ethical culture gospel was preached; yea, let us grant all this, the inquiry will still be pertinent: Did Jesus' affections, as defined and traced in the gospels, transcend the limits of nationality? If this impeachment of Judaism is true—which it is not—did he rise in this above the religion of his times? If Judaism did not, he did not. "Cast not your pearls before the swine," he says; "give your bread to the children of Israel." According to the gospel of St. Matthew, he shared all the prejudices of the Jews in this regard; he would not traverse Samaria, because Samaria was for the Jew defiled. He sends his disciples to the lost sheep of the house of Israel. In one word, he is always national; Jew first, if not all the time. Nevertheless it is a myth that the synagogue in the days of Jesus was deaf to all calls for a broader universalism. Jesus was a Jew, but being such his Judaism did flood beyond the narrow bounds of nationality. In the ethical maxims of the rabbis we have the Leitmotif of the unended melody of a united humanity. For philanthropy, the distinction between sons of Abraham and sons of other nations is obliterated. The poor by their poverty are made the wards of the Jew; the weak by their weakness are made the brother of the strong Jew; the dead of all nations must be buried, the hungry of all nations must be fed, and the suffering and the slaves of all nations must be freed, is rabbinical ethics, and has been the practice of Judaism from time immemorial to this present day.

If the synagogue, then, is narrow, would that the world were as narrow; if this means national exclusiveness, Jesus was nationally exclusive. There were some undoubtedly, among the ancient Jews of those times, as there are some today, who were not up to their Judaism; but in judging of principles, those that lagged behind in the onward realization of fundamental propositions must not be considered. In principle Judaism is universal; in principle Jesus was Jew and universal at one and the same time. His universalism does not go beyond the universalism of the synagogue of that day, of this day, or of any time. Did not the Jew recognize that those who observed the seven laws of Noah, the fundamental laws of morality, are entitled to all the privileges which await the pious Jews in Heaven. The righteous of all nations shall enter into kingdom come; and, mark you well! the world to come of righteousness to be, is the fundamental pillar in the eschatology of the Jewish synagogue. Is this nationalism, or is this universalism? That the Thorah was the book of the "generation of *man*," constituted the joy of the best among the sages of Israel. But, it is said to prove that Jesus introduced a new religious idea, he calls himself the "son of man." "Son of man" means, if it means anything, as every Semitic philologist must concede, one who is human. In the phraseology of the Semitic dialects, the word son is always used where in English or modern languages we employ an adjective. Son of man, means one with human attributes; son of strength means strong; son of wisdom, means wise. The phrase "Ben Adam" or even "Ben Ha-Adam," "Ben-Enosh" equal to Aramaic "Bar-Nash," if Jesus employs it to designate himself could have conveyed to himself and to his disciples simply the notion that he was a man, a typical man with none but human attributes. No other sense but this can be imputed to the passages where the term occurs in the Old Testament, not even to the verse Daniel vii. 13. A careful analysis of the context, of all the verses in which in the Synoptic Gospels—for John must be excluded for well known reasons—the phrase is found, leads to no other conclusion. Perhaps—I, at least, always have had the feeling that—Jesus in so characterizing himself meant to imply that in the new order of things it was possible for man to be simply man. One conversant with rabbinic thought will remember that the generation which was fed by manna was regarded by the sages as the only one which could be loyal to the study of the law, because free from the distraction necessitated by the struggle for bread. Something of the same thought must have been uppermost in the mind of Jesus in the use of the phrase "Son of Man."

The future was to bring about conditions such as rendered possible a simply *human* existence, free from the hunger and anxiety for wealth which now exists. Man, this may have been his hope, shall be in a position to live the naturally human life, as does now the animal the naturally animal. In other words, Jesus may have contrasted the natural lot of man with that of the beasts, of whom one rabbi observes "I have never seen the deer hunt, the lion carry loads, and the fox engage in mercantile ventures, and yet they are fed. But the son of man hath not where to lay his head; while the fox has his lair and the birds find their nest." If it means aught else, Ezekiel claims priority. Ezekiel calls himself "Ben-Enosh," therefore this old Ezekiel, priest and prophet, Jewish nationalist and Jewish priest, did address himself as man; so Judaism must have attained the level of this humanity; it did not have to wait for Jesus to bring to it this new light.

But was not Jesus the first to teach that the forms of religion are secondary, while the essence of religion lies in the pure heart, in the clean hand, in the righteous soul, in the hunger after justice, in the kindly deed, in the humble service, in the charity in secret? Jesus taught all these things, and still—his own words are corroborative of this—he did not depart one iota from the ritual of the old synagogue. "Think ye not," says he, according to Matthew, "that I am come to destroy the law; I am come to fulfill the law; not a jot nor a tittle of the law shall pass away until all things be accomplished." What does he mean by the latter phrase? Nothing more than what was even a platitude in the mouth of the rabbis, that in the Messianic age all ritual practices will be set aside; no sacrifices will be offered, no Sabbath day will be kept; all the "Mizwoth" will be set aside in this world to come; that is what Jesus means by "until all things be accomplished, until the end come," the end, another term for the Messianic age, for *'Olam Haba* in the phraseology of the rabbis. And his other phrase: "I am not come to destroy the law, but to fulfill the law," has an equivalent in your own daily prayer book. "To keep all the commandments," is the original of the words here rendered to "fulfill," just as we pray in the old liturgy. Jesus used the identical words "I am come not to destroy," but to learn, to teach, to observe, and to fulfill *Lekayem,* all the words (of the instruction) of the law. He thus avowed himself in this respect a loyal Jew. But did he not preach against the hypocrites, did not he protest against the wearing of phylacteries and of outward display; against fasting and ceremonies; did he not with words of bitter scorn address those that stood at the corner of the streets to be seen of men constantly inquiring whether there be something neglected by them, while their hand was soiled with the blood of innocence, and their pouch filled with ill-gotten gains through oppression of the poor? Yea, he did; but so did the prophets of old; they all cry out: Shame, shame upon you that merely keep the shell of religion while the kernel is lost to you; woe unto you "whose interior does not tally with the exterior." Does not Isaiah, even, castigate those whose hearts are rankling with hatred of the brother? Do not the rabbis insist that the mere doing of ceremonial alone does not suffice? This is the position of Jesus; it is the position of the best in the synagogue. Not an advance, but a correspondence of views, therefore, we have in these utterances. Did he not set aside the Sabbath; did he not say the Sabbath is made for man, and not man for the Sabbath? For us, it is strange that the Jews of modern time have forgotten this doctrine of Jesus. I say forgotten, for it is the doctrine of the old synagogue, that the Sabbath was made for man, and not man for the Sabbath.

If Jesus should come back today, he would rub his eyes in utter astonishment at seeing that the synagogue had forgotten what he taught and what he had learned from his teachers. The identical phrase is found in the Mekhilta, (Ki Thisa) a rabbinical commentary on the book of Exodus. It is given to you but you are not given over to it. "Make thy Sabbath like a common day," says another rabbinical dictum, "and do not fall, in consequence of your keeping the Sabbath day, into the necessity of receiving alms;" Work on the Sabbath day, if by keeping it you make yourself dependent on others. So Jesus did not teach in regard to the Sabbath aught that transcended the doctrine of the synagogue; a correspondence again, not an advance. For that to save life the Sabbath may be violated is a well established maxim of rabbinical casuistry. It is curious to note that in Jalkut on I Sam. xxi. 7, the same appeal to the occurrence related in the verse is found as is in the second chapter of the Gospel of St. Mark.

In many non-Jewish prints—and their authors are by no means recruited from the camp of orthodoxy—one may run across the statement that Jesus was among Jews certainly the first to emphasize an altruistic view of religion and life, as he was the first to teach the "golden rule." Great as is the assurance of those who ask credence for this opinion, even so weak is the basis of fact upon which it rests. Before Jesus, the "golden rule" was one of the household sayings of Israel. It is certain that Hillel—some of our modern Jewish preachers are in the habit of calling him "Rabbi" Hillel;—who is by about thirty years at least the senior of Jesus, taught that the fundamental principle of the law and of the prophets is: Love thy neighbor like thyself, and what thou wouldst not have thy neighbor do to thee do not unto thy neighbor: Whatever is hateful to thee, do not do unto thy neighbor. But is this not the distinction between Jesus and Hillel that the former gave the "rule" its positive form while the Jew merely reached the negative? Much ink has been wasted in arguing this fine point. Calmly considered and without bias, the negative form is certainly the more natural; the positive smacks of a selfish motive; if we are to press the words to their utmost, we border in the positive statement on selfish calculation of profit to self in our conduct toward the neighbor. What did the Jew understand by neighbor? Around this question has raved these many years a bitter controversy, revived but recently in Germany, in which even liberal German Christians . . . have entered the lists to contend that Hillel as every other Jew only deemed the Jew and none other his associate and neighbor. How untenable this proposition is appears at once, if the situation is remembered, when and to whom Hillel so formulated the essence of his religion. For mind, and this is the point regularly overlooked by our critics, Hillel tells this to a non-Jew who wishes to become a Jew, on condition that Judaism be made plain to him during the time he is able to stand on one foot. For this non-Jew the word neighbor could certainly have had no "Jewish" significance and limitation. . . . In this connection the question must be considered, is the supposed antithesis of Jesus to "them of old" especially in reference to the inculcation of love for enemy, while the Jew would hate him, at all real? Certain it is that nowhere in the Old Testament or anywhere else in Jewish literature is found such a law. Jesus could, for Jewish and rabbinical ethics urges as emphatically as he does regard for the enemy, not have uttered the sentiment. How would you then explain this discrepancy? One familiar with rabbinical dialectics and brachylogy will soon find the key to this mystery. The phrase "and hate thine enemy" must be taken as the question of an assumed interlocutor. You have heard that it was said, "Thou shalt *love* thy neighbor." Does this imply "and thou shalt *hate* thine enemy?" No, the neighbor embraces even the enemy. The *political* enemy, the heretic, the traitor conspiring with the Romans, moreover, are in all probability those covered by the term, not personal enemies, for these to love, *i.e.* to serve and not to hate, the Jewish "Law and Prophets" always enjoined.

Did not Jesus teach a new way of prayer? Was it not he who first led man to appeal to "our Father which is in Heaven?" And indeed that prayer which is remembered as *the* prayer of Jesus, is of all prayers the most prayerful. Miracles it has accomplished. It has welcomed the new-born babe at the threshold of life with a consecration which it alone on mother's lips could confer; it has given hope to the despondent; it has made death even radiant with beauty: it has steeled hearts that were on the verge of despair: it has taught modesty to minds that were carried away by arrogance; that prayer indeed has rightly become the universal appeal, but it is and was an anthology of Jewish prayers. It is a pearl necklace each pearl taken from the jewel casket of old matron Judaism, not a single phrase but is found in our prayer book.

These correspondences are well known. I may therefore be allowed to pass on to the consideration of one other point. It is generally held that Jesus taught the absolute burdensomeness of wealth; that he, in other words, attempted to establish a communistic society. Men cannot, he says, serve God and Mammon; the rich man cannot enter into kingdom come. We cannot understand this, unless we be familiar with contemporaneous Jewish history. Against whom are these pointed remarks against wealth directed? Against the priests. They were the rich who tried to serve Mammon and God alike, and had a monopoly in the Temple by which they made money, "big money" out of their sacred offices. The doctrine of non-resistance which seems to be preached in the sermon on the mount, is either an eastern hyperbole, or a warning against bringing Jewish disputes before the forum of the Romans. Who was the oppressor? Who took the outer garment? The Roman. Who compelled service, such as running errands for two thousand miles? The Romans. Jesus takes the stand that patience is meet. For the short lived triumph of violence is the surest indication that the hour of reckoning is near. In the Messianic age, the day will dawn when the Romans will no longer be the rulers of the country. This is Jesus's advice: Be rather among the persecuted than among the persecutors; rather bear injury and insult, than be among those that join insult to injury.

Thus, in his doctrines, Jesus is the best exponent of the thoughts, the moral ideas and the religious aspirations of the Judaism of his time. Such a mind as was his, however, leaves its imprint on whatsoever it touches. He took the crude material from the great mine of Judaism, but under his treatment the ore changed into ready coin, each coin bearing the stamp and die of a high value. He was original, not so much in the discovery of new thoughts as in the presentation of old thoughts. This much must be said, and none may dispute it, in the form which Jesus gave to these old Jewish maxims they were given a force and directness and pithiness that the rabbinical maxims of equal tenor almost altogether lack. Herein consists his originality. His words became the ready moral currency of the world; his words were carried out into the broad world, and wherever his voice was heard, willing ears were led to listen to the call for a higher life, and even those less eager were won to heed a message of better things. Through *his* words, Judaism was carried into the world; by his name Judaism knocked for admission at the gate of the nations. This he accomplished; the presentation of our old ideas, by his touch remodeled, conquered the Roman Empire for the light. He was of us; he is of us. We quote the rabbis of the Talmud; shall we then, not also quote the rabbi of Bethlehem? Shall not he in whom there burned, if it burned in any one, the spirit and the light of Judaism, be reclaimed by the synagogue? Yea, he hath been reclaimed; the old mother clasps him today to her bosom as he lays at her feet the fruitage of his work in the world, and old mother Judaism lifts her hand and blesses him who was her child, and blesses also those who though they thought they had accepted him, had heaped injury upon the old mother. Happy this day when Judaism finds again her son, the son comes back to the mother laden with the rich reward of his quest. The New Testament in the gospels presents Jewish thought, Jewish religion, Jewish universalism. Not an advance beyond Judaism, but a correspondence with Judaism, we have in the doctrine of Jesus, who was Jew and man; and because man, son of God; man, therefore divine—as you are, as every man is son of God even by the spirit of truth which links dust to God, and earth to Heaven.

13   The Question of the Messiah

A central point of controversy in the centuries old dispute between Christianity and Judaism has been the question of the messiah. In the pamphlet, "Why Do the Jews Not Accept Jesus as Their Messiah?," Bernhard Felsenthal argues against the messiahship of Jesus. He based his argument on four points: 1) there are others besides the Jews who deny the messiahship of Jesus, including millions of nominal Christians; 2) Christian belief in the messiahship of Jesus is predicated on a faulty evaluation of human nature, viewing it as essentially corrupt and in need of atonement from an outside source; 3) the miracles performed by Jesus which Christians claim as proof of Jesus' messiahship cannot be authenticated with any more certainty than those claimed for Mohammed or the saints of the Roman Catholic church; 4) Christians have misunderstood the Old Testament messianic passages, and have failed to understand that the New Testament used these passages in a homiletic manner in the same way that Rabbinic literature had done with innumerable Old Testament verses.

Felsenthal's lecture was delivered to a conference of Christians and Jews held at the First Methodist Church in Chicago on November 24–25, 1890.

WHY DO THE JEWS NOT ACCEPT JESUS
AS THEIR MESSIAH?

I have been requested to give, from my own Jewish standpoint, an answer to the question, "Why do the Jews not accept Jesus at their Messiah?" The question should have been amplified; some other questions should have been connected therewith and should have been added thereto. For instance: Why do the Unitarians refuse to acknowledge Jesus as their Messiah, as their savior and redeemer, and why are they so decidedly opposed to adore him as a divine being, as the second person in the holy trinity, aye, as a God himself, as a God incarnate? And you might further ask: Why do the members of Free Religious Associations and those who have joined Ethical Culture Societies totally ignore Jesus, and why are they so bold and so outspoken in their antagonism and opposition to the Christology of the orthodox Christian denominations?

You who ask the Jew for his reasons why he does not accept Jesus as his Messiah, and who are so anxious for the salvation of his soul, you might even go out into still larger circles, you might ask the tens of thousands, aye, the hundreds of thousands and the millions, who are Christians in name only, but who in reality are as far from acknowledging Jesus as a Redeemer of mankind and as a Savior of the world as the strictest Jew is from such an acknowledgment. You can find such "Christians"—in reality only nominal Christians, but essentially, to use one of your own terms, perfect heathens—in exceedingly large numbers almost everywhere,—in our United States, in Canada, in the British Isles, on the European Continent, everywhere. Chicago is full of them. *And their number is daily growing.* Now go and approach them and ask them your question, "Why, friends, do you not accept Jesus as your Messiah? O, we pray you, come to Jesus! Believe in him! Your salvation depends on that belief."

You will be astonished at the answers you will receive from those whom you address in such words—from those physicians, and lawyers, and teachers, and merchants, and bankers, and mechanics, and clerks, and others; from gentlemen and from ladies of good education and in various positions of life and of standing in society; provided that they have the leisure and the inclination to listen to your questions and exhortations, and are candid enough to reveal to you their real honest opinions regarding your Christian system of creed and its various dogmas.

"Please don't bother us"—so they will say—"don't bother us with your antiquated superstitions, with your irrational notions, with your obsolete Christian scholasticism and mysticism, which may have appeared acceptable enough in the Dark Ages, but which are certainly out of time in our nineteenth century; please let us alone." And if you continue to press them for further answers and ask them to state more in particular their religious views, the one will probably say, "I am a Deist;" and the next one, "I am a Theist;" and the third one, "I am a Monist;" and others, "We are Pantheists"—or Agnostics—or Buddhists—or Darwinian evolutionists—or adherents of some other philosophical or theological system. The one will continue stating that he is just as much of an orthodox Christian and just as much a believer in the messiahship and divinity of Jesus as Thomas Jefferson was, or as Charles Sumner, or William Ellery Channing, or Theodore Parker, or Ralph Waldo Emerson, and a number of other most eminent men and women in our land have been. Others will confess themselves as sharing the un-Christian views of Herbert Spencer, of Professor Huxley, of John Stuart Mill, of Immanuel Kant, of Benedict Spinoza, and other philosophers and thinkers of our own age and of former ages. You see here you have a large field for your missionary efforts, for your endeavors to convert and to "save" your infidel gentile brethren, and you ought indeed first try to reconquer these unbelieving sons and daughters of Christian parents and to bring them back to the Christian fold, before you proceed with your missionary work among these obstinate and benighted Jews—"these obstinate and benighted Jews," as you, in your amiable *façon de parler,* are used to call them.

Yes, my dear orthodox Christian friends, you to whom the conversion of the unbelievers to the belief in the messiahship and divinity of Jesus is the holiest and most exalted work you can conceive, yes, you ought to convert your own backsliders first, and you ought to try with all your might to stem, *if you can,* the disintegrating process now going on within your own Christian churches. Go to the preachers and teachers in the Unitarian churches here; go to the flourishing independent congregations here who are not connected with any "church;" go to the unbelieving masses of ladies and gentlemen who fill their churches and lecture halls whenever they ascend their pulpits or come forward on their platforms; go to the tens of thousands of the unchurched ones, go to them, move among them, preach your gospel among them, and convert them. Try to bring them back to your fold. The game is numerous, and it is noble game, and it is worth that you should try to catch it. And after you have succeeded in "saving" them, then, dear friends, will it be time enough to "save" us stiffnecked and obstinate Jews.

I may be interrupted here, and I may be requested to keep more closely to the question proposed to me—to the question: "Why do the Jews not accept Jesus as their Messiah?" But as in the main the Jews have the same reasons for the non-acceptance of Jesus as a Messiah as so large numbers of non-Jews have, I thought it proper to show by what I have said thus far that it would have been more logical to have the wording of the question amended and to have it read: Why do so many millions of people, Jews and Gentiles, Semites and Aryans, refuse to acknowledge Jesus as the Messiah of the world, as the Redeemer of mankind? But let this pass now, and as you explicitly desire me to give the reasons why the Jews do not accept Jesus as their Messiah, I shall now stick more closely to the question, though the same is so imperfect and faulty.

However, before I proceed, I must again point out another illogical feature in the question. The question presupposes correctly the fact that the Jews do not accept Jesus as their Messiah, and it demands that we should give our reasons and our proofs for our non-believing. But how can we prove a negative? One who is familiar with the A B C of the science of logic knows that the burden of proof lies upon him who makes a positive assertion, and not upon him who negatives the same. If anyone in conversation with me should tell me that upon the moon a kind of human beings are living, each one of whom is four feet high, white as snow, and provided with a pair of large wings, I should in all likelihood answer, "I don't believe that." If now my friend, who has told me so, is otherwise of a sane mind, who, in his reasonings, consciously or unconsciously, is governed by logic, do you think he would now turn to me and say, "Why don't you believe that? Why will you not accept what I said as a truth? Come forward with your arguments and your proofs for not believing me." Certainly he would not make such a foolish demand that I should prove a negative. But he would acknowledge it as perfectly correct and justified if I would ask him that he should prove what he said, that he should demonstrate the truth of it, and that he should make it convincingly clear to me that the moon is inhabited by winged human beings, each one of whom is four feet high and as white as snow.

The same logical law applies here. I am asked to give the reasons why the Jews do not believe in the Christian Messiah dogma. But I come with a more logical counter-question and with a more proper counter-request. I say to my Christian interlocutor, "Why do you believe that a certain Jew, named Jesus, who lived in Palestine, and died there about 1860 years ago, was a messiah, a savior and redeemer of all mankind from the consequences of sin? What are your reasons for such a belief? What are your supports and your proofs for such assertions? Let us hear your arguments; let me examine your supports, so that I may know whether these arguments are strong or weak, and whether these supports are sound or rotten."

Yes, sir, it is I who proposes now a question, and it is you from whom I expect a logical and rational answer. My question, I repeat it, is, Why do you, my Christian friend, believe that the Jew Jesus is your savior and the savior of all the generations of men?

———

Do not trouble yourself, however, with formulating an answer. My question is after all but a rhetorical question, and in reality I have neither a taste nor a willingness to enter into dogmatical discussions with confessors of another religion. Your religious convictions, my friend, are sacred to me, and far is it from me to disturb you in your faith and in your convictions so dear and precious to you. And I sincerely wish that all the Christians, without exception, would also regard as sacred and inviolable my religious convictions and the religious convictions of my Jewish coreligionists, and would not offend us by sending to us their missionaries and converting agents and by attempting to entice us, by means fair and foul, to renounce our Judaism and to become Christians . . .

But I do confess, my heart is not with such conferences in which articles of faith are discussed by confessors of different religious systems. For it is not to be expected that by such conferences we all, Jews and Christians, should come to a peaceful agreement as to the truth or untruth of the dogmas under discussion. Such a final outcome should not be thought of. Religious dogmas do not belong to the realm of exact science, and they cannot be proven and their truth cannot be demonstrated as a mathematical problem can.

Therefore different opinions concerning them will prevail among men as long as men shall live upon earth. It is for this reason easy to understand why now-a-days so many educated people think that such public discussions between Jews and Christians are perfectly out of times in our age. Some of this class of people mock at such conferences, others remain totally indifferent towards them and take not the least notice of them. As for me, I am free to say that such conferences appear to me—how shall I say? Comical? Humorous? Involuntarily I am reminded here of the great "Disputation" in Toledo, of which the poet Heine sang in one of his ballads. And if a second Heine would arise and would sing of the disputation which took place on the 24th and 25th of November, in the year 1890, *"in der Aula zu Chicago,"* he would earn the plaudits of many. Friends, what we need are conferences of another kind and for other purposes, and not such which will remain resultless and which may become irritating, peace-disturbing, harmful, if the speakers and listeners, one and all, are not beforehand honestly agreed to disagree.

———

Without waiting for anyone coming forward and stating the substance of the doctrine of the messiahship of Jesus and the essential parts of the whole Christological system, of which system the dogma that Jesus was and is the Messiah is but a single part, I shall now proceed to examine briefly the Christological points coming here into consideration. I shall try to be fair, just, and fully impartial.

According to the theology of the orthodox Christian churches the Messiah is a superhuman being, and Jesus is this Messiah. He is not merely the theocratic king of the Jews, but he is the Messiah and Redeemer of each human being and of the entire human race. He died at the cross as a vicarious sacrifice for the sinful human family, and by his self-sacrification he effected atonement for the sins of men and redeemed men from the eternal punishment which otherwise an offended God in his wrath would have visited upon them. Christ has saved us— so it is claimed—he has redeemed us, and by his having died for us he continues to save us and redeem us and those that will come after us, *provided we believe in him.*

This is the central idea of Christianity and the head and cornerstone upon which, if I am not mistaken, the whole structure of Christianity is reared. It contains several presuppositions, for which the claim is raised that they must be accepted as firmly established facts and as eternal and unshakable truths. What are these pre-suppositions?

The first one is: Man is morally rotten to the core and saturated with sinfulness so deeply rooted and so full of strength that he, by his own powers and exertions, cannot get rid of this state of sinfulness. The second pre-supposition is: Atonement for our sins can be had only and exclusively by a vicarious sacrifice; such a sacrifice alone will effect it that the wrath of God is appeased.

If we now look a little closely into the face of these presumed facts and alleged truths, we come to the conclusion that they are not in agreement with well-established Jewish doctrines; that, on the contrary, they are heathenish.

Is it true that all men are indeed impregnated with sin in such a high degree so that it is not possible for them to free themselves from it and to rise above it by their own endeavors? Did the Creator befoul man's nature by incorrigible wickedness and moral rotteness from the beginning? Did he, whom we call our Father, soil and spoil the nature of man, even before man was born? No, not exactly so, we are answered by orthodox Christianity. Adam, the first of men, was made and put into the world pure and sinless. But he fell from the state of purity after he had been tempted by the serpent and had committed what Christian theologians call the Original Sin. Thereby his whole moral being became deteriorated, and he descended into such a low depth of sinfulness that he could not rise again. And still more. "By Adam's fall we sinned all." By Adam's fall all the descendants of Adam became miserable hopeless sinners; for they all inherited sin from the first man. Even the babe does not see the light of the world as an innocent child. As a sin-laden and vile being it comes into the world, and if it should die one day old, its lot would be eternal damnation if it were not baptized in the name of Christ and saved by Divine grace. And so all men would fall a prey to eternal perdition, if God, the Father, had not sent into the world his only begotten son, his divine son who took upon himself the sins of the world, and who died a vicarious death, in order to save and redeem mankind from sin and its consequences.

A God died for wicked men, or rather for those among them who believe in him! (May the God of truth, of love, and of justice pardon us for the utterance of such awful blasphemies!) A God died for the elect ones, for the believing ones, and saves them! The others, the Jews and the others who nod to believe—well, it is awful to think of their future. But it serves them right. Why do the Jews not accept Jesus as their Messiah? Why do the infidels among the Gentiles reject Jesus, who was a ransom for them too, and who appeased the wrath of the angry Monarch in heaven by sacrificing himself?

Within the time allotted to me it is impossible that I should enter at length into a critical examination of such redemption theories. A few brief counter-statements must be sufficient. And so I say: If a human being, endowed with reason and possessed of the faculty to think rationally, a being who never went into a Christian Sabbath-school, and never read the writings of orthodox Christian theologians, and never listened to the sermons and exhortations of orthodox Christian preachers, would descend today from heaven and would hear for the first time an exposition of the Christian dogmas concerning Messiah and Redeemer and a wrathful God and a crucified God and of whatever is connected with these dogmas—this being would wonderingly shake his head, and would say, "This is the most confounded mysticism and the most irrational religious philosophy which I ever heard." I think that many of my Christian friends, who believe that they believe, would also never have come to assent to such unintelligible ideas, if such ideas had not been instilled into their minds since the days of their childhood from without—in the Sabbath schools they visited, in the churches they attended, in the books and papers they read.

To such an expression as I laid just now into the mouth of my supposed visitor from heaven, a Jew would probably add: The theory that sin is inborn in man and inherited from Adam is not only mystical and against all reason, it is also decidedly un-Jewish, and it has no support in my Bible. The Jewish theory is, Man has a natural inclination to sin, but he has also the power to master this inclination. And when he has sinned, he has the power and the duty to repent, to forsake the evil paths, to return to the ways of righteousness and holiness, and thus to regain moral purity and to reconquer the heights of a virtuous and blameless life. No ransom can be paid for him, no one else can die in his stead if he is guilty; he must be his own redeemer, he must repent and return, and he can then come without a mediator to the Heavenly Father, who is the Father of love and of mercy, and is not like a cruel earthly king, or like a revengeful Asiatic despot, who first must see blood before he becomes pacified and satisfied. Furthermore, the theory that sin can be effaced and blotted out by sacrifice only, is un-Jewish and has no support in my Bible. No ram and no bullock, no human and no divine being can die a vicarious death for me. In the sacrificial cult of the Jerusalem temple the sacrifices had only an allegorical meaning, and were admitted only as helpful to awaken in the Israelites the consciousness of having committed sins, to cause them to repent, and to strengthen them in their endeavors to return to moral purity.

To this it must be added that, according to numerous Bible passages, the sacrifices in the Mosaic cult were only suffered to be retained among the ancient Israelites, because the Israelites in yonder times were not yet ripe enough to conceive a worship possible without sacrifices, and were not yet able to understand that "God desires mercy, and not sacrifice, and the knowledge of God more than burnt offerings." (Hosea vi, 6; Psalm xl, 6; ibid., li-, 16, 17; Micah vi., 6, 7, 8; *comp.* also Jeremiah vii., 22, 23, and many other Bible passages.)

I am well aware that my orthodox Christian friend will not admit readily that the Jews' conception and understanding of the Old Testament is correct. He probably will try to explain the Bible otherwise. In this short hour I cannot enter more deeply into the subject. It would require more than an hour—it would require many weeks to do full justice to the matter.

One point, however, I shall unhesitatingly admit here, if my Christian antagonist should raise that point. It is true that a few isolated passages found in the Talmudical literature and a few mystical books written by some Jewish Kabbalists, that is, by some Jewish cultivators of mysticism and of "the Occult Science," contain views somewhat similar to the Christian sin and redemption theories and to the Christian conception of sacrifices. But these passages are isolated and these books are but few, and, as a whole, Judaism was not much tainted thereby.

Some of these un-Jewish ideas can be proven to have been transplanted into the Jewish fields in consequence of the mutual contact between Jews and Christians. On the other side, in the Christian church un-Christian ideas have been taking root, which, by such intercourse with Judaism, had been learned and borrowed from the synagogue. But the un-Jewish ideas within Judaism remained foreign plants on Jewish soil and would not flourish there. And, furthermore, has Christianity alone the privilege of being mystic? Has all the mysticism in the world been taken possession of by members of the Christian church alone? There are also some Jewish mystics. But while in Judaism mysticism remained a foreign, uncongenial growth, in Christianity mysticism was overshadowing all theological thinking, and Christianity and mysticism are almost synonymous terms.

I cannot let you go yet, continues my Christian friend. What do you, Jew, say to the miracles worked by Jesus? And are these miracles not proof enough that Jesus was the Messiah?

I again respond with a counter-question. What are your evidences for the truth of these miracle stories?

"Why," I am answered, "here are my witnesses—St. Matthew, St. Mark, St. Luke, St. John, St. Paul."

And this you call good evidence? There is good reason for saying that the books ascribed to the men whom you have just named have been written a great many years after the death of Jesus, and that their authors offer, therefore, only hearsay evidence. Such hearsay evidence is ruled out in every court of justice as inadmissible. And if you insist that the testimony of those five or six men, who wrote the gospels and the epistles, should be admitted as classical evidence, then I will ask you, Why don't you believe in the miracles said to have been effected by the holy waters at Lourdes, in France, in our own days? Not only five men came forward who report from hearsay that these waters in Lourdes are wonder-working, but thousands of men, who have been there themselves as pilgrims and who claim to have seen the wonders by their own eyes and to have heard the voice of the Holy Virgin by their own ears, will step before you and bear witness to the truth of what they say. The words of these thousands of living, contemporary witnesses should, according to all laws of evidence, be considered as far better evidence than the words of those five New Testament writers who, many years after the death of Jesus, repeated the legendary stories concerning him, which were in those days circulating among women, children, and uneducated, credulous country people. And are the stories as to the miracles of Muhammed and of the saints of the Roman Catholic Church not just as well "authenticated" by men and by books? Why, then, do you reject them?

———

Another support for your assertion that Jesus was our Messiah will probably be pointed out by you by your referring us to numerous so-called Messianic passages in the Old Testament. Your own sacred scriptures, so you will say to the Jew, contain in large numbers predictions and prophesies which point clearly to Jesus the Messiah. There are types in large numbers to which Jesus is the great antitype. There is the Shiloh clearly spoken of, and the Immanuel, and the Man of Sorrow, who bore our sins and died for our sins, and all that. Will you Jews still remain blind enough and close wilfully your eyes before the glaring light shining out of these Bible words?

No, the Jew will not shut his eyes, but he will see with open eyes that you read the Bible without understanding it. You take verses out of their context and then explain them most arbitrarily. You read the thoughts of the Bible not out of the Bible, but you read your own thoughts into the Bible. There is no book in the world that has suffered so much by false interpretations as the Bible has. For every philosophical or theological system, for every heresy, for every nonsense, for every crooked idea entertained by Jew, by Christian, or by Muhammedan, support was found in Bible words. And it is astonishing, in hundreds of cases the very same Old Testament passages are explained by different parties in different manners. "The desire of all the nations," who, according to an old Jewish prophet, will come, is understood by a New Testament writer as having reference to Jesus, and in the Koran it is explained as being a prediction of Muhammed, and by Jewish commentators it is taken neither in the New Testament sense nor in the Koran sense, but is interpreted by them in a way differing from both. The verse Haggai ii. 7 is translated by them, "The desirable things of all the nations shall come," etc.; and this is, as your own professors of Hebrew will corroborate, a correct translation; the Hebrew verb in that sentence is in the plural; "*they* shall come," it reads, and not "*he* shall come."

Yes, I say, not only Bible expositors of later times, but also your New Testament itself cannot be excepted from the charge of interpreting the Old Testament wrongly. Open, for instance, the Gospel according to St. Matthew, and look over the very first leaf of the New Testament. It is said there that Mary was to bring forth a son whose name will be Jesus and who will save his people from their sins. Now all this was done, St. Matthew continues, that it might be fulfilled what the Lord said by the prophet, Behold, a virgin shall be with child and shall bring forth a son, and they shall call his name Immanuel. If we open now the book of Isaiah and read this passage quoted therefrom in its connection with what precedes it and what follows it, we shall find that it does not in the least refer to a Messiah in a distant future, nor to Jesus especially. You certainly do not expect that in the few minutes I have yet at my disposal, I should give you a correct explanation of the chapter in Isaiah, in which the quoted verse is to be found. Such is not possible in so short a time. Only brief statements can be made here and all lengthy proofs for them I must necessarily omit. Read your Bible yourself, however, without any preconceived notion, and the true sense of the oracle of the prophet will become clear to you. And if you should not consider yourself able and competent to understand that chapter correctly, then ask any scholarly Christian pastor, or any teacher of Hebrew, and you will learn what was meant by Isaiah's words.

We go on for a few moments with looking up a few more Old Testament quotations in the beginning of St. Matthew's gospel. In the second chapter of this gospel it is reported that Joseph took his wife and his young child and departed into Egypt and was there until the death of Herod, "that it might be fulfilled what was said by the Lord, Out of Egypt I have called my son." In the book of the prophet Hosea, where the original passage is found, the Israelites who were taken out from Egyptian bondage were spoken of. The verse is here homiletically applied as having been fulfilled by the return of Joseph and his family—not from bondage, but from a place of safety in Egypt. Immediately after this the evangelist, St. Matthew, speaks of the massacre of the babes in Bethlehem by Herod, and that "then was fulfilled what was said by Jeremiah: In Ramah a voice was heard, lamentation, and weeping, and great mourning, Rachel weeping for her children," and so forth. Every unbiased and impartial Bible reader must admit that this is a very forced application, not to say a very unmistakable misunderstanding, of a verse in the Old Testament. In general, the passages from the Old Testament quoted in the New Testament were applied in a homiletical or a so-called Midrashic method, and a true exegesis of the quoted verses, in the modern sense of the word exegesis, was never intended. In a similar way, innumerable Old Testament verses were quoted and applied in the Talmudic and Midrashic literature of the Jews in the first centuries after Christ, and in a similar way applications of Bible words are made now-a-days in the sermons of modern preachers.

By the scholars among Christian theologians—and there are very learned, very upright, and very noble ones among them—such misunderstandings by the New Testament writers of the original sense of Old Testament passages are now pretty generally admitted, even by conservative scholars who know what they are talking about. But in order to support the Christian doctrines, these orthodox, or rather half-orthodox, scholars say that there were deeper meanings in the prophetic words, of which even the prophets themselves who uttered them had not the remotest idea, and these deeper meanings were, by virtue of inspiration, clothed into such a form that by the facts in the life of Jesus they became finally lucid and clear. Undoubtedly there are some who are satisfied with such subtle and illusive reasoning. Others, and we Jews among them, are not. And among these others who dissent are also great Bible scholars. The German Julius Wellhausen, and the Frenchman Ernest Reman, and the Dutchman Abraham Kuenen, and the Englishman Robertson Smith, and many others, are also entitled to be heard when Bible questions are discussed.

———

I would like to continue and to say something more. Especially I would have liked to give you the Jewish conception of the messiah-idea and the history of this idea among our people since it germinated in the days of the prophets until the present times. But I must drop the

subject here, and concerning this Jewish messiah-idea I shall but remark that never, never was the Messiah understood by Jews as a superhuman being; that never, never a divine character was attributed to
him; that never, never was he said to be able to forgive sins and
to redeem fallen mankind from sins, and so forth, and so forth.

If we would have fuller and more reliable records, regarding the
life of Jesus than we really have, then each one of us would admit that
the great man of Nazareth himself had religious ideas and convictions
which decidedly differed from the ideas and teachings of many in our
own days, who call themselves his followers and his disciples. The religion of Christ and the Christian religion are not identical. More than
a hundred years ago Lessing already—Lessing the man of the clearest
mind and of the noblest heart, the man before whom, whenever his
name is mentioned, let us all take off our hats—has taught us to make
a distinction between the religion of Christ and the Christian religion.
The religion of Christ was no doubt the religion of the Jewish prophets. The religion of Christ was the religion of the Pharisees, freed from
some untenable outgrowths of the times and from the overburdenings
with ceremonies which had become meaningless and were practiced
mechanically. The religion of Christ has a future; the Christian religion
has not.

I must refrain from all further remarks, as I must not occupy more
time and must not further tire you. Only one word more I beg to say
before I conclude. It is a Jew who, upon request, has spoken to you
and before you, and I trust that you will have listened to him with
indulgence and in kindness. Jews and Christians differ in some articles
of creed. Let us consider these articles of creed on which we disagree as
personal opinions, and let both parties agree to work, each one with
all his means and all his power, for the firmer establishment and for the
more rapid spreading of peace and of harmony, of truth and of righteousness, of mental and of moral culture among the human family.

14 A Jewish Attack
on Tendentious
Christian Scholarship

Nineteenth-century Jewish writers maintained that a proper historical under-
standing of Jesus and his teachings required knowledge of Rabbinic sources that
were contemporaneous with him. A comparison of these sources with the teachings
of Jesus would show that Jesus was a product of his Jewish environment and
that his message is largely unoriginal. Many Christian scholars, however, ignored
Rabbinic sources. Others, who did refer to them, often distorted their meaning
in order to demonstrate how the message of Jesus differed from and excelled that
of the Judaism of his day. In "The Attitude of Christian Scholars Toward
Jewish Literature," Kaufmann Kohler attacks this tendentious scholarship.

THE ATTITUDE OF
CHRISTIAN SCHOLARS TOWARD
JEWISH LITERATURE

Goethe says: "When you draw the picture of an angel, omit not by
way of contrast the one of the devil." I have no angels for my subject,
but scholars who are not always angelic, and I feel that by way of contrast I ought to begin with such Christian scholars as are, or were,
eager to sit at the feet of the Jew, though most of them do not belong
to that class. "The Jew," says Geiger, "is, as a rule, wise, inasmuch as
he always endeavors to acquire wisdom from non-Jewish sources."
Probably the fact of his being in the minority ever awakened the desire
in him of knowing what the other side thinks, though the regard of
other people's opinion has always guided his footsteps. The Christian,
on the other hand, has the majority and an iron-cast creed on his side;
why should he care about the Jew's opinion concerning him?

There are a number of Christian scholars who deserve an honor-
able mention for earnestly wishing to see the Christian horizon enlarged by the study of Judaism. Foremost among them is E. Schuerer,

whose history of the Jews in New Testament times was a revelation to many Christian scholars, and is, indeed, an indispensable work for the Jewish student, whatever its shortcomings may be. It is written from the angular point of the New Testament, and therefore loses sight of the inner and fuller life of Judaism, . . .

Far more biased, or tendenz-ful, is Das System der altsynagogalen Theologie, by Weber, a pupil of Franz Delitzsch, who was a friend of the Jews, but at the same time a worker for Christian conversionism. The writer shows a tolerable acquaintance with the Agadic literature in Talmud and Midrash, but he wrote for the purpose of showing the inferior character of Jewish to New Testament teachings, and therefore he not only gives as a system of theology what he happens to find in Jewish sources where the very idea of system does not exist, each opinion expressed being more or less an individual one and of no authoritative character, but he frequently forces occasional utterances into harsh principles, and narrows broader views voiced so as to suit his purpose. He is unjust and unreliable, because he is constantly guilty of sins of omission and commission. Let me, because it is a storehouse of Jewish learning for Christian theologians, give you a few specimens. . . . Very characteristic is the following sin of omission. In order to show the worthlessness of the heathen world in the eyes of God and Israel, he quotes a number of passages from the late Midrashim, in which a share in the world to come is denied to the Gentiles, omitting the overwhelmingly large number of older utterances stating that 'the righteous among the Gentiles have a share in the future world,' which have been collected by Zunz in his Geschichte und Literatur, and which have been accepted by the leading rabbinical authorities. There are hundreds of such willful misrepresentations in Weber's book. But he wrote in the service of the Church, and has no doubt been accorded a choice seat in the Christian heaven.

Really fair-minded is Professor Wuensche in Dresden, another pupil of Delitzsch. His translation of the larger part of all the Midrashim is of great help to those who cannot read the original, and I believe there are some such rabbis in this country. Poor man! his "Erlaeuterungen der Evangelien, aus Talmud und Midrash" which is a modest way of explaining the New Testament sayings by Rabbinical parallels and without which many a lecture on Jesus and the Talmud by our popular rabbis would never have been written, marred his professional success, because official Christianity dares not draw such comparisons. Professor Strack of Berlin, another pupil of Delitzsch, was somewhat more cautious in his love for Talmudical studies. He translated a number of Mishnaic treatises, wrote instructive articles on the Talmud and reviewed works of Jewish scholars, but left New Testament theology severely alone. He nobly defended the Jews against the horrible blood accusations, and we are grateful for little favors received.

Last, but not least on the honor roll, stands Isaac Taylor, of Cambridge, England, a pupil of Professor Schechter, whose work on Pirke Abot, The Ethical Sayings of the Fathers, may be called classical. The notes and the appendix offer a mine of information to the student of Talmud and New Testament literature. So, for instance, it shows the Rabbinic origin of the so-called Lord's Prayer, upon which Harnack bases half of his theory of the unique greatness of Jesus Christ.

It is, however, a great mistake to ascribe broad-mindedness to the Christian theology of our age. The Reformation owes a great deal of its liberating power to the impulse given by the study of Hebrew literature. Reuchlin, in 1520, was the first in Germany to point out its importance. He, the great defender of the Talmud against the assaults of Pfefferkorn, the Jewish renegade, and the Dominican monks, loved Rabbinical literature, if only because its Cabbala seemed to explain to him the mysteries of Christian dogma. At any rate the Reformers welcomed the aid of the Jews, by which to unlock to them those treasures of the Bible, to which the Church had for centuries closed the eyes of all. Luther's Bible and the King James version inaugurated a new era for Hebrew studies as well as for popular education through the vernacular. The end of the sixteenth and the seventeenth century produced the greatest students of Rabbinical literature Christendom ever had, our own time included.

Foremost among these was Johannes Buxtorf, whose Hebrew (that is, Biblical) and Rabbinical (that is, Chaldaean) Dictionary, his Concordance and Synagogua Judaica, furnished learned Christendom with the means of penetrating into the secluded chambers of Jewish learning. A professor at the University of Basle, not forty years after Servetus had been burned at the stake on account of his Unitarian heresy, Buxtorf had the courage to associate and correspond with every Jewish scholar he could lay hold of, in order to be able to present the first rudiments of Jewish learning to the Christian world. Reuchlin, Sebastian Muenster, and Buxtorf were the morning stars that drew the night of mediaeval ignorance and stupor to its close by illumining the path of Hebrew study. England had its John Smith; its John Lightfoot in 1655, a Cambridge professor, whose Harmony of the New Testament with the Old, or, more correctly, whose illustrations of New Testament utterances by Rabbinical parallels are an admirable effort for a pioneer worker, and upon them Wuensche's work is based; its John Selden, whose works on the Jewish woman and the Synhedrion are still consulted as standard works.

Holland was next in order. This enterprising cosmopolitan people produced some of the greatest Bible commentators since the Spanish and French Jews had ceased interpreting Scriptures on a scientific system, and it was owing to them that our modern era of exegesis began taking the dusty Hebrew folios down from the shelves. Surenhuys translated the Mishna, Vitringa opened a new path for Bible exegesis, and then came the Orientalists ushered in by Albert Schultens.

Those sixteenth and seventeenth century scholars, while Christian believers, were sincere seekers after truth—no anti-Semites, no Jew-haters, like so many of the leading Christian theologians to-day, who have a different measurement for Jewish and for Christian writings, while pretending to follow scientific methods. All our Bible critics, Old Testament critics like Reuss and Wellhausen, and New Testament critics like Harnack, Holzman and Canon Farrar, with very few exceptions—Cornill, for instance—are Christians only in so far as they hate whatever is Jewish. Like the dog in the fable, who, seeing his own picture reflected in the water, casts off the piece of meat in his mouth in order to seize upon that held by his supposed rival in the water, so do all these famous scholars cast away whatever is Jewish in Jesus and the New Testament, in order to make the Christ of their own fancy rise who has nothing in him of the Jew. They see not that Apollo and the Muses, whose kinship they claim rather than that of Sinai's God and the Hebrew covenant people, have nothing in common with the man of Golgotha.

Against these influences, which are of far more pernicious character than the summer hotel or similar ostracism the common crowd complain of with such bitterness, we Jews have to contend to-day, and this is why I think two great American movements have begun at the right time—the Jewish Encyclopedia, which is to open the eyes of Jew and Gentile of the doings of Judaism throughout the ages, and Schechter's coming here, to raise the standard of rabbinical education by insisting on something more than Fourth-of-July oratory. We need men conversant with the entire Jewish literature to map out for us a system of Jewish theology which challenges the Christian dogma after truly scientific methods. This has hardly been begun as yet.

As to the Jewish Encyclopedia, I cannot help saying that when starting this great work both editors and publishers had a right to expect a large number of subscribers from among Christian readers who ought to be interested in having Jewish life and literature portrayed to them, and, above all, the Old and New Testament presented to them by the kinsmen of Jesus and the Apostles, but we were disappointed. Our Christian confreres, theologians and laymen, do not care to hear the other side. They do not believe in Lessing's beautiful dictum: "If God in His right hand would offer me the truth, and nothing but the truth, and in the other the longing after truth with the possibility of error, yet, with the incessant eagerness of coming near and ever nearer the truth, I would seize upon God's left hand and say, 'O Father, give me this, for the full truth is for Thee alone!' " Liberal Christian professors have neither the time nor the mind to read Jewish works which render their position only all the harder. A Christian layman occasionally ascertains the Jewish view regarding the origin of Christianity; a Christian theologian never, and he is probably right or wise in doing so.

Of all Christian theologians, the finest and most liberal one in America is, I think, Professor Toy, of Cambridge, Massachusetts, and yet, even he could not overcome the bias of the school. In his Judaism and Christianity he says: "We are not to regard the transition from Judaism to historical Christianity as the substitution of a perfect for an imperfect form of religion, but as an advance from an imperfect to a less imperfect form, the one which permitted the moral, spiritual truth, which is the germ of all religions, to assert itself with greater freedom, and exert its true influence more completely. For the Jewish scheme of obedience to a mass of precepts"—you see, he uses the stock-in-trade of all Christian theologians, ... "Paul substituted faith in Jesus as Redeemer—a vastly higher and freer conception." Strangely enough, Prof. Toy here forgot what he wrote in the earlier part of the work on Antigonus of Soko's well-known saying: "Be not like servants who merely wait on their master with the view of getting a piece from their master's table"—that virtue should spring from love of right and be accepted as its own sufficient reward. "This is an utterance which has no parallel in the Old Testament or the New." And yet, Paul's system, which renders religion a service for reward in heaven, and of fear of hell, a faith which turned God into the most cruel tyrant that ever ruled over men, is claimed to be more perfect than the Jewish! Is this cant, hypocrisy or narrowmindedness? Let Prof. Toy read a little less of Christian cheap talk and apply himself to the study of Rabbinical treatises, and he will find that the 'greater freedom' is not in the religion in which he has been reared.

Much stronger is the contrast between Judaism and Christianity presented by Prof. Harnack, the leading Church theologian of Germany, whose lectures on Das Wesen des Christenthums before cultured Berlin created a stir on account of their liberal ideas. Mark well, he no longer believes in miracle, in the resurrection, although, as he himself says, historical Christianity rests on this vision of an entranced class of people, but he must have a dark background to make the portrait of Jesus shine forth as a God in heavenly lustre. So Pharisaism must be painted all black, Jesus represented as the preacher of a higher righteousness, as the one who revealed God as Father, and Paul, the founder of the Church dogma, as the one whose bright side was Greek, and whose dark side was Pharisean Judaism. The whole picture is untrue, because the background is covered with nothing but the dark and flimsy material of fiction and falsehood, of ignorance and prejudice. Would Harnack from sincere love of truth have familiarized himself with the facts of Jewish history and literature, as he is at home in Church history and literature, his picture would have dissolved itself into a Fata Morgana; he would have seen that Jesus was a Jew of lofty aspirations, yet nothing but a Jew.

In fact, no real comprehension of Jesus' sayings in the New Testament is possible without a thorough familiarity with the Talmud and Midrash. . . There is an exquisite saying of the Rabbis: "The Bible has been written down, and is in the hand of Jew and non-Jew, but the key to the Bible is the tradition that has been handed only to the Jew." That is to say: The Christians, in using the Bible, made it serve purposes altogether different from its original design, a dogmatic chain to fetter the intellect; the Jews use the Bible freely and rationally, because they are in possession of the key which does not idolize every word, but applies it to various needs in accordance with the varying time. The best utterances of Jesus find their explanation in the Agadah. Take, for instance, the beautiful saying of Jesus: "Behold the birds of heaven! They sow not, neither do they reap, yet your heavenly Father feedeth them. Are ye not of much more value than they? Behold the lilies of the field; they toil not, neither do they spin; yet I say unto you that even Solomon in all his glory was not arrayed like one of these. But if God so clothes the grass of the field, shall He not much more clothe you, oh men of little faith." As soon as you compare it with an almost identical saying concerning the beasts and the birds in the Mishna, of the men that lack Emunah, 'faith,' and then take into consideration that the name of the purple lily in Palestine was 'the king's lily,' you recognize at once that the saying did not originate with one man, but with the whole class of Hasidim, whose chief teaching was trust in God, who gave the Manna as daily bread even in the wilderness, and not to give a thought to to-morrow's cares and troubles. The Midrash to Parshat ha-Man offers the key to this saying. So does the New Testament story of the widow's mite as being more than all the gifts of the rich find not only its parallel, but also its explanatory origin in the Midrash where the Biblical word *ve'im Nefesh ki takrib,* If a soul or person brings a sacrifice, is explained by the story of the widow who with her little gift offers her very soul.—You see here that as Agadist or expounder of a Biblical text, Jesus, or whosoever first offers the beautiful parable, taught the lesson in question. A few more of these New Testament sayings placed in the right light will convince you or any one who wishes to be enlightened, that their source is Synagogue teaching. What does it mean: "When thou givest alms sound not a trumpet before thee as the hypocrites do in the Synagogue! Let not thy left hand know what thy right hand doeth, but let thine alms be in secret." The almsbox in the Temple, and also in the Synagogue, was called Shofar, trumpet, because it was bent shofar-like, so that money could be cast in but not taken out. So the teaching is, Do not cast your money with such ostentation into the Shofar as to make it sound before all, and remember that "An abomination of God is the proud in heart, if he offers a gift from hand to hand he will not be free from punishment (Prov. XVI, 5) that is, the right hand should not see what the left hand doeth."

The other day I related in a sermon the Midrash story of Moses carrying the sheep that had gone astray on his shoulders back to the fold; after the sermon a lady came up to me and in the simplicity of her heart said: "I always thought that only Jesus was regarded as the good shepherd." I have since found that the Essenes had the story of the good and the bad shepherd well developed out of the well-known chapter of Ezekiel, long before the New Testament characters made their appearance.

And so I might go through the four Gospels and find without difficulty the Rabbinical parallels and originals to all the teachings and doings of Jesus. How can Christians with any sense of right speak of the Jews as having rejected Christ, if the Jews recognize Jesus as one amongst their hundreds of rabbis, even though he was in one direction or another more powerful or more interesting a personality than many of them? Let our Christian friends study the Jewish sources, and they will think and judge better of Judaism and also more humanly or sensibly of Jesus.

The other day a Christian theologian of my own city spoke of woman in the usual strain, as having been lifted by Christianity to the position which is hers by right and dignity. Of course, he spoke belittlingly of the women in the Old Testament, also of the 'Song of the Virtuous Woman' in Proverbs. I gave him an article of mine on The Jewish Woman in Post-Biblical Times, and he thanked me heartily for the new light offered. What a pity, then, that such opportunities are not sought for and solicited. They would be beneficial for both sides, Jew and Christian.

Let me close with a subject of more general interest. It is one of the axiomatic beliefs of Christianity that all the institutions of charity are the fruit of Jesus' teachings, who first made the care of the forsaken, the sick and the stranger, a duty of the community, and so on and so on. Accordingly we are told by Lecky that hospitals were unknown before Christianity. "Christianity for the first time made charity a rudimentary virtue, giving it a leading place in the moral type and in the exhortations of its teachers. It effected a complete revolution by representing the poor as the special representatives of the Christian Founder, and thus making the love of Christ rather than the love of man the principle of charity" (Hist. of Europ. Morals, ii, 84). And Uhlhorn, who made a special study of the Christliche Liebesthaetigkeit, 1882, and wrote the article on Wohlthaetigkeit in Herzog's Encyclopedia, writes: "Organized charity is not known in Israel; almsgiving, but not institutions of benevolence, existed in post-exilic Judaism. Love in its true humane and universal sense was given to the world only by Christ. The founder of the Church not only taught and commanded, but practiced true love and thus became the personal founder of a life of love. Until then there was but a world without love." These assertions, repeated in a thousand different books and addresses, are totally untrue.

Helene of Adiabene, in time of a great famine in Palestine, furnished the people of Jerusalem with ship-loads of corn and fruit, and her son, Izates, with money. These things were given, says Josephus, in charge of the first men of Jerusalem; that is to say, they were the charity administrators. An ancient Mishna says that those whose fathers have been administrators of charity need no further examination as to noble birth, and may marry into the highest priestly families. And in the face of such clear statements, that go back to pre-Christian times, high-ranking Christian writers assert that the church first organized the work of charity. But that is not all. All the Christian historians state it as an undisputed fact that the hospital is a Christian institution; that a certain Roman lady, Fabiola, a Christian convert, was the immortal founder of the first hospital, and a friend of hers and of St. Jerome soon afterwards founded an Inn for Strangers. What puzzled me when reading this in Uhlhorn's and Haeser's work on Christian charity was a strange remark of St. Jerome, the friend of the two so-called founders of the first hospital and poorhouse in the West: "Thou hast now," he writes to his friend, "transplanted a branch of the terebinth of Abraham to the shores of the Ansonian river," that is Italy. Only acquaintance with Rabbinical literature, such as St. Jerome possessed, who had a rabbi, Bar Hanina, as teacher, explains this mysterious utterance. The rabbis say that the terebinth, which Abraham planted at Bersheba, as well as the oak tree at Mamre, was turned into a Pandokeion, that is, inn for strangers, so that every needy and helpless one found relief and comfort under the shadow of that tree. In other words, the hospital planted by St. Pammachius and Fabiola under St. Jerome's influence in the West, originated in ancient Jewish practice traced back to Abraham. In fact, the whole East was dotted with such poorhouses, used now for the sick, and then for other classes of needy and distressed. In the West, where wealthy Roman women and men donated large amounts of money to the church for such purposes, there sprang up all sorts of asylums altogether new in their destination and character. In the East, the old form was retained, and the poorhouse used for all purposes. The work done by these institutions in the East was such that the Emperor Julian writes: "The Jews and the Christians put us heathens to shame. The Jews so provide for their own that there is no poor Jew found anywhere begging alms, and those Galileans take care even of the Gentile poor." Of these Christian charity institutions we learn that Jews have been found imposing upon them by allowing themselves to be converted over and over again only to obtain money. This, mind you, occurred in the fourth Christian century, not in 1902!

You observe, then, that the Jews had charitable institutions of their own like the Christians, only the latter did as they do to-day, made charity the means of conversion, and so extended it to outsiders; the Jews provide both for their own and for their Gentile fellowmen who appealed to their sympathy as townsmen. The Church pursued a policy of pauperizing the people by giving to the undeserving; the Jews already in Talmudical times, made charity a system of helpfulness, as can be learned from the old sources. But we are in the position to prove that already in the New Testament time the work of charity was ramified and the branches of helping were diversified. Read the words put into the mouths of the Jews in Matt. 25, 35: "I was hungered and ye gave me meat; I was thirsty and ye gave me drink; I was a stranger and ye took me in; naked and ye clothed me; I was sick and ye visited me; I was in prison and ye came unto me. Verily, inasmuch as ye did it unto the least of my brethren, ye have done it unto me."

Now these very ideas are taken from the synagogue again. The Midrash Shir hashirim Zutta, ed. Schechter, says: "My Corban, my bread. Does God need bread or a Corban? when you give to the poor, My friends, you give unto Me." So the seven kinds of good deeds, the feeding of the hungry, the visiting of the sick, the donating of the clothing, the burying of the dead, the dowering of the poor brides, the redemption of the captives—are Jewish. To them the Hasidim or Essene saints of each town devoted their whole time and labor. Only from this point of view the saying of Jesus is understood. Christianity is an outgrowth of the Essene fraternity. The Essene developed the whole system, and the Church adopted it.

I might go further into detail and show how the whole organization of the Church with its systematic provision for the poor and needy was derived from the Essene fraternities, who appear in Rabbinical and other writings as occupied exactly as the early Christians were with works of redeeming love and of feeling. But I had better bring my remarks to a close.

The Old Testament exegesis, with its higher criticism, has been placed upon a scientific basis only since Christian scholarship began to study Jewish literature and the Jewish grammarians, lexicographers and commentators, many of whom wrote in Arabic. The New Testament exegesis will never attain a truly scientific character unless Rabbinical literature is thoroughly studied and consulted as to the meaning and purpose of the various sayings and teachings of Jesus and the apostles, and as to the historical perspective from which alone the work of the nascent Christian sect can be understood.

Perhaps, after all, Christian theologians leave Jewish studies alone, or else their views might be radically changed and their trinitarian belief be affected, the consequence of which would be that the Christian heaven would be shut to them, and as we Jews as lost souls have no Jewish heaven, they might be compelled to wander about until they settled down as members of the Church Universal, which is neither Jewish nor Christian, but which knows only of God's children.

15　An Anthology of
　　　Jewish Views of Jesus

Reform writings on Jesus elicited the hope among some Christians that the Jews would accept Jesus as something more than a gifted teacher. In 1899, the publisher I. K. Funk undertook to survey contemporary Jewish views of Jesus. He received a large number of responses from European and American Jewish public figures, and he published twenty-six of them in an appendix to George Croly's 1901 edition of Tarry Thou Till I Come. *Presented here are the responses of the American Jews that Funk published along with his own remarks on their meaning.*

JESUS OF NAZARETH FROM THE
PRESENT JEWISH POINT OF VIEW

In this age and land, Jew and Christian seem destined at last to give one another the glad hand. The old spirit of misunderstanding and often of hate (which to our shame—more to the shame of the Christian than of the Jew—has now lasted nearly a score of centuries), in this light of noon, now and here, is intolerable. At the dawn of the twentieth century, antisemitism in America, even the feeblest whisper of it, is an anachorism, and an anachronism of the grossest sort.

　That spirit was natural enough with the church of the early ages, for the church, nearly all of it, was simply the pagan tiger baptized, and labels changed, but not the nature of the beast. The Christ that was presented to the Jew the Jew did well to hate, for he was a Christ of barbaric cruelty, a monster who drove millions of Jews through fire and starvation, out of the world, and this entire people for ages from their homes and countries. If the Jews had not hated and spit on the very name of that Christ, they had been more or less than human.

　Among this people the ties of kinship are especially strong, so that when a wrong is done to one, no other flame is needed to make the blood of all boil. With the million of fires burning to death their martyred brethren, quite naturally the air grew too thick with smoke, and their eyes too sore with weeping, for them to see any of the beauty of the Cross. Talk of the sweetness of that Christ was hideous mockery to them. I too would join with them and spit on such a Christ. But now the smoke is getting out of the air, and the Jew, like the rest of us, is beginning to see the real Jesus of the Gospels, and he also, like the rest of us when we see Him aright, can not but respect, admire, love Him—claim Him as one of his own people, saying, with Rabbi Henry Berkowitz, of Philadelphia, this Jew, Jesus, "is the greatest, noblest rabbi of them all," and as the famous Jewish writer, Max Nordau, touchingly says, "He is one of us."

Yes, we are living in a better land and in a better time. Here both Christian and Jew clasp the folds of the same flag and say, Our Country, and both look up to the one God, the God of Abraham, Isaac, and Jacob, and say, Our Father; and may not both, by and by, look to this Jew, Jesus of Nazareth, and say, Our Brother?

Within the past two years I have written to a number of representative Jews, residing in different parts of the world, asking the question, *WHAT IS THE JEWISH THOUGHT TODAY OF JESUS OF NAZARETH?* The inquiry was accompanied with a copy of the letter from Dr. Kohler, which is here published as the first of the series. There are utterances in some of these published replies that may strike strangely and discordantly on orthodox Christian hearts. It will be well for all such to ponder the following letter, here given as prefatory to the other replies. It is from the pen of Dr. Singer, a well-known Jewish scholar, the originator and now the managing editor of the Jewish Encyclopedia:

A LETTER FROM ISIDORE SINGER, Ph.D.

"It has been both a privilege and a pleasure to me to examine in the original manuscript the letters which are printed on the following pages. They are all from representative Jewish scholars, theologians, historians, and philosophers, well and most favorably known in the scientific world of Europe and America. Where it has been necessary to abbreviate for lack of space, I find that the work has been done in a way that does no injustice to the writer. No one is made to say, by faulty translation, or abridgment, or otherwise, what he does not intend to say. It is my hope and most ardent desire that these utterances may greatly help to make known to the Christian world the real heart and mind of my brethren. I am glad to be permitted to add a thought or two of my own.

"I regard Jesus of Nazareth as a Jew of the Jews, one whom all Jewish people are learning to love. His teaching has been an immense service to the world in bringing Israel's God to the knowledge of hundreds of millions of mankind.

"The great change in Jewish thought concerning Jesus of Nazareth, I can not better illustrate than by this fact:

"When I was a boy, had my father, who was a very pious man, heard the name of Jesus uttered from the pulpit of our synagog, he and every other man in the congregation would have left the building, and the rabbi would have been dismissed at once.

"Now, it is not strange, in many synagogs, to hear sermons preached eulogistic of this Jesus, and nobody thinks of protesting,—in fact, we are all glad to claim Jesus as one of our people.

"ISIDORE SINGER"

New York, March 25, 1901.

From KAUFMANN KOHLER, Ph.D., Rabbi of Temple Beth-El, New York:

The true history of Jesus is so wrapped up in myth, the story of his life told in the gospels so replete with contradictions, that it is rather difficult for the unbiased reader to arrive at the true historical facts. Still the beautiful tales about the things that happened around the lake of Galilee show that there was a spiritual daybreak in that dark corner of Judea of which official Judaism had failed to take sufficient cognizance. "The stone that the builders rejected has become the cornerstone" of a new world.

It is assumed by entire Christendom that the Jews in rejecting Jesus Christ brought upon themselves everlasting doom, the inexorable fate of exile, persecution, and hatred. This view is based upon the crucifixion story in the gospel records, which, while shielding the Romans, maligns the Jews, and is incompatible with the simple facts of the Jewish law, the older Christian tradition, with common sense, and with the established character of Pontius Pilate, a very tiger in human shape. Surely the records of the trial demand a revision.

"DID THE JEWS REJECT CHRIST?" Most assuredly the weird and visionary figure of the dead and rerisen Christ, the crucified Messiah lifted up to the clouds there to become a partaker of God's nature—a metaphysical or mythological principle of the cosmos—the Jews did reject. They would not, let it cost what it may, surrender the doctrine of the unity and spirituality of God. Jesus, the living man, the teacher and practiser of the tenderest love for God and man, the paragon of piety, humility, and self-surrender, whose very failings were born of overflowing goodness and sympathy with the afflicted, the Jews had no cause to reject. He was one of the best and truest sons of the synagog. Did he not say, "I have not come to destroy the law, but to fulfill it"? What reason had the Jews for hating and persecuting him who had nothing of the rigidity of the schoolman, none of the pride of the philosopher and recluse, nor even the implacable zeal of the ancient prophet to excite the popular wrath; who came only to weep with the sorrowing, to lift up the downtrodden, to save and to heal? He was a man of the people; why should the people have raised the cry. "Crucify him!" against him whose only object in life was to bring home the message of God's love to the humblest of his children? Nor, in fact, was he the only one among the popular preachers of the time who in unsparing language and scathing satire exposed and castigated the abuses of the ruling priesthood, the worldly Sadducees, as well as the hypocrisy and false piety of some of the Pharisean doctors of the law. His whole manner of teaching, the so-called Lord's Prayer, the Golden Rule, the code of ethics expounded for the elect ones in the Sermon on the Mount, no less than his miraculous cures, show him to have been one of the Essenes, a popular saint.

But he was more than an ordinary teacher and healer of men. He went to the very core of religion and laid bare the depths of the human soul. As a veritable prophet, Jesus, in such striking manner, disclaimed allegiance to any of the Pharisean schools and asked for no authority but that of the living voice within, while passing judgment on the law, in order to raise life to a higher standard. He was a bold religious and social reformer, eager to regenerate Judaism. True, a large number of sayings were attributed to the dead master by his disciples which had been current in the schools. Still, the charm of true originality is felt in these utterances of his when the great realities of life, when the idea of Sabbath, the principle of purity, the value of a human soul, of woman, even of the abject sinner, are touched upon. None can read these parables and verdicts of the Nazarene and not be thrilled with the joy of a truth unspelled before. There is wonderful music in the voice which stays an angry crowd, saying, "Let him that is without sin cast the first stone!" that speaks the words, "Be like children, and you are not far from the kingdom of God!"

"DID THE JEWS REJECT CHRIST?" Jesus anticipated a reign of perfect love, but centuries of hatred came. Could the Jews, victims of Christian intolerance, look with calmness and admiration upon Jesus, in whose name all the atrocities were perpetrated? Still, the leading thinkers of Judaism willingly recognized that the founder of the Christian Church, as well as that of Islamism, was sent by divine Providence to prepare the pagan world for the Messianic kingdom of truth and righteousness.

The Jew of to-day beholds in Jesus an inspiring ideal of matchless beauty. While he lacks the element of stern justice expressed so forcibly in the law and in the Old Testament characters, the firmness of self-assertion so necessary to the full development of manhood, all those social qualities which build up the home and society, industry and worldly progress, he is the unique exponent of the principle of redeeming love. His name as helper of the poor, as sympathizing friend of the fallen, as brother of every fellow sufferer, as lover of man and redeemer of woman, has become the inspiration, the symbol, and the watchword for the world's greatest achievements in the field of benevolence. While continuing the work of the synagog, the Christian Church with the larger means at her disposal created those institutions of charity and redeeming love that accomplished wondrous things. The very sign of the cross has lent a new meaning, a holier pathos to suffering, sickness, and sin, so as to offer new practical solutions for the great problems of evil which fill the human heart with new joys of self-sacrificing love.

All this modern Judaism gladly acknowledges, reclaiming Jesus as one of its greatest sons. But it denies that one single man, or one church, however broad, holds the key to many-sided truth. It waits for the time when all life's deepest mysteries will have been spelled, and to the ideals of sage and saint that of the seeker of all that is good, beautiful, and true will have been joined; when Jew and Gentile, synagog and church, will merge into the Church universal, into the great city of humanity whose name is "God is there."
August 23, 1899.

From MORRIS JASTROW, Jr., Ph.D., Professor of Semitic Languages, University of Pennsylvania, Philadelphia, Pa.:

From the historic point of view, Jesus is to be regarded as a direct successor of the Hebrew prophets. His teachings are synonymous with the highest spiritual aspirations of the human race. Like the prophets, he lays the chief stress upon pure conduct and moral ideas, but he goes beyond the prophets in his absolute indifference to theological speculations and religious rites. It is commonly said that the Jews rejected Jesus. They did so in the sense in which they rejected the teachings of their earlier prophets, but the question may be pertinently asked. Has Christianity accepted Jesus? Neither our social nor our political system rests upon the principles of love and charity, so prominently put forward by Jesus.

The long hoped-for reconciliation between Judaism and Christianity will come when once the teachings of Jesus shall have become the axioms of human conduct.
November 6, 1899.

From MARCUS JASTROW, Ph.D., Rabbi Emeritus of Rodeph-
Shalom Congregation, Philadelphia, Pa., Author of the "Dic
tionary of the Talmud," etc.:

The thoughtful Jews of all days, and especially of modern tendency of thought, see in Jesus, as depicted in the New Testament, the
exponent of a part of the ethics of Judaism, and more especially of its
milder side—love and charity. The ethical sayings of Jesus reflect the
conception of Judaism in his own period, as it was current among its
spiritual leaders, such as Hillel, Rabbi Akiba, Ben Zoma, and others.
To a heathen world merged in vice and crime, to a civilization that led
the thoughtful among Romans and Greeks toward the abyss of pessimism and despair, Christianity offered the bright prospect of forgiveness and reconciliation with goodness. For the Jews it had no mission,
no new gifts to offer. Its ethics appear to the modern Jew one-sided
and exaggerated; the sense of justice appears to be pushed into the
background in favor of an unrealizable ideal of love.

Judaism prohibits revenge and the bearing of grudge, commands
the assistance of an enemy in distress, but "to love one's enemy" appears to the modern Jew a somewhat morbid philanthropy that could
never have been seriously meant. To bear indignities with patience, "to
be of the insulted and not of the insulters," is a Jewish principle, but to
offer the right cheek to him who slaps you on the left, to offer the
undergarment to him who takes away your cloak—no, we will not
and we can not do it. Hence it is that we Jews, of our modern days,
speak of Jesus with that respect which all high-minded dreamers of all
ages and nations inspire, even though we can not accept all their ideas
and ideals, and are mindful of the fact that it is to noble dreamers that
humanity is indebted for its most precious possessions.
September 4, 1899.

From HENRY BERKOWITZ, D. D., Rabbi of Rodeph Shalom Congregation, Founder and Chancellor of the Jewish Chautauqua
Society, Philadelphia, Pa.:

. . . To me one of the saddest and most tragic facts in history is
this, that Jesus, the gentlest and noblest rabbi of them all, should
have become lost to his own people by reason of the conduct of those
who called themselves his followers. In Jesus there is the very flower-
ing of Judaism. What pathos, then, in the fact that his own people have
been made to shun his very name; that even to-day they speak it with
bated breath, because it has been made to them a symbol and a synonym of all that is unjewish, unchristian—irreligious. . . .
November 1, 1899.

From the late JAMES H. HOFFMAN, Founder and first President of
the Hebrew Technical Institute, New York City:

. . . I revere him (Jesus) for having brought home by his own life
and his teachings, to the innermost hearts and souls of mankind, of all
times, in every station, the eternal truths as first embodied in the Mosaic code and proclaimed in undying words by the prophets. I recognize in him the blending of the divine and human, the lofty and lowly,
showing the path for the dual nature of man, by divine aspirations to
gain the victory over the earthly life, tending to draw him down-
ward—the Son of God triumphing over the child of the earth. . . .
October 6, 1899.

From JACOB H. SCHIFF, New York City:

We Jews honor and revere Jesus of Nazareth as we do our own
prophets who preceded him. By his martyrdom, his teachings have
been emphasized, and these are to this day I believe often better practised by the descendants of the race he sprang from than by those who
have become the followers of Christ in name, but not in spirit, else the
prejudice practised by the latter against Jews would not exist. . . .
September 5, 1899.

From SIMON WOLF, LL. D., former Consul of the United States to
Egypt. Vice-President of Order B'ne B'rith, Washington, D.C.:

I have not had the time nor the desire to investigate the alleged
divinity of the Christian Savior. I have, however, recognized the great
influence his character and labors have exercised throughout the
world. If properly understood and if properly construed, I have no
doubt whatsoever that what he aimed at and labored for would prove
of great benefit to every human being. I look upon him, in short, as a
great teacher and reformer, one who aimed at the uplifting of suffering
humanity, whose every motive was kindness, mercy, charity, and justice, and if his wise teaching and example have not always been followed, the blame should not be his, but rather those who have claimed
to be his followers. I have the very highest regard for him as a man
who reflects in his sayings the divine Spirit, which after all is nothing
more or less than a reflex of the Jewish ethics in which he was so well
grounded.
October 9, 1899.

From H. WEINSTOCK, Sacramento, Cal. Extract from a letter to
Dr. K. Kohler:

[The letter urges reasons why the life and sayings of Jesus should
be taught in Jewish Sabbath-schools. Dr. Kohler approves of the
suggestion.]

With the growing enlightenment and the broadening atmosphere
under which the modern Jew lives, the progressive Jew looks upon the
Nazarene as one of Israel's great teachers, who has a potent influence
on civilization, whose words and deeds have left an undying imprint
upon the human mind, and have done heroic work toward universal-
izing the God of Israel and the Bible. This change of sentiment toward
Jesus is largely due to the intelligent and progressive preaching of our
modern rabbis, who seem to appreciate the glory Jesus has shed upon
the Jewish name, and the splendid work he did in broadening the influence of the Jewish teachings. But, despite all this, the fact remains,
that, so far as I know, not one Jewish Sabbath-school in the land
teaches a single word concerning Jesus of Nazareth.

To maintain a continued silence in the Jewish Sabbath-school on
Jesus would seem a grave error. . . .

The influence of "Jesus the Christ" may be diminishing in the rational world, but the influence of "Jesus the Man" is increasing daily
the world over, and no Jewish education can be complete that does not
embody within it a comprehensive knowledge of Jesus the Jew, his life,
his teachings, and the causes which led to his death. . . .

It would seem to be in the highest interest of the modern Jew and
Judaism that the curriculum of at least every reform Jewish Sabbath-
school should, from a purely historical standpoint, embrace a simple
yet comprehensible history of the life of Jesus, and its wonderful moral
and religious influence, in order that the rising Jews may be able to
appreciate better the powerful influence Judaic teachings and the Bible
have had upon civilization, and the exalted place given by the world to
one of their teachers and brethren, who lived a purely Jewish life and
taught only Jewish precepts. . . .
September 26, 1899.

From GUSTAV GOTTHEIL, Ph.D., Rabbi Emeritus of Temple
Emanu-El, New York:

The keynote of prophetic religion of the Jewish prophets was holiness of life and purity of heart. Love and mercy shown by men, one
to another, make up the acceptable worship of the Holy One of Israel.

To place the Master of Nazareth by their side can surely be no dis-
honor to him, nor can it dim the luster of his name. If he has added to
their spiritual bequests new jewels of religious truth, and spoken words
which are words of life, because they touch the deepest springs of the
human heart, why should we Jews not glory in him? Show us the
man, help us to understand his mind, draw from his face the thick veil
behind which his personality has been buried for the Jewish life by the
heartless zeal of his so-called followers, and you will find the Jewish
heart as responsive to truth and light and love as that of all other nations. The question whether Jesus suffered martyrdom solely for his
new teachings or for other causes, we will not discuss. The crown of
thorns on his head makes him only the more our brother. For to this
day it is borne by his people. Were he alive to-day, who, think you,
would be nearer his heart—the persecuted or the persecutors?
October 24, 1899.

From DAVID PHILIPSON, D. D. Professor in Hebrew Union College, Rabbi of Mound Street Temple, Cincinnati, Ohio:

There is no backwardness nor hesitancy on the part of modern
Jewish thought in acknowledging the greatness of the teacher of Nazareth, the sweetness of his character, the power of his genius. But, as a
matter of course, we accord him no exceptional position as the flower
of humanity, the special incarnation of the Divinity. Judaism holds that
every man is the son of God. Jesus was a Jew of the Jews. The orthodox Christianity of to-day he would scarcely recognize, as its chief
dogmas were unknown to him.
September 19, 1899.

From EMIL G. HIRSCH, Ph.D., LL.D., L.H.D., Rabbi of Sinai Congregation, Professor of Rabbinical Literature in Chicago University, Chicago, Ill.:

. . . For me Jesus is an historical reality. To understand his work
and correctly to value his mission, one must bear in mind his own
time. Galilean as he was, he must have grown up under influences
making for an intense Jewish patriotism.

. . . Under close analysis, his precepts will be found to contain
nothing that was new. There is scarce an expression credited to him
but has its analogon in the well-known sayings of the rabbis. He did
not pretend to found a new religion. The doctrines he developed were
the familiar truths of Israel's prophetic monotheism. Nor did his ethical proclamation sound a note before unknown in the household of the
synagogue or in the schools. He was in method a wonderfully gifted

Haggadist. His originality lies in the striking form which he understood to give to the old vitalities of his ancestral religion. He moved the heart of the people.

. . . The Jews of every shade of religious belief do not regard Jesus in the light of Paul's theology. But the gospel Jesus, the Jesus who teaches so superbly the principles of Jewish ethics, is revered by all the liberal expounders of Judaism. His words are studied; the New Testament forms a part of Jewish literature. Among the great preceptors that have worded the truths of which Judaism is the historical guardian, none, in our estimation and esteem, takes precedence of the rabbi of Nazareth. To impute to us suspicious sentiments concerning him does us gross injustice. We know him to be among our greatest and purest.

January 26, 1901.

MEMORANDUM JOTTINGS

Here are some of the jottings which I find on my memorandum pad, suggested by the reading of these Jewish letters—letters which it would be difficult to read without feeling that at last Jew and Christian, after a horrible nightmare of misunderstandings centuries long, are coming to see that after all they are first cousins, if not actually brothers.

1. Right nobly is it in some of these Jewish writers to say that Jesus is not to be blamed for those awful persecutions committed for ages in His name, and in reverse of His teachings. As He foretold, many were called by His name whom He knew not, and who knew not Him—false prophets who came in sheep's clothing, but were, within, ravening wolves. Sometimes these wolves tore the Jews, sometimes they tore one another, and sometimes they tore the real Christians. But we live, all of us, in a better time. The glowing sky is not sunset, but is sunrise—sunrise of a glorious day that is to reveal a far wider brotherhood than the world ever heretofore has known.

2. Jewish friends, "Let the dead past bury its dead." All the world is bound to realize sooner or later that your history has been of inestimable advantage to the world. Turn your faces to that rapidly advancing future. The divine reason will appear for all the sorrows of the past ages, for all the persecutions, misapprehensions, including the errors into which you and we have fallen—largely *because* of these, not in spite of them, the Jewish race will arise a purified flame.

Look the future in the face. As Shelley has put it: "The past is dead, and the future alone is living." Why not, all of us, permit the ashes to grow over the embers of hate, and let the rawness of all wounds, real or imaginary, heal over? Distance now gives a wider survey and a juster survey to both Jew and Christian.

Waste no time in denying hostility to Jesus nineteen hundred years ago. Who alive to-day is to be blamed for that any more than for the forty years of rebellion in the wilderness? No more are you to be blamed for the death of Jesus than are we to-day to be blamed for Washington having held slaves, and for the slave auction-block in the Nation's capital, and for the slave lash a generation ago.

3. The Mosaic system of ceremonies, as seen before the destruction of Jerusalem, was beautiful. How mournfully are Jewish eyes still fixed upon the broken shell. Friends, lift your eyes and see what came out of that shell; see in the boughs above, the singing-bird of the civilization of to-day. Claim it all, for God has given it to the world through your people.

From the matrix of the Jewish soul sprang Christianity. Heine, the great Jewish writer of the last century, has wittily put it: Half the civilized world worships a Jew, the other half a Jewess.

4. Come, children of the prophets, your home, for a season at least, is in the West, not in the East. Let not your hearts longer be troubled. Cease dragging about with you that monstrous corpse of memory—the persecutions committed against you, no matter how frightfully you have been misunderstood and wronged.

Above all let it never be truly said that the Jew has suffered so much, and come so far, now only to reap despair and bitterness. There are two Jewish tendencies to-day, one to cold materialism, the motto of which is "make money, eat, drink, be merry, to-morrow ye die"; the other is upward, the path the prophets walked. This latter tendency must be made to dominate. The time will come, with many already here, when the Jew will turn again to his sublime mission and say, like Agassiz, "I have not time to make money."

Surely, the Jew of America is to be a regenerating educational force to the Jews of all the world, and not to the Jews only. It does not yet appear fully what he shall be; but in some way it will appear that this mass of concentrated human energy will arise above the commercial, the material, the sordid, which so dominates much of the so-called Christian world. The Jewish genius is essentially religious. The Jew will again come to himself and find his center, and God will vindicate His purpose through this wonderful people from Abraham's time to the present.

The Jew has grown strong by the law of the survival of the fittest. For eighteen centuries he has not known what security is, always living by his resource of keenest wit—the feeblest dying out. Those who were physically strong enough and mentally clever enough, escaped destruction, and these became the parents of the new and stronger generation. Thus the law of compensation works justice. For ages the Jew was compelled to be a money-lender as the business of such an one was held to be disreputable for Christians. Thus the Jew mastered the problems of finance, and now when finance rules the world, the Jew is naturally on the throne. The whirligig of time is twirled by a hand that cares for justice.

5. How unseemly, impossible, that it should prove in the end that they who have been to the world messengers of God, whose feet have been beautiful upon the mountain-tops and who did eat the bread of angels, should now forget their prophets and their God and grovel in materialism, and seek to satisfy their hunger with husks. No; this can not be. This people have done too glorious things for humanity, for such an ending. They have in them the nobility that will assert itself. They are born for great things yet to be; they have been made in large molds. They, like the best of us, have often slipped, but are now coming to themselves. For one I am glad, and thank God for it.

Now will the Christian Church permit a friendly exhortation: You have tried everything to get the Jewish people to understand Jesus of Nazareth, except one thing, *love*. Try that, for they believe in love; and you believe in love. Let both Jew and Christian get on this common ground, and have respect for the honest convictions of one another, and then both may clasp hands and look into each other's eyes, and repeat the words uttered alike by Moses and by Jesus:

"THE LORD OUR GOD IS ONE GOD. AND THOU SHALT LOVE

Notes

CHAPTER 1

1. For information on the issues involved in the Christian-Jewish debate, cf. Frank Talmage, *Disputation and Dialogue: Readings in the Jewish-Christian Encounter* (New York, 1975); David Berger, *The Jewish-Christian Debate in the High Middle Ages* (Philadelphia, 1979); and Hans Joachim Schoeps, *The Jewish-Christian Argument: A History of Theologies in Conflict* (London, 1963).

2. *The American Jewish Experience* edited by Jonathan D. Sarna (New York, 1986), p. 296.

3. Winthrop S. Hudson, *American Protestantism* (Chicago, 1961), p. 66.

4. Ibid., p. 86.

5. Robert T. Handy, *A Christian America: Protestant Hopes and Historical Realities* (New York, 1971), p. 33.

6. Quoted in Oliver W. Elsbree, *The Rise of the Missionary Spirit in America, 1790–1815* (Williamsport, 1928), p. 128. See also Robert T. Handy, *A Christian America: Protestant Hopes and Historical Realities* (New York, 1971), chapter 2, and Ernest R. Sandeen, *The Roots of Fundamentalism* (Chicago, 1970), pp. 42–58. For a full exposition of American millenarianism in the nineteenth century, see Leroy E. Froom, *The Prophetic Faith of Our Fathers* (Washington, DC, 1954).

7. Elsbree, *Rise of the Missionary Spirit*, p. 129.

8. Ibid., p. 132.

9. Yona Malachy, *American Fundamentalism and Israel* (Jerusalem, 1978), p. 22. See also, Lorman Ratner, "Conversion of the Jews and Pre-Civil War Reform," *American Quarterly*, 13 (Spring 1961), p. 49.

10. John McDonald, *Isaiah's Message to the American Nation* (Albany, 1814), p. 15. Cf. also, Peter Grose, *Israel in the Mind of America* (New York, 1983), pp. 9–10.

11. McDonald, *Isaiah*, p. 27.

CHAPTER 2

1. David Max Eichhorn, *Evangelizing the American Jew* (New York, 1978), pp. 18–73; Lee M. Friedman, "The American Society for Meliorating the Condition of the Jews and Joseph S. C. F. Frey" in *Early American Jews* (Cambridge, Mass., 1934), pp. 96–112; Lorman Ratner, "Conversion of the Jews and Pre-Civil War Reform," *American Quarterly* 13 (1961), pp. 43–54; George L. Berlin, "Joseph S. C. F. Frey, the Jews, and Early Nineteenth Century Millenarianism," *Journal of the Early Republic* 1 (Spring, 1981), pp. 27–49; Joseph S. C. F. Frey, *Narrative* (New York: 1817). The constitution of the ASMCJ stated that: "The object of this Society shall be to invite and receive, from any part of the world, such Jews as do already profess the Christian Religion, or are desirous to receive Christian Instruction, to form them into a settlement, and to furnish them with the ordinances of the Gospel and with such employment in the settlement as shall be assigned them; but no one shall be received, unless he comes well recommended for morals and industry, and without charge to this Society, and both his reception and continuance in the settlement, shall be at all times at the discretion of the Directors." *Israel's Advocate,* January, 1823, p. 7; June, 1823, p. 99; Morris U. Schappes, *A Documentary History of the Jews in the United States 1654–1875* (New York, 1971), p. 606, n. 4. More generally, on Christian missionary work among Jews in America, see Charles L. Chaney, *The Birth of Missions in America* (Pasadena, 1976); A. E. Thompson, *A Century of Jewish Missions* (Chicago, 1902); Max Eisen, "Christian Missions to the Jews in North America and Great Britain," *Jewish Social Studies* 10 (1948), pp. 31–66; Marshall Sklare, "The Conversion of the Jews", *Commentary* 56 (September, 1973), pp. 44–53.

2. Jacob Nikelsburger, *Koul Jacob in Defense of the Jewish Religion: Containing the Arguments of the Rev. C. F. Frey One of the Committee of the London Society for the Conversion of the Jews and Answers Thereto* (New York, 1816), pp. 10–11.

3. Gaylord P. Allbough, "Anti-Missionary Movement in the United States" in Vergilius T. A. Ferm, ed., *An Encyclopedia of Religion* (New York, 1945), pp. 27–28; Jonathan D. Sarna, "American Christian Opposition to Missions to the Jews 1816–1900," *Journal of Ecumenical Studies* 23 (Spring, 1986), pp. 225–238.

4. *Tobit's Letters to Levi* (New York, 1816), p. 58.

5. Ibid., pp. 23, 28.

6. Ibid., p. 41.

7. Ibid., pp. 15, 41–42.

8. Ibid., pp. 21–23.

9. Ibid., pp. 25, 27.

10. Ibid., p. 46.

11. Ibid., p. 36.

12. *Israel Vindicated being a Refutation of the Calumnies Propagated respecting the Jewish Nation: in which the Objects and Views of the American Society for Ameliorating the Condition of the Jews are Investigated* (New York, 1820); Jonathan Sarna, "The Freethinker, the Jews, and the Missionaries: George Houston and the Mystery of *Israel Vindicated*," *AJS Review,* 5 (1980), pp. 101–114.

13. The full title was *The Jew: Being a Defence of Judaism Against all Adversaries and Particularly Against the Insidious Attacks of Israel's Advocate.* The publisher was Louis Emmanuel. Sarna, "The Freethinker", cites an antimissionary pamphlet written by Abraham Collins prior to the *Jew.* The pamphlet was entitled *The Voice of Israel, Being a Review of Two Sermons Preached in the City of New York, by the Rev. Mr. Spring, and the Rev. P. N. Strong. Also an examination of the Principles and Effects of the Christian Religion.* (1823).

14. *Universal Jewish Encyclopedia,* 6, p. 4; Malcolm H. Stern, *First American Jewish Families* (Cincinnati, 1978), p. 130; Hyman B. Grinstein, *The Rise of the Jewish Community of New York 1654–1860* (New York, 1945), pp. 43, 79, 116, 214, 218, 255, 385; Joseph L. Blau and Salo W. Baron, *The Jews of the United States, 1790–1840. A Documentary History* (New York, 1963), vol. 3, pp. 691; 963–964.

15. *The Jew,* March, 1823, p. viii; "A Unique Jewish Document of a Century Ago", *The Jewish Exponent* 85 (October 25, 1929), p. 8. Jackson's hardhitting approach may be contrasted with that of his contemporary, Mordecai Manuel Noah, the journalist and politician and leading American Jewish figure of his time. Noah assumed a considerably more moderate stance in his statements about Christianity than did Jackson. While he spoke against the missionaries and their tactics, he never attacked Christianity. Cf. Jonathan D. Sarna, "The Impact of Nineteenth-Century Christian Missions on American Jews", *Jewish Apostary in the Modern World* edited by Todd M. Endelman (New York, 1987), pp. 232–254.

16. Jackson was mistaken. Isaac Orobio de Castro did not suffer because of his polemical writings which were written after he had moved to Amsterdam and reverted openly to Judaism. Earlier, he had been imprisoned by the Inquisition in Salamanca on the suspicion that he was secretly practicing Judaism. It was Yom Tov Lippman Mullhausen who barely escaped physical harm because of his polemical works.

17. In the first issue of *The Jew* Jackson promised that "*The Jew* will be conducted with candor, temper and moderation; the language to be always such as should not offend. Derision will never be admitted." Jackson repeated this pledge in subsequent issues; *The Jew,* June, 1823, pp. 62–66; July, 1823, p. 75.

18. *Ibid.,* July, 1824, pp. 355–356.

19. *Ibid.,* July, 1824, pp. 342–344.

20. S. Joshua Kohn, "Mordecai Manuel Noah's Ararat Project and the Missionaries," *American Jewish Historical Quarterly,* 55 (1963), pp. 162–196; *Israel's Advocate,* January, 1823, pp. 4ff; Eichhorn, *op. cit.,* pp. 38–44.

21. *The Jew,* March, 1823, p. 6. Not all members of the ASMCJ supported the settlement plan either. Dr. John H. Livingston, one of the vice-presidents of the ASMCJ, opposed it. Blau and Baron, *op. cit.,* vol. 3, pp. 747–757.

22. *The Jew,* June, 1823, pp. 67–69.

23. *The Jew,* September, 1823, pp. 143–149; for Jadownicky's role, cf. *First Report of the American Society for Meliorating the Condition of the Jews* (May, 1823), pp. iii ff. See also, Eichhorn, *op. cit.,* p. 49.

24. *The Jew,* July, 1823, pp. 80–83; January, 1824, pp. 225–228.

25. *Ibid.,* November, 1823, pp. 192–193. Cf. also Sarna, "American Christian Opposition to Missions", p. 234.

26. Of the clergymen who were officers of the ASMCJ, Alexander McCleod, Ashbel Green, and Samuel H. Cox were Presbyterians. Philip Milledoler and John H. Livingston were Dutch Reform, and Jeremiah Day was a Congregationalist; *Israel's Advocate,* December, 1824.

27. *The Jew,* June, 1823, p. 55.

28. *Ibid.,* November, 1823, pp. 172; 178–187; March, 1825, p. 480. An American edition of David Levy's *Letters to Dr. Priestly* was published in New York in 1794, and an American edition of his *Defence of the Old Testament* was published in New York in 1797. A second edition of the latter work was published in Philadelphia in 1798. Mendelssohn's *Letter to Deacon Lavater* was published in New York in 1821; Sarna, "The Freethinker . . . ", pp. 106–109.

29. *The Jew,* August, 1823, pp. 121–122; September, 1823, pp. 142–143; November, 1823, pp. 187–191; December, 1823, pp. 217–219; February, 1824, pp. 245–248.

30. *Ibid.,* July, 1823, pp. 85–95; August, 1823, pp. 115–122; September, 1823, pp. 136–139; October, 1823, pp. 159–165; December, 1823, pp. 207–217; February, 1824, pp. 239–244; April, 1824, pp. 279–286; May, 1824, pp. 309–316; June, 1824, pp. 336–344; September, 1824, pp. 364–368; December, 1824, pp. 419–427; January, 1825, pp. 430–438; February, 1825, pp. 453–458; Benjamin Dias Fernandes, *A Series of Letters on the Evidences of Christianity* (Philadelphia, 1859).

31. *The Jew,* July, 1823, pp. 2–3.

32. *Ibid.,* May, 1824, pp. 299–309.

33. *Ibid.,* January, 1824, pp. 440–441; November, 1824, pp. 398–407; December, 1824, pp. 427–429; and January, 1825, pp. 440–452 continued in February, 1825, pp. 450–452.

34. *Ibid.*, February, 1825, pp. 462–465, and March, 1825, pp. 466–476.

35. *Ibid.*, October, 1824, p. 397; March, 1825, pp. 480–481; *The Second Report of the American Society for Meliorating the Condition of the Jews* (Princeton, 1824), p. 20.

CHAPTER 3

1. For overviews of Leeser's life and work, cf. Mayer Sulzberger, "The Late Reverend Isaac Leeser," *Occident* 25 (1868), pp.593–611, republished in *American Jewish Archives* 21 (1969), pp. 140–148; Bertram W. Korn, "Isaac Leeser: Centennial Reflections," *American Jewish Archives* 19 (1967), pp. 127–141; Henry Englander, "Isaac Leeser," *Central Conference of American Rabbis Yearbook* 28 (1918), pp. 213–252; Maxwell Whiteman, "Isaac Leeser and the Jews of Philadelphia," *Publications of the American Jewish Historical Society* 48 (1959), pp. 207–244; Idem, "The Legacy of Isaac Leeser" in Murry Friedman, ed., *Jewish Life in Philadelphia, 1830–1940* (Philadelphia, 1983), pp. 26–47. Abraham Sutro was an opponent of Reform, but open to some modern influences. He was one of the earliest rabbis to preach in German and he favored occupational training for Jews. For information on Sutro and his influence on Leeser, cf. Lawrence Grossman, "Isaac Leeser's Mentor: Rabbi Abraham Sutro, 1784–1869" in Leo Landman ed., *Rabbi Joseph H. Lookstein Memorial Volume* (New York, 1980), pp. 151–162.

2. Maxwell Whiteman has written aptly that "The years of American Jewish history from 1830 until the close of the Civil War are, in fact, the 'Age of Leeser.' " Korn enumerates Leeser's "firsts" in American Jewish history as follows: "the first volumes of sermons delivered and published by an American Jewish religious teacher (1837); the first complete American translation of the Sephardic prayer book (1837); the first Hebrew primer for children (1838); the first Jewish communal religious school (1839); the first successful American Jewish magazine-news journal (1843); the first American Jewish publication society (1845); the first Hebrew-English Torah to be edited and translated by an American Jew (1845); the first complete English translation of the Ashkenazic prayer book (1848); the first Hebrew "high school" (1849); the first English translation of the entire Bible by an American Jew (1853); the first Jewish defense organization—the Board of Delegates of American Israelites (1859); the first American Jewish theological seminary—Maimonides College (1867). Korn, *Isaac Leeser*, p. 133.

3. Isaac Leeser, *Discourses on the Jewish Religion* (Philadelphia, 1867), vol. 8, p. 93; *Occident,* 15 (September 1857), pp. 291–295. Cf. also, Naomi W. Cohen, "Pioneers of American Jewish Defense," *American Jewish Archives* 29 (1977), pp. 125–128; Idem, *Encounter with Emancipation: The German Jews in the United States 1830–1914* (Philadelphia, 1984), pp. 72–108.

4. *Occident* 3 (May, 1845), pp. 64–65.

5. Leeser, *Discourses,* vol. 1, pp. 260–261; vol. 4, pp. 10–11; vol. 5, p. 28; vol. 6, pp. 131–132, 330–333; vol. 7, pp. 46–48, 231–232, 391–392; vol. 9, p.

120; *Occident* 2 (March, 1845), pp. 600–606; 3 (September, 1845), pp. 265–275; 22 (April, 1864), p. 12. Cf. also, Maxine S. Seller, "Isaac Leeser's Views on the Restoration of A Jewish Palestine,"*American Jewish Historical Quarterly* 58 (September, 1968), pp. 118–135 and Jonathan D. Sarna, *Jacksonian Jew: The Two Worlds of Mordecai Noah* (New York, 1981), pp. 152–157.

In one sermon, Leeser expressed the view that many Christians favored granting freedom to the Jews in order to make their conversion easier. Leeser, *Discourses,* vol. 8, p. 93.

6. Leeser frequently stressed the necessity for American Jews to maintain traditional religious practice. He explained that the social aloofness resulting from traditional practice was not due to anti-Christian sentiments, and that decent Christians would understand this. Leeser, *Discourses,* vol. 4, pp. 139–140; vol. 10, p. 115; *Occident* 1 (June, 1843), pp. 113–120. Traditional practice was the only sure way of preserving Judaism and keeping the Jews a separate people so that they could bring the word of God in its pure form to mankind.

7. Isaac Leeser, *The Jews and the Mosaic Law* (Philadelphia, 1833), pp. v–vi.

8. Isaac Leeser, *The Claims of the Jews to an Equality of Rights* (Philadelphia, 1841), p. 12.

9. Leeser, *Jews and the Mosaic Law,* pp. v–vii. It seems likely that the prominent Richmond Jew Jacob Mordechai helped to foster Leeser's interest in polemics. Mordechai had composed a polemical tract in 1827 in order to convince Jews, including members of his own family, not to convert to Christianity. This unpublished work was called *Introduction to the New Testament.* Myron Berman, *Richmond's Jewry, 1769–1976* (Charlottesville, 1979), pp. 120–124.

10. *Occident* 2 (April, 1844), p. 5; (September, 1844), p. 279; Leeser, *Discourses,* vol. 2, pp. 49ff.; vol. 3, p. 45; vol. 4, p. 109; vol. 8, pp. 131–133, 341–343.

11. Leeser, *Jews and the Mosaic Law,* p. 237.

12. Leeser, *Discourses,* vol. 4, p. 143. By late 1858, Leeser was having second thoughts on this. He advised Jews in small towns where no synagogue existed to refrain from going to churches, even out of curiosity. He feared that their presence in churches would be misunderstood as demonstrating a Jewish interest in Christianity, and that this would only serve to encourage the missionaries. He cited the example of Chicago's reverend Robert Patterson who had claimed that Jews were visiting churches and that this showed their interest in converting to Christianity. *Occident* 16 (December, 1858), pp. 438–445; (January, 1859), pp. 467–475.

Indicative of Leeser's more aggressive tone is his statement in response to an article in the *Episcopal Recorder* urging the Jews to convert. Leeser remarked that in responding to missionary attempts, Jews may "freely employ invective as the only legitimate reply, especially when we can do so and utter the plain uncontrovertible truth, which history and experience so fully confirm." *Occident* 9 (October, 1851), p. 370.

13. *Occident* 7 (January, 1850), pp. 481–495. For Presbyterian interest in converting the Jews, cf. Max D. Eichhorn, *Evangelizing the American Jew* (New York, 1978), pp. 115–118; 155–157.

14. *Occident* 7 (January, 1850), p. 485. For other examples of Leeser's triumphalist hope that the Gentiles would one day accept the teachings of Judaism, cf. Leeser, *Discourses,* vol. 4, p. 79; vol. 8, pp. 335–338; vol. 10, p. 280; *Occident* 2 (May, 1844), p. 124.

15. *Occident* 8 (July, 1850), pp. 185–193; (August, 1850), pp. 232–237; (September, 1850), pp. 287–297; (November, 1850), pp. 398–405; (January, 1851), pp. 509–514; (March, 1851), pp. 594–599; Matthew R. Miller, *The Identity of Judaism and Christianity* (New York, 1850). Peynado's response was published in the *Asmonean* 3 (October 25, 1850), pp. 1–2.

In December 1846, the New York presbytery established a Jewish mission in New York and Miller served as its first missionary until 1852. Eichhorn, *Evangelizing the American Jew,* p. 115. Miller's attempts to convince the Jews that trinitarian doctrine was implied in the Hebrew Bible were not confined to his *Identity of Judaism and Christianity.* He later carried on a debate on this subject with Rabbi Aaron Guinzburg in the pages of the *Israelite.* Miller published his part of the correspondence in *The Luminous Unity; or letters Addressed to the Rev. A. Guinzburg, a rabbi of Boston, Mass., from the Rev. M. R. Miller, on the question, Is Unitarianism, as opposed to Trinitarianism, a principle of heathenism, rather than of specific Judaism* (Philadelphia, 1874).

16. *Occident* 8 (September, 1850), pp. 297–306; (October, 1850), pp. 348–354; (December, 1850), pp. 459–464; (January, 1851), pp. 514–519. Cf. also Miller's letters responding to Schlessinger in *Occident* (January, 1851), pp. 496–509; (February, 1851), pp. 545–552. The *Asmonean* also contained a series of articles refuting Miller's pamphlet. *Asmonean* 2 (June 21, 1850), pp. 68–70; (July 12, 1850), pp. 93–94; (July 26, 1850), pp. 108–109.

17. Jacob Mordechi's *Introduction to the New Testament* was a book by book analysis of the New Testament which questioned both the historicity of the New Testament and the existence of Jesus. Berman, *Richmond's Jewry,* p. 121.

18. Leeser, *Discourses,* vol. 5, pp. 51–52. Cf. however, Leeser's remark that the only sources that discuss Jesus were composed by his followers, and that since they contradict one another they are unreliable. *Occident* 6 (December, 1848), pp. 450–451. Leeser's Reform contemporary, Isaac M. Wise, expressed similar concern about New Testament criticism. In the *American Israelite* of January 9, 1880, Wise wrote "Ever since Strauss and Renan have run the dissenter's knife into the body of the New Testament, other parties have adopted the decision of Solomon, to cut in twain both the dead and the living child, and they run the dissenter's knife also into the body of the Old Testament." Quoted in Andrew F. Key, *The Theology of Isaac Meyer Wise* (Cincinnati, 1962), p. 15.

19. *Occident* 2 (April, 1844), pp. 3–4; Leeser, *Discourses,* vol. 7, p. 356; vol. 8, p. 130.

20. Leeser, *Discourses,* vol. 2, pp. 85–86; vol. 5, p. 236; vol. 6, pp. 198–199; vol. 7, pp. 298–299; vol. 8, pp. 112–113, 341–356; *Occident* 1 (May, 1843), pp. 71–72.

21. Leeser, *Discourses,* vol. 2, p. 281.

22. Leeser, *Discourses,* vol. 4, pp. 116–121; vol. 8, pp. 346–356.

23. *Occident* 2 (August, 1844), pp. 217–221; Leeser, *Discourses,* vol. 7, pp. 33–36.

24. *Occident,* 2 (May, 1844), pp. 123, 159; Leeser, *Discourses,* vol. 2, p. 269; vol. 10, p. 63.

25. Leeser, *Discourses,* vol. 2, pp. 253–372. Cf. also *Occident* 1 (March, 1844), pp. 609–610 and 8 (October, 1851), pp. 365–372.

26. Leeser, *Discourses,* vol. 4, pp. 363–386.

27. Leeser, *Discourses,* vol. 1, pp. 352–355; vol. 2, pp. 91ff; vol. 4, pp. 125–126; vol. 8, p. 127.

28. Robert T. Handy, *A Christian America: Protestant Hopes and Historical Realities* (New York, 1971), p. 28.

29. *Occident* 9 (June, 1851), p. 242; Leeser, *Discourses,* vol. 5, pp. 390–394; vol. 6, p. 198; vol. 7, pp. 85, 160, 255; vol. 8, pp. 3–4, 10–11, 37–39.

30. *Occident* 1 (February, 1844), p. 519; Leeser, *Discourses,* vol. 5, p. 321; vol. 6, pp. 75–76; vol. 7, p. 160.

31. *Occident* 6 (December, 1848), p. 450; 9 (January, 1851), pp. 499–500. Cf. also Leeser, *Discourses,* vol. 6, p. 108; vol. 8, pp. 130, 154, 335–337; vol. 9, pp. 50–51, 169–170, 223; vol. 10, p. 303. Mordecai M. Noah also praised Christianity as the religion that spread monotheism. Cf. Jonathan D. Sarna, *Jacksonian Jew: The Two Worlds of Mordecai Noah* (New York, 1981), p. 131. For similar Reform views, see below chapter 4.

32. Leeser, *Discourses,* vol. 10, p. 303.

33. Leeser, *Discourses,* vol. 9, p. 223.

34. See Leeser's exchange with reverend J. F. Halsey of Perth Amboy, New Jersey, *Occident* 2 (April, 1844), pp. 40–46; (May, 1844), pp. 154–159. Barbara Tuchman summarizes the view of the English millenarians towards the Jews in the following words: " . . . the Jews were simply the instrument through which Biblical prophecy would be fulfilled. They were not a people, but a mass Error that must be brought to a belief in Christ in order that the whole chain reaction leading to the Second Coming and the redemption of mankind might be set in motion." Barbara Tuchman, *Bible and Sword: England and Palestine from the Bronze Age to Balfour* (New York, 1956), p. 178.

35. Leeser, *Claims of the Jews,* pp. 37–40. The background for this project is discussed in Tuchman, *Bible and Sword,* pp. 113–133. Cf. also, John S. Conway, "The Jerusalem Bishopric: A 'Union of Foolscrap and Blotting Paper,'" *Studies in Religion* 7 (Summer, 1978), pp. 305–315, and idem, "Protestant Missions to the Jews 1810–1980 Ecclesiastical Imperialism or Theological Aberration?", *Holocaust and Genocide Studies* 1 (1986), pp. 130–131.

36. Leeser was careful to note that belief in the divinity of Jesus constituted idolatry only for Jews. Gentiles, however, were allowed to associate another being with God since their perception of the religious truth of God's unity was not as pure as that of the Jews. *Occident* 8 (January, 1851), pp. 499–500. For comments on the Unitarians, cf. *Occident* 3 (July, 1845), pp. 177–189, and (September, 1845), p. 293.

37. *Occident* 8 (July, 1850), pp. 187–193. For the English proponents of this idea, cf. Mel Scult, *Millennial Expectations and Jewish Liberties: A Study of the Efforts to Convert the Jews in Britain, up to the Mid Nineteenth Century* (Leiden, 1978), pp. 38–41, 69, 84. Cf. also *Occident* 1 (October, 1843), pp. 354–357.

38. Leeser, *Jews and the Mosaic Law,* pp. 249–261.

39. Leeser, *Discourses,* vol. 4, p. 116; vol. 7, p. 255; vol. 8, pp. 3–4.

40. *Occident* 1 (May, 1843), p. 67; (September, 1844), p. 281.

41. *Occident* 3 (May, 1845), pp. 98–100; Leeser, *Discourses,* vol. 6, p. 158; vol. 8, pp. 220ff.

42. Leeser, *Equality of Rights,* pp. 15–17, 32–33; *Occident* 1 (April, 1843), pp. 43ff; 2 (December, 1844), pp. 428–429; 5 (December, 1847), p. 462–463; (March, 1848), pp. 585–593; 6 (May, 1848), pp. 98–103; (October, 1848), pp. 359–366; 20 (March, 1863), pp. 529–543; Leeser, *Discourses,* vol. 8, pp. 92–93. Cf. also Leeser's statement in reference to the missionaries: "Ours is a constant state of warfare with all around." Ibid., p. 130.

43. Leeser's translation was meant to free Jews from reliance on the Authorized Version. While declaring in his preface that he had "thrown aside all bias, discarded every preconceived opinion, and translated the text . . . without regard to the result thence arising for his creed," Leeser followed the traditional Jewish understanding of the Bible and emphasized the literal meaning of the text. *The Twenty-Four Books of the Holy Scriptures Carefully Translated According to the Massoretic Text on the Basis of the English Version after the Best Jewish Authorities and Supplied with Short Explanatory Notes* by Isaac Leeser (New York, 1922), p. iii. Leeser criticized Christian Biblical interpreters for distorting the text by applying allegorical interpretations to it. He also, however, occasionally departed from the literal sense of a verse when the literal sense seemed to buttress the Christian interpretation. On Leeser's translation, cf. Matitiahu Tsevat, "A Retrospective View of Isaac Leeser's Biblical Work," *Essays in American Jewish History* (Cincinnati, 1958), pp. 295–313, and Lance J. Sussman, "Another Look at Isaac Leeser and the First Jewish Translation of the

Bible in the United States," *Modern Judaism* 5 (May, 1985), pp. 159–190. Cf. also, Leeser, *Equality of Rights,* p. 37; *Occident* 2 (February, 1845), p. 519; Leeser, *Discourses,* vol. 5, pp. 41–46; vol. 8, pp. 263–273; vol. 10, pp. 301, 305, 319. Sussman points to another important factor that led Leeser to translate the Bible. He realized that Bibliocentrism was crucial to American Protestantism and was, therefore, a major characteristic of American religious life. Leeser wanted to make it possible for Jews to adapt to this Bibliocentrism without falling prey to Christological Biblical interpretations.

44. On Jewish resentment of Christian missionary proclamations of love for the Jews, cf. Jonathan D. Sarna, "Jewish-Christian Hostility in the United States: Perceptions from a Jewish Point of View," F. E. Greenspahn ed., *Uncivil Religion* (New York, 1987), pp. 5–22.

45. Leeser, *Equality of Rights,* p. 9; *Occident* 6 (May, 1848), p. 100. Cf. also, Jonathan D. Sarna, "The American Jewish Response to Nineteenth Century Christian Missions," *The Journal of American History* 68 (June, 1981), p. 50. If Jews were to missionize, it would not have alleviated the conditions that left Jews open to Christian missionaries. Christian missionaries exploited points of vulnerability in the Jewish community such as ignorance, poverty, and the isolation of Jews living in small communities. In fact, Christian missionary efforts stimulated Jewish communal efforts to overcome those conditions within the Jewish community that left some Jews vulnerable to the missionaries. Cf. Jonathan Sarna, "The Impact of Nineteenth Century Christian Missions on American Jews," *Jewish Apostasy in the Modern World* edited by Todd M. Endelman (New York, 1987) pp. 232–254.

CHAPTER 4

1. Donald T. Hagner, *The Jewish Reclamation of Jesus: An Analysis and Critique of Modern Jewish Study of Jesus* (Grand Rapids, 1984), p. 52.

2. Abraham Geiger, *Judaism and its History,* translated from the German by Maurice Mayer, (New York 1865); Samuel Hirsch, *Die Religionsphilosophie der Juden* (Leipzig, 1842). For an analysis of nineteenth century European Jewish writings on Jesus and Christianity, cf. Walter Jacob, *Christianity Through Jewish Eyes: the Quest for Common Ground* (Cincinnati, 1974).

3. William R. Hutchison, *The Modernist Impulse in American Protestantism* (Cambridge, 1976), pp. 76–144.

4. Ibid., pp. 119; 133.

5. Ibid., pp. 129–132. Cf. also David W. Lotz's article on Harnack in *The Encyclopedia of Religion* (New York, 1987) 6, pp. 198–199, and James Turner, *Without God, Without Creed: The Origins of Unbelief in America* (Baltimore, 1985), pp. 141–202.

6. For the development of Reform Judaism in America in the nineteenth century and the problems that it confronted, cf. David Philipson, *The Reform*

Movement in Judaism (New York, 1967), pp. 329–381; Marc Lee Raphael, *Profiles in American Judaism: The Reform, Conservative, Orthodox and Reconstructionist Traditions in Historical Perspective* (San Francisco, 1984), pp. 3–78; Naomi W. Cohen, *Encounter with Emancipation: the German Jews in the United States 1830–1914* (Philadelphia, 1984), pp. 159–194, and Moshe Davis, *The Emergence of Conservative Judaism* (Philadelphia, 1963), pp. 200–228.

7. Isaac M. Wise, *The Origin of Christianity and a Commentary to the Acts of the Apostles* (Cincinnati, 1868), p. vi. Cf. also, Emil G. Hirsch, "My Religion and the Religion of Jesus" in *My Religion and the Crucifixion Viewed from a Jewish Standpoint* (New York, 1973), pp. 32ff and Kaufmann Kohler, "The Attitude of Christian Scholars Toward Jewish Literature," *Menorah* 33 (August, 1902), pp. 91–101.

8. Abraham Geiger, *Judaism and its History*, pp. 214–220.

9. Wise wrote extensively on Jesus and Christianity. Although at first he doubted the historicity of Jesus, he later modified his position. His major works on the subject are: *The Origin of Christianity and a Commentary to the Acts of the Apostles* (Cincinnati, 1868); *Three Lectures on the Origins of Christianity* (Cincinnati, 1873); *The Martyrdom of Jesus of Nazareth: a Historic-Critical Treatise on the Last Chapters of the Gospel* (Cincinnati, 1874); *History of the Hebrews' Second Commonwealth with Special Reference to its Literature, Culture, and the Origin of Rabbinism and Christianity* (Cincinnati, 1880); *Judaism and Christianity, Their Agreements and Disagreements* (Cincinnati, 1883); *A Defense of Judaism Versus Proselytizing Christianity* (Cincinnati, 1889). Cf. also, Samuel Sandmel, "Isaac Mayer Wise's 'Jesus Himself,' " *Essays in American Jewish History*, edited by J. R. Marcus and A. J. Peck, (Cincinnati, 1958), pp. 325–358 and James G. Heller, *Isaac M. Wise: His Life, Work and Thought* (New York, 1965), pp. 623–657.

10. Kaufmann Kohler, *The Origins of the Synagogue and the Church* (New York, 1929), pp. 211–240; idem, "Jesus of Nazareth—In theology," *The Jewish Encyclopedia* 7 (New York, 1904), pp. 166–170; idem, "Christianity in its Relation to Judaism," *The Jewish Encyclopedia* 4 (New York, 1903), pp. 49–59; idem, "Jesus of Nazareth," *Jewish Times* 6 (January 22, 1875), pp. 755–756.

11. *American Hebrew* 42 (April 4, 1890), pp. 165–195.

12. Ibid., p. 170.

13. Isaac M. Wise, *The Martyrdom of Jesus*, p. 81.

14. Ibid., pp. 22–41; 103–105.

15. Emil G. Hirsch, *The Crucifixion Viewed from a Jewish Standpoint* (New York, 1908); idem, "The Crucifixion," *Reform Advocate* 3 (February 20, 1892), pp. 5–15. For an analysis of modern Jewish views of Jewish responsibility for the crucifixion see David R. Catchpole, *The Trial of Jesus: A Study in the Gospels and Jewish Historiography from 1770 to the Present Day* (Leiden, 1971).

16. Joseph Krauskopf, *A Rabbi's Impressions of the Oberammergau Passion Play* (Philadelphia, 1901), pp. 63–83.

17. Gustav Gottheil based his defense of the Jews on neither of these grounds. He wrote that the Jews could not be held accountable for the death of Jesus since most Jews at that time did not live in Palestine and, therefore, never knew or even heard of Jesus. Gustav Gottheil, "Jesus was not Rejected," *Menorah* 14 (1894), pp. 177–178.

18. *Reform Advocate* 10 (December 21, 1895), p. 745. For similar Reform expressions of this theme, cf. J. Krauskopf, *A Rabbi's Impressions*, p. 152; Gustav Gottheil, "The Great Refusal," *Unitarian Review* 27 (January, 1887), pp. 11–12; *Bernhard Felsenthal, Teacher in Israel: Selections from His Writings with Biographical Sketch and Bibliography by His Daughter Emma Felsenthal* (New York, 1924), p. 203. Cf. also Emil G. Hirsch's contrast of the martyrdom of Jesus with that of Rabbi Akibah, the prototypical martyr in Jewish tradition. E. G. Hirsch, "My Religion and the Religion of Jesus," p. 46.

19. *Reform Advocate* 18 (October 28, 1899), p. 313.

20. Emil G. Hirsch, "My Religion and the Religion of Jesus," pp. 34–40; idem, *The Doctrines of Jesus* (Chicago, 1894); J. Krauskopf, *A Rabbi's Impressions*, pp. 182–191. Cf. also, Joseph Stoltz, "Jesus and the Jews," *Reform Advocate* 5 (May 20, 1893), pp. 262–265; Kaufmann Kohler, "The Inadequacy of Christian Ethics," *Reform Advocate* 7 (March 17, 1894), pp. 69–71.

21. Emil G. Hirsch, "The Ethics of Jesus," *Reform Advocate* 8 (January 26, 1895), pp. 367–370.

22. Kaufmann Kohler, "Three Discourses on Jewish Ethics," *Studies, Addresses, and Personal Papers* (New York, 1931), pp. 236–242. These discourses were delivered at the Fifth Annual Session of the Summer Assembly of the Jewish Chautauqua Society in Atlantic City, July, 1901. Cf. Also his "Synagogue and Church in their Mutual Relations Particularly in Reference to their Ethical Teachings," Ibid., pp. 251–265. Kohler delivered this address to the Jewish Denominational Congress at the World's Parliament of Religions in Chicago on August 27, 1893.

23. Idem, "Three Discourses," pp. 242–247. Here, Kohler was repeating the Reform emphasis on the consonance of Jewish and American ideals, especially ethical ideals. Over two decades earlier, Isaac M. Wise had given striking expression to this belief when he predicted that the essence of Judaism would become the religion of most intelligent Americans before the end of the nineteenth century. Benny Kraut, "Judaism Triumphant: Isaac Mayer Wise on Unitarianism and Liberal Christianity," *AJS Review* 7–8 (1982–1983), p. 194, no. 46. Cf. also Andrew F. Key, *The Theology of Isaac Meyer Wise* (Cincinnati, 1962), p. 43 for Wise's statement "that the government of the United States in principle and form is identical with the Mosaic State as laid down in the Pentatench." Kohler was expressing the same attitude when he declared that the

words "American Judaism spell the triumph of the world's two greatest peoples and ideals." Arnold M. Eisen, *The Chosen People in America: A Study in Jewish Religious Ideology* (Bloomington, 1983), p. 20. By emphasizing that Jewish and American ethical ideals were in agreement, the Reformers sought to counter antisemites who held the Jews collectively guilty for the unethical acts of individual Jews, and they also hoped to show that Judaism should not be held responsible for the misdeeds of Jewish miscreants. Most important of all, by asserting that Jewish rather than Christian ethical ideals were more in tune with the American spirit, the Reformers were making their strongest argument for insider status in America. Cf. *Bernard Felsenthal, Teacher in Israel*, pp. 265–266.

24. Emil G. Hirsch, "The Jews and Jesus," *Reform Advocate* 5 (May 6, 1893), pp. 222–226.

25. Kaufmann Kohler, *Studies, Addresses, and Personal Papers*, pp. 248–250.

26. Emanuel Schreiber, "Jesus of Nazareth," *Menorah* 7 (1889), p. 88.

27. E. G. Hirsch, "The Doctrines of Jesus," (Chicago, 1894), p. 27.

28. K. Kohler, *Origins of the Synagogue*, p. 27; idem, "Jesus of Nazareth," *Jewish Times* 6 (January 22, 1875), pp. 755–756.

29. *Selected Works of Hyman G. Enelow* (Kingsport, Tennessee, 1935), vol. 3, p. 466.

30. Ibid., p. 430.

31. Ibid., pp. 438–442. For similar views of Jesus as a proto Reform Jew, cf. for example, I. M. Wise, *Three Lectures on the Origin of Christianity*, pp. 18–22, E. Schreiber, "Jesus of Nazareth," p. 85, and *Bernhard Felsenthal, Teacher in Israel*, pp. 29–30.

32. On the Pittsburgh platform and its aftermath, cf. David Philipson, *The Reform Movement in Judaism* (New York, 1967), pp. 355–357 and Moshe Davis, *The Emergence of Conservative Judaism*, pp. 216–228. For an example of the traditionalist attack on Reform as Paulinian, see Solomon Solis Cohen, "Under Which Flag?", *American Hebrew* 31 (July 22, 1887), p. 163. Cf. also rabbi Joseph Silverman's rebuttal of the claim put forth by both traditionalist Jews and liberal Christians that Reform represented a breakup of Judaism and a turning to Christianity. In a speech to the Jewish Religious Congress at the World's Parliament of Religions, Silverman declared that Reform strengthened Judaism by making it possible to retain within the Jewish fold people who otherwise would have gone over not to Christianity, but to atheism. John H. Burrows ed., *The World's Parliament of Religions* (Chicago, 1893), 2, pp. 1120–1122. Cf. also, *Reform Advocate* 6 (September 6, 1893), pp. 75–78.

33. *Reform Advocate* 14 (February 5, 1898), p. 834.

34. *Reform Advocate* 17 (March 4, 1899), pp. 71–72. See also, D. Einhorn, "Dogmatical Differences Between Judaism and Christianity," *Jewish Times* 1

(June 18, 1869), p. 2 for David Einhorn's assertion that orthodoxy was closer to Christianity than Reform.

35. *Reform Advocate* 13 (February 27, 1897), p. 19.

36. *Bernhard Felsenthal, Teacher in Israel*, p. 29. Felsenthal went on to state that "The religion of Christ is essentially identical with the religion of Israel. Paradoxical as it may sound, it is nevertheless true that the Jews are the true Christians, and that the so-called Christians are not Christians, inasmuch as they profess a number of doctrines totally foreign to the religion of Christ," p. 265. For an example of the liberal Protestant claim that Paul's ideas were rooted in Judaism, see the exchange between R. Heber Newton and the editors of the *American Hebrew*, 42 (February 14, 1890), p. 22; (February 28, 1890), pp. 62–63; (March 28, 1890), pp. 142–144.

37. K. Kohler, *The Origins of the Synagogue and the Church*, pp. 260–270. Cf. also, Kohler's article "Saul of Tarsus," *The Jewish Encyclopedia* 11 (1905), pp. 79–87. In contrast to Kohler and Hirsch, Max Schlessinger wrote that Paul based himself on Jewish ideas but transformed them into a form of heathenism. Max Schlessinger, *The Historical Jesus of Nazareth* (New York, 1876), pp. 88–98.

38. Emil G. Hirsch, "Paul, the Apostle of Heathen Judaism or Christianity," *Reform Advocate* 7 (June 30, 1894), pp. 356–359. Also, idem, "My Religion and Dogmatic Christianity" in *My Religion*, pp. 47–64.

39. I. M. Wise, *The Origin of Christianity*, pp. 311–535.

40. J. Krauskopf, *A Rabbi's Impressions*, pp. 207–208.

41. Ibid., p. 216.

42. Many late nineteenth century liberal Protestants and Reform leaders shared the hope for a universal religion. However, each identified his own religion with the new universal one. The failure of liberal Protestants to acknowledge that Judaism was a religion that retained religious value after the coming of Jesus and the growth of antisemitism in America contributed to a lowering of Reform hopes that Judaism would become the universal religion anytime in the near future. Cf. for example, the attitude of Isaac Mayer Wise in Benny Kraut, "Judaism Triumphant: Isaac Mayer Wise on Unitarianism and Liberal Christianity" *AJA Review* 7–8 (1982–1983), pp. 179–230. Some of the more radical Reformers carried the idea of a universal religion to an extreme. Solomon Schindler, rabbi of Boston's congregation Adath Israel, envisioned a future universal religion which would "be neither specifically Jewish nor Christian nor Mohammedan." It would be an entirely new religion "in which the immortal parts of all the present religions will be represented, but at the same time so equally balanced that none will dare to claim superiority." He went on to say that "A messianic period with one of the present religious systems dominating is an absurdity, and a contradiction of itself." Schindler felt that Judaism, because of its rationality and flexibility, would find it easy to

flow into the religion of the future. Solomon Schindler, *Messianic Expectations and Modern Judaism* (Boston, 1886), p. 166. In order to ease the way to the new religion, Schindler encouraged intermarriage between liberal Christians and liberal Jews. This caused a split between him and his congregation and he left Adath Israel in 1893. In 1911, Schindler recanted his earlier extremism in a sermon entitled "Mistakes I Have Made." Schindler's successor at Adath Israel was Charles Fleischer, and he proved to be even more radical than his predecessor. Fleischer, too, urged Jews to intermarry, and in 1911 he left Adath Israel (then called Temple Israel) to establish a nonsectarian religious congregation known as the "Sunday Commons." He advocated a religion of progress and American democracy which was heavily influenced by the Transcendentalist thought of Theodore Parker and Ralph Waldo Emerson. Cf. Arthur Mann, "Charles Fleischer's Religion of Democracy: an Experiment in American Faith," *Commentary* 17 (1954), pp. 557–565. On the other hand, some Reformers were altogether skeptical about the possibility or advisability of a universal religion. Bernhard Felsenthal believed that a "universal church is but a dream—a dream which will never be realized." Instead, the future would see a variety of national churches, the Jewish church being one of them. The world would eventually accept the principles of Judaism, but the Jewish religion with its own calendar, Sabbaths, and other institutions and ceremonies would remain the religion of the Jews alone. *Bernhard Felsenthal, Teacher in Israel*, pp. 188–194. See also rabbi Louis Grossman's critical reference to rabbis who were eager for what he called a "premature universalism." Quoted in Rebecca T. Alpert, "Jewish Participation at the World's Parliament of Religions, 1893," Ronald Brauner ed., *Jewish Civilization* (Philadelphia, 1979), p. 115. For Hirsch's reservations about a universal religion, see below, pp. 67–68. For Maurice Harris's negative view of the concept of a universal religion, cf. his "The Spirit of Judaism," *Selected Addresses* third series (New York, 1896), pp. 45–46.

43. Robert Andrew Everett, "Judaism in Nineteenth Century American Transcendentalist and Liberal Protestant Thought," *Journal of Ecumenical Studies* 20 (Summer, 1983), pp. 396–414; Benny Kraut, "Francis E. Abott: Perceptions of a Nineteenth century Religious Radical on Jews and Judaism," *Studies in the American Jewish Experience* edited by J. R. Marcus and A. J. Peck, (Cincinnati, 1981), pp. 90–113. Cf. also, Kaufmann Kohler's review of C. H. Toy's *Judaism and Christianity,* in *Jewish Messenger* 69 (February 13, 1891), pp. 4–5; (March 6, 1891), p. 4.

44. Washington Gladden, "The Children of the Ghetto," *American Hebrew* (November 13, 1896), pp. 40–42; (November 20, 1896), pp.87–89; idem, "Can Jews be Christians?", *American Hebrew* (December 11, 1896), pp. 174–175. See also the editorial response of the *American Hebrew,* "Need We be Christians?" (December 18, 1896), p. 196.

45. Benny Kraut, *From Reform Judaism to Ethical Culture: the Religious Evolution of Felix Adler* (Cincinnati, 1979), pp. 219–220. Cf. also idem, "Unitarianism on the Reform Jewish Mind," *Proceedings of the Eighth World Congress of*

Jewish Studies Division B The History of the Jewish People (Jerusalem, 1982), pp. 91–98 and idem, "The Ambivalent Relations of American Reform Judaism with Unitarianism in the Last Third of the Nineteenth Century," *Journal of Ecumenical Studies* 23 (Winter, 1986), pp. 58–68. For information on Sonneschein, cf. idem, "A Unitarian Rabbi? The Case of Solomon H. Sonneschein," *Jewish Apostasy in the Modern World* edited by Todd M. Endelman, (New York, 1987), pp. 272–308.

46. Maurice Harris, "Judaism and Unitarianism from a Jewish Standpoint," *Selected Addresses*, pp. 3–16. Cf. also, Benny Kraut, "Judaism Triumphant" for an analysis of Isaac M. Wise's changing attitude towards Unitarianism. Through the 1870's Wise stressed the commonalities between the two religions, however, from the 1880's he emphasized the differences.

47. Conrad Wright, ed., *A Stream of Light: A Sesquicentennial History of American Unitarianism* (Boston, 1975), pp. 67–74.

48. *Reform Advocate* 6 (February 3, 1894), pp. 398–400.

49. Emil G. Hirsch, "Universal Religion and Judaism," *Reform Advocate* 6 (October 13, 1893), p. 140.

50. *American Hebrew* 63 (May 20, 1898), pp. 74–75.

51. Emil G. Hirsch, "Are the Jews the Chosen People?", *Reform Advocate* 5 (April 15, 1893), pp. 162–165.

52. Benny Kraut, *From Reform Judaism to Ethical Culture*, pp. 169–172.

53. Ibid., pp. 150–168.

54. Josephine Lazarus, *The Spirit of Judaism* (New York, 1895).

55. Ibid., pp. 22–27.

56. Ibid., pp. 45–50.

57. Ibid., pp. 104–105.

58. Ibid., pp. 193–202.

59. *Reform Advocate* 10 (December 21, 1895), pp. 744–746. Grace Aguilar (1816–1847) was an English Jewish author of Portuguese Marrano descent. She wrote novels and religious books. Among her important works are her translation from the French of the apologetic work of the ex-Marrano Orobio de Castro *Israel Defended* (1838); *The Spirit of Judaism: In Defense of Her Faith and its Professors* (1842), and *The Jewish Faith* (1846). Uriel Da Costa (1585–1640) was born into a Marrano family in Portugal. He reverted to Judaism after studying the Bible and fled to Amsterdam. There he became disillusioned with Judaism because of its ritualism and its doctrine of immortality which he rejected. Da Costa was excommunicated, but later recanted and rejoined the Synagogue. However, he once again became dissatisfied with Judaism as he

came to doubt the divine authority of the Torah. He gave up Jewish practice and was once again excommunicated. Some years later, he sought to rejoin the Synagogue and was subjected to a humiliating public recantation of his views. Shortly thereafter, he committed suicide. Dorothea Mendelssohn (1765–1839), eldest daughter of the famous German Jewish philosopher Moses Mendelssohn, married the poet Friedrich Schlegel and converted to Protestantism. Later, both she and Schlegel became Catholics.

60. *Reform Advocate* 10 (January 4, 1896), pp. 786–789.

61. *An Address to the Members of Central Conference of American Rabbis* (Sacramento, 1900).

62. Harris Weinstock, *Jesus the Jew* (New York, 1902).

63. Ibid., p. 30.

64. Ibid., p. 15.

65. *Central Conference of American Rabbis Yearbook* 11 (1901), p. 86.

66. *An Address,* pp. 8–20.

67. Cf. for example, A. E. Thompson, author of *A Century of Jewish Missions,* who welcomed Weinstock's proposal and the Central Conference's response as evidence of a "radical change" in the disposition of the Jews towards Jesus. Writing of the Central Conference's response, Thompson noted, "There is a studied indefiniteness about this pronouncement which speaks plainly of the trend of opinion. It is definite enough as regards the divinity of Christ, which the American Rabbis are not yet prepared to concede. But what council of Rabbis a hundred years ago would have allowed a free discussion of the merits and claims of the founder of Christianity, or have given a moment's consideration to the question of the advisability of giving the teachings of Jesus a place in a school curriculum?" *A Century of Jewish Missions* (Chicago, 1902), pp. 50–51. Cf. also, Isaac K. Funk's introductory remarks to his 1899 survey of Jewish views of Jesus published as an appendix to George Croly, *Tarry Thou till I Come* (New York, 1901), pp. 551–573, and Isidore Singer, "The Attitude of the Jews Toward Jesus," *North American Review* 191 (1910), pp. 128–134.

68. Israel Goldstein, *Jesus of Nazareth: An Authentic Ancient Tale* (New York, 1866).

69. *Reform Advocate,* 5 (May 6, 1893), p. 222.

70. See also the later controversy aroused by Stephen S. Wise's December 20, 1925 sermon "A Jew's View of Jesus." Wise reiterated the main points of the nineteenth century Reform position on Jesus and was denounced by many, especially the orthodox. The storm erupted now rather than in the nineteenth century because of the influence that east-European orthodoxy had gained in the community as a result of the east-European immigration, and also because

Stephen S. Wise was generally recognized as the leading figure in American Jewry, a stature which none of the nineteenth century figures had attained. Cf. Melvin I. Urofsky, *A Voice that Spoke for Justice: The Life and Times of Stephen S. Wise* (Albany, 1982), pp. 194–202.

Bibliography

Adler, Cyrus, comp. *Catalogue of the Leeser Library*. Philadelphia, 1883.

Ahlstrom, Sydney E. *A Religious History of the American People*. New Haven, 1972.

Allbough, Gaylord P. "Anti-Missionary Movement in the United States." *An Encyclopedia of Religion*, ed. by Vergilius T. A. Ferm, (New York, 1945): 27–28.

Alpert, Rebecca Trachtenberg. "Jewish Participation at the World's Parliament of Religions, 1893." *Jewish Civilization*, ed. by Ronald A. Brauner, (Philadelphia, 1979): 111–121.

Barrows, John H., ed. *The World's Parliament of Religions*. Chicago, 1893.

Benjamin, Walter. *Christianity Through Jewish Eyes: The Quest for Common Ground*. Cincinnati, 1974.

Bennett, Ephraim. *An Evaluation of the Life of Isaac Leeser*. Ph.D. Dissertation, Yeshiva University, 1959.

Berger, David. *The Jewish-Christian Debate in the High Middle Ages*. Philadelphia, 1979.

Berlin, George L. "Joseph S. C. F. Frey, the Jews, and Early Nineteenth Century Millenarianism." *Journal of the Early Republic* 1 (Spring, 1981): 27–49.

———. "Solomon Jackson's *The Jew*: An Early American Jewish Response to the Missionaries." *American Jewish History* 71 (September, 1981): 10–28.

Berman, Myron, *Richmond's Jewry, 1769–1976*. Charlottesville, 1979.

Bernhard Felsenthal. Teacher in Israel: Selections from His Writings with Biographical Sketch and Bibliography by His Daughter Emma Felsenthal. New York, 1924.

Blau, Joseph L., and Baron, Salo W. *The Jews of the United States, 1790–1840, A Documentary History*. New York, 1963.

Blau, Joseph L. *Judaism in America: from Curiosity to Third Faith.* Chicago, 1976.

Borden, Morton. *Jews, Turks, and Infidels.* Chapel Hill, 1984.

Catchpole, David R. *The Trial of Jesus: A Study in the Gospels and Jewish Historiography from 1770 to the Present Day.* Leiden, 1971.

Chaney, Charles L. *The Birth of Missions in America.* Pasadena, 1976.

Cohen, Naomi W. *Encounter with Emancipation: the German Jews in the United States 1830–1914.* Philadelphia, 1984.

————. "Pioneers of American Jewish Defense." *American Jewish Archives* 29 (November, 1977): 116–150.

Conway, John S. "The Jerusalem-Bishopric: 'A Union of Foolscrap and Blotting Paper'." *Studies in Religion* 7 (Summer, 1978): 305–315.

————. "Protestant Missions to the Jews 1810–1980: Ecclesiastical Imperialism or Theological Aberration?" *Holocaust and Genocide Studies* 1 (1986): 127–146.

Davis, Moshe. *The Emergence of Conservative Judaism.* Philadelphia, 1963.

Dobkowski, Michael N. *The Tarnished Dream: the Basis of American Anti-Semitism.* Westport, 1979.

Eichhorn, David M. *Evangelizing the American Jew.* New York, 1978.

Einhorn, David. "Dogmatical Differences Between Judaism and Christianity." *Jewish Times* (June 18–August 20, 1869), passim.

Eisen, Arnold M. *The Chosen People in America: A Study in Jewish Religious Ideology.* Bloomington, 1983.

Eisen, Max. "Christian Missions to the Jews in North America and Great Britain." *Jewish Social Studies* 10 (1948): 31–66.

Elsbree, Oliver W. *The Rise of the Missionary Spirit in America, 1790–1815.* Williamsport, 1928.

Enelow, Hyman G. *Selected Works.* Kingsport, Tennessee, 1935.

Englander, Henry. "Isaac Leeser." *Central Conference of American Rabbis Yearbook* 28 (1918): 213–252.

Everett, Robert Andrew. "Judaism in Nineteenth Century American Transcendentalist and Liberal Protestant Thought." *Journal of Ecumenical Studies* 20 (Summer, 1983): 396–414.

Felsenthal, Bernard. *Why Do the Jews Not Accept Jesus as their Messiah?* Chicago, 1890.

Fernandes, Benjamin Dias. *A Series of Letters on the Evidences of Christianity.* Philadelphia, 1859.

First Report of the American Society for Meliorating the Condition of the Jews. May, 1823.

Freeland, John C. "The Jewish Estimate of Jesus of Nazareth." *American Catholic Quarterly Review* 36 (1911): 730–753.

Frey, Joseph Samuel C. F. *The Converted Jew.* Boston, 1815.

———. *Narrative.* New York, 1817.

Friedman, Lee M. "The American Society for Meliorating the Condition of the Jews and Joseph S. C. F. Frey." *Early American Jews* (Cambridge, Massachusetts, 1934): 96–112.

Froom, Leroy E. *The Prophetic Faith of Our Fathers.* Washington, D.C., 1954.

Funk, I. K. "Jesus of Nazareth From the Present Jewish Point of View." Appendix to George Croly, *Tarry Thou Will I Come.* (New York, 1901): 551–570.

Geiger, Abraham. *Judaism and Its History;* trans. by Maurice Mayer. New York, 1865.

Gladden, Washington. "Can Jews be Christians?" *American Hebrew* (December 11, 1896): 174–175.

Glick, Wayne G. *The Reality of Christianity; A Study of Adolf von Harnack as Historian and Theologian.* New York, 1967.

Gottheil, Gustav. "The Great Refusal." *Unitarian Review* 27 (January, 1887): 1–12.

———. "Jesus was not Rejected." *Menorah* 14 (1894): 176–180.

Grinstein, Hyman B. *The Rise of the Jewish Community of New York 1654–1860.* Philadelphia, 1947.

Grose, Peter. *Israel in the Mind of America.* New York, 1983.

Grossman, Lawrence. "Isaac Leeser's Mentor: Rabbi Abraham Sutro, 1784–1869." *Rabbi Joseph H. Lookstein Memorial Volume,* ed. by Leo Landman, (New York, 1980): 151–162.

Hagner, Donald A. *The Jewish Reclamation of Jesus: An Analysis and Critique of Modern Jewish Study of Jesus.* Grand Rapids, 1984.

Handy, Robert T. *A Christian America: Protestant Hopes and Historical Realities.* New York, 1971.

Harris, Maurice H. "Judaism and Unitarianism from a Jewish Standpoint." *Selected Addresses,* Third Series (New York, 1896): 3–17.

———. "The Spirit of Judaism." *Selected Addresses,* Third Series (New York, 1896): 37–46.

Healey, Robert M. "From Conversion to Dialogue: Protestant and American Mission to the Jews in the Nineteenth and Twentieth Centuries." *Christian Jewish Relations* 15 (September, 1982): 18–30.

Heller, James G. *Isaac M. Wise: His Life, Work and Thought.* New York, 1965.

Hirsch, Emil G. "Are the Jews the Chosen People?" *Reform Advocate* 5 (April 15, 1893): 162–165.

———. "The Crucifixion." *Reform Advocate* 3 (February 29, 1892): 5–15.

———. *The Crucifixion Viewed from a Jewish Standpoint.* Chicago, 1892.

———. *The Doctrines of Jesus.* Chicago, 1894.

———. "The Ethics of Jesus." *Reform Advocate* 8 (December 29, 1894): 301–303.

———. "Jesus, His Life and His Times." *Reform Advocate* 7 (May 19, 1894): 214–217.

———. "Jewish View on Jesus." *Reform Advocate* 1 (February 27, 1891): 48.

———. "The Jews and Jesus." *Reform Advocate* 5 (May 6, 1893): 222–226.

———. "Moses and Jesus: or Reform Judaism and Unitarianism." *Reform Advocate* 9 (July 29, 1895): 345–348.

———. *My Religion.* New York, 1925.

———. "Paul, the Apostle of Heathen Judaism or Christianity." *Reform Advocate* 7 (June 30, 1894): 356–359.

———. *Reform Judaism and Unitarianism.* Chicago, 1905.

———. "Universal Religion and Judaism." *Reform Advocate* 6 (October 14, 1893): 137–140.

Hirsch, Samuel. *Die Religionsphilosophie der Juden.* Leipzig, 1842.

———. "Judaism and Christianity." trans. by Emil G. Hirsch, *Jewish Times* 9, (August 27—December 17, 1869), passim.

Hudson, Winthrop S. *American Protestantism.* Chicago, 1961.

Hutchison, William R. *The Modernist Impulse in American Protestantism.* Cambridge, 1976.

Israel Vindicated being a Refutation of the Calumnies Propogated respecting the Jew-ish Nation: in which the Objects and Views of the American Society for Amelio-rating the Condition of the Jews are Investigated. New York, 1820.

The Jew. New York, 1823–1825.

Jew and Gentile Being a Report of a Conference of Israelites and Christians Regard-ing their Mutual Relations and Welfare. Chicago, 1890.

Jick, Leon. *The Americanization of the Synagogue, 1820–1870.* Hanover, New Hampshire, 1976.

Key, Andrew F. *The Theology of Isaac Mayer Wise.* Cincinnati, 1962.

Kohler, Kaufmann. "The Attitude of Christian Scholars Toward Jewish Liter-ature." *Studies, Addresses, and Personal Papers* (New York, 1931): 413–425.

———. "Christianity in its Relation to Judaism." *Jewish Encyclopedia* 4 (1903): 49–59.

———. "The Inadequacy of Christian Ethics." *Reform Advocate* 7 (February, 1894): 69–71.

———. "Jesus of Nazareth." *Jewish Times* 6 (January 22, 1875): 755–756.

———. "Jesus of Nazareth—In Theology." *Jewish Encyclopedia* 7 (New York, 1904): 166–170.

———. "The Jewish and Christian Liturgy and their Common Essene Or-igin." *Hebrew Union College and other Addresses* (Cincinnati, 1916): 17–31.

———. "Moses and Jesus." *Menorah* 12 (March, 1892): 158–168.

———. *The Origins of the Synagogue and the Church.* New York, 1929.

———. "Saul of Tarsus." *Jewish Encyclopedia* 11 (New York, 1905): 79–87.

———. "Synagogue and Church in Their Mutual Relations, Particularly in Reference to Their Ethical Teachings." *Studies, Addresses, and Personal Pa-pers* (New York, 1931): 251–265.

———. "Three Discourses on Jewish Ethics." *Studies, Addresses, and Personal Papers* (New York, 1931): 236–250.

Kohn, Joshua S. "Mordecai Manuel Noah's Ararat Project and the Missionar-ies." *American Jewish Historical Quarterly* 55 (1963): 162–196.

Korn, Bertram W. *Eventful Years and Experiences.* Cincinnati, 1954.

———. "Isaac Leeser: Centennial Reflections." *American Jewish Archives* 19 (1967): 127–141.

Krauskopf, Joseph. *A Rabbi's Impressions of the Oberammergau Passion Play.* Philadelphia, 1901.

———. *Jesus—Man or God?* Cincinnati, 1911.

Kraut, Benny. "A Unitarian Rabbi? The Case of Solomon Sonneschein," *Jewish Apostasy in the Modern World* edited by Todd M. Endelman. New York, 1987: 272–308.

———. "The Ambivalent Relations of American Reform Judaism with Unitarianism in the Last Third of the Nineteenth Century." *Journal of Ecumenical Studies* 23 (Winter, 1986): 58–68.

———. "Francis E. Abbott: Perceptions of a Nineteenth Century Religious Radical on Jews and Judaism." *Studies in the American Jewish Experience* 1, ed. by J. R. Marcus and A. J. Peck, (Cincinnati, 1981): 90–113.

———. *From Reform Judaism to Ethical Culture: The Religious Evolution of Felix Adler.* Cincinnati, 1979.

———. "Judaism Triumphant: Isaac Mayer Wise on Unitarianism and Liberal Christianity." *AJS Review* 7–8 (1982–1983): 179–230.

———. "Unitarianism on the Reform Jewish Mind." *Proceedings of the Eighth World Congress of Jewish Studies, Division B, The History of the Jewish People* (Jerusalem, 1982): 91–98.

Latourette, Kenneth Scott. *A History of Christianity.* New York, 1953.

Lazarus, Josephine. *The Spirit of Judaism.* New York, 1895.

Leeser, Isaac. *The Claims of the Jews to an Equality of Rights.* Philadelphia, 1841.

———. *The Jews and the Mosaic Law.* Philadelphia, 1833.

Levy, David. *Defence of the Old Testament.* New York, 1797.

———. *Letters to Dr. Priestly.* New York, 1794.

Lindeskog, Gosta. *Die Jesusfrage im neuzeitlichen Judentum.* Uppsala, 1938.

Malachy, Yona. *American Fundamentalism and Israel.* Jersualem, 1978.

Martin, Bernard. "The Religious Philosophy of Emil G. Hirsch." *American Jewish Archives* 4 (June, 1952): 66–82.

———. "The Social Philosophy of Emil G. Hirsch." *American Jewish Archives* 6 (June, 1954): 151–165.

McDonald, John. *A New Translation of Isaiah, Chapter XVIII.* Albany, NY 1814.

Miller, Matthew R. *Identity of Judaism and Christianity.* New York, 1850.

————. *The Luminous Unity or Letters Addressed to the Rev. A. Guinzburg, A Rabbi of Boston, Mass., From the Rev. M. R. Miller on the Question is Unitarianism, as Opposed to Trinitarianism, A Principle of Heathenism Rather than of Specific Judaism*. Philadelphia, 1874.

Moore, Laurence, R. *Religious Outsiders and the Making of Americans*. New York, 1986.

"Need We be Christians?" *American Hebrew* (December 18, 1896): 196.

Newman, Selig. *The Challenge Accepted: A Dialogue Between A Jew and A Christian: the Former Answering A Challenge Thrown Out by the Latter Respecting the Accomplishment of the Prophecies Predictive of the Advent of Jesus*. New York, 1850.

Nikelsburger, Jacob. *Koul Jacob in Defense of the Jewish Religion: Containing the Arguments of the Rev. C. F. Frey One of the Committee of the London Society for the Conversion of the Jews and Answers Thereto*. New York, 1816.

The Occident and American Jewish Advocate. Philadelphia. 1843–1868.

Philipson, David. *The Reform Movement in Judaism*. New York, 1967.

Plaut, Gunther W. *The Growth of Reform Judaism*. New York, 1965.

————. *The Rise of Reform Judaism*. New York, 1963.

Raphael, Marc Lee. *Profiles in American Judaism: the Reform, Conservative, Orthodox, and Reconstructionist Traditions in Historical Perspective*. San Francisco, 1984.

Ratner, Lorman. "Conversion of the Jews and Pre-Civil War Reform". *American Quarterly* 13 (Spring, 1961): 43–52.

Rosenwaike, Ira. *On the Edge of Greatness: A Portrait of American Jewry in the Early National Period*. Cincinnati, 1985.

Rubinstein, Aryeh. "Isaac Mayer Wise: A New Approach". *Jewish Social Studies* 39 (Winter-Spring, 1977): 53–74.

Sandeen, Ernest R. *The Roots of Fundamentalism*. Chicago, 1970.

Sandmel, Samuel. "Isaac Mayer Wise's 'Jesus Himself'." *Essays in American Jewish History* (Cincinnati, 1958): 325–358.

————. "Isaac Mayer Wise's *Pronaos to Holy Writ*." *A Bicentennial Festschrift for Jacob Rader Marcus*, ed. by Bertram W. Korn, (New York, 1976): 517–527.

Sarna, Jonathan D. "American Christian Opposition to Missions to the Jews— 1816–1900." *Journal of Ecumenical Studies* 23 (Spring, 1986): 225–238.

————, ed. *The American Jewish Experience*. New York, 1986.

————. "The American Jewish Response to Nineteenth Century Christian Missions." *Journal of American History* 68 (June, 1981): 35–51.

————. "The Freethinker, the Jews, and the Missionaries: George Houston and the Mystery of Israel Vindicated." *AJS Review* 5 (1980): 101–114.

————. "The Impact of Nineteenth-Century Christian Missions on American Jews." *Jewish Apostasy in the Modern World* edited by Todd M. Endelman. New York, 1987: 232–254.

————. *Jacksonian Jew: the Two Worlds of Mordecai Noah.* New York, 1981.

————. "Jewish-Christian Hostility in the United States: Perceptions from a Jewish Point of View." *Uncivil Religion,* ed. by F. E. Greenspahn, (New York, 1987): 5–22.

————. "The Mythical Jew and the Jew Next Door in Nineteenth Century America." *Anti-Semitism in American History,* ed. by David A. Gerber, (Urbana, 1986): 57–78.

Schappes, Morris U. *A Documentary History of the Jews in the United States 1654–1875.* New York, 1971.

Schindler, Solomon. *Messianic Expectations and Modern Judaism.* Boston, 1886.

Schlessinger, Max. *The Historical Jesus of Nazareth.* New York, 1876.

Schoeps, Hans Joachim. *The Christian-Jewish Argument: A History of Theologies in Conflict.* London, 1963.

Schreiber, Emanuel. "Jesus of Nazareth." *Menorah* 7 (1889): 80–88.

Scult, Mel. *Millennial Expectations and Jewish Liberties: A Study of the Efforts to Convert the Jews in Britain, up to the Mid Nineteenth Century.* Leiden, 1978.

Seller, Maxine. *Isaac Leeser: Architect of the American Jewish Community.* Ph.D. dissertation, University of Pennsylvania, 1965.

————. "Isaac Leeser's Views on the Restoration of a Jewish Palestine." *American Jewish Historical Quarterly* 58 (September, 1968): 118–135.

Silverman, Joseph. "Popular Errors about the Jews." *Reform Advocate* 6 (September 6, 1893): 75–78.

Sklare, Marshall. "The Conversion of the Jews." *Commentary* 56 (September, 1973): 44–53.

Stern, Malcolm H. *First American Jewish Families.* Cincinnati, 1978.

Sussman, Lance J. "Another Look at Isaac Leeser and the First Jewish Translation of the Bible in the United States." *Modern Judaism* 5 (May, 1985): 159–190.

——. *Confidence in God: the Life and Preaching of Isaac Leeser (1806–1868)*. Ordination thesis, Hebrew Union College—Jewish Institute of Religion, 1980.

——. "Isaac Leeser and the Protestantization of American Judaism." *American Jewish Archives* 38 (April, 1986): 1–21.

The Second Report of the American Society for Meliorating the Condition of the Jews. Princeton, 1824.

Talmage, Frank. *Disputation and Dialogue: Readings in the Jewish-Christian Encounter*. New York, 1975.

Tarshish, Allan. "Jew and Christian in a New Society: Some Aspects of Jewish-Christian Relationships in the United States, 1848–1881." *A Bicentennial Festschrift for Jacob Rader Marcus,* ed. by Bertram W. Korn (New York, 1976): 565–583.

Temkin, Sefton D. "Isaac Mayer Wise: A Biographical Sketch." *A Guide to the Writings of Isaac Mayer Wise* (Cincinnati, 1981): 5–53.

Thompson, A. E. *A Century of Jewish Missions*. Chicago, 1902.

Toy, Crawford H. *Judaism and Christianity: a Sketch of the Progress of Thought from Old Testament to New Testament*. Boston, 1891.

Tobit's Letters to Levi; or A Reply to the Narrative of Joseph Samuel C. F. Frey. New York, 1816.

Tsevat, Matitiahu. "A Retrospective View of Isaac Leeser's Biblical Work." *Essays in American Jewish History* (Cincinnati, 1958): 295–313.

Tuchman, Barbara W. *Bible and Sword: England and Palestine from the Bronze Age to Balfour*. New York, 1956.

Turner, James. *Without God, Without Creed: the Origins of Unbelief in America*. Baltimore, 1985.

The Twenty-Four Books of the Holy Scriptures Carefully Translated According to the Massoretic Text on the Basis of the English Version after the Best Jewish Authorities and Supplied with Short Explanatory Notes by Isaac Leeser. New York, 1922.

Urofsky, Melvin I. *A Voice that Spoke for Justice: The Life and Times of Stephen S. Wise*. Albany, N.Y., 1982.

Weinstock, Harris. *Jesus the Jew*. New York, 1902.

Wise, Isaac M. *A Defense of Judaism versus Proselytizing Christianity*. Cincinnati, 1889.

———. *History of the Hebrews' Second Commonwealth with special Reference to its Literature, Culture, and the Origin of Rabbinism and Christianity.* Cincinnati, 1880.

———. *Judaism and Christianity, Their Agreements and Disagreements.* Cincinnati, 1883.

———. *The Martyrdom of Jesus of Nazareth: a Historico—Critical Treatise on the Last Chapters of the Gospel.* Cincinnati, 1874.

———. *The Origin of Christianity and a Commentary to the Acts of the Apostles.* Cincinnati, 1868.

———. *Reminiscences.* trans. by David Philipson. Cincinnati, 1901.

———. "The World of My Books." trans. by Albert H. Friedlander, *American Jewish Archives* 6 (June, 1954): 107–148.

———. *Three Lectures on the Origins of Christianity.* Cincinnati, 1873.

Whiteman, Maxwell. "The Legacy of Isaac Leeser." *Jewish Life in Philadelphia 1830–1940* (Philadelphia, 1983): 26–47.

Wolf, Edwin and Whiteman, Maxwell. *The History of the Jews of Philadelphia from Colonial Times to the Age of Jackson.* Philadelphia, 1957.

Wolfson, Harry A. "How the Jews Will Reclaim Jesus." *Judaism and Christianity: Selected Accounts, 1892–1962,* ed. by Jacob B. Agus, (New York, 1962).

Wright, Conrad. *A Stream of Light: A Sesquicentennial History of American Unitarianism.* Boston, 1975.

Index